Developing Reflective Practice

Developing Reflective Practice

A guide for beginning teachers

Edited by Debra McGregor and Lesley Cartwright

McGraw Hill Open University Press

Open University Press
McGraw-Hill Education
McGraw-Hill House
Shoppenhangers Road
Maidenhead
Berkshire
England
SL6 2QL

email: enquiries@openup.co.uk
world wide web: www.openup.co.uk

and

Two Penn Plaza, New York, NY 10121-2289, USA

Open University Press 2011

Copyright © Debra McGregor & Lesley Cartwright 2011

A catalogue record of this book is available from the British Library

ISBN10: 0-33-524257-X (pb) 0-33-524258-8 (hb)
ISBN13: 978-0-33-524257-3 (pb) 978-0-33-524258-0 (hb)
eISBN: 978-0-33-524259-7

Library of Congress Cataloging -in-Publication Data
CIP data has been applied for

Typeset by Aptara Inc., India
Printed in the UK by Bell & Bain Ltd, Glasgow

Fictitous names of companies, products, people, characters and/or data that may be used herein (in case studies or in examples) are not intended to represent any real individual, company, product or event.

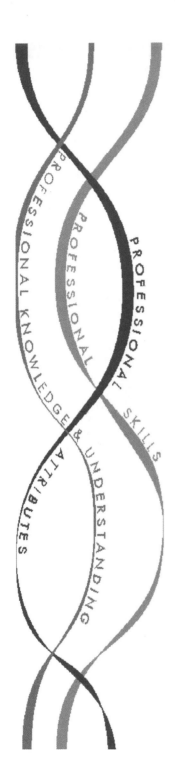

Comments from OfSTED (2010) regarding the teacher education programmes at the University of Wolverhampton :

'the cohesive nature of the course which combines school and centre-based training and opportunities for trainees to develop into highly reflective practitioners very well, through:

- the use of research
- highly reflective tasks and assignments
- the outstanding use of a wide range of resources
- excellent opportunities to prepare trainees to teach in a diverse range of
- schools' (p. 5)

'trainees put theory into practice well and develop into highly reflective practitioners. From beginning the programmes with a wide variety of starting points, they make at least good progress and emerge as predominantly good and increasingly outstanding trainees' (p.6)

'exemplary tracking of trainees' progress and reflective practice' (p. 10)

'The quality of trainees' self-reflection is consistently strong, analysing their impact on the progress of individuals or groups in order to differentiate starting points' (p. 12)

'The development of trainees' skills in reflective practice is high' (p. 20)

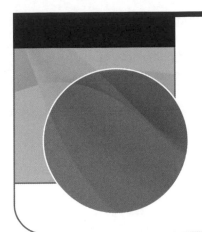

Contents

Notes on contributors

Lesley Cartwright began her career as a modern languages teacher and was Secondary Partnership Director, Initial Teacher Education (ITE), at the University of Wolverhampton from 2004 to 2009. As well as her role in training teachers, she has taught on the MA in Education with a specific focus on mentoring and coaching. She has played a key role in academic and curriculum development for ITE at the University of Wolverhampton, where the underpinning principles include a strong emphasis on informed reflective practice. Currently an education consultant, she works actively to support the professional growth of both trainee teachers and their mentors.

Dr Linda Devlin (Professional Learning Research Cluster Leader) is an experienced research coordinator working within the School of Education at the University of Wolverhampton. She worked in secondary schools for 12 years and during this time was responsible for trainee and newly qualified teachers. She has worked in higher education for 16 years embracing a range of roles in teacher education at Keele, Manchester Metropolitan and Wolverhampton universities. She has also worked with local authorities to provide accredited training opportunities for teachers in their first five years of teaching.

Mary Dunne (Senior Lecturer and Pathway Leader for Secondary English) worked as a secondary school English teacher and head of department for 24 years before moving to the University of Wolverhampton to set up an English PGCE course. She also runs the English pathway for the graduate teacher programme and is currently the external examiner for employment based initial teacher training (ITT) at Canterbury Christ Church University. Her main research interests are in the graduate teacher programme, improving the quality of school-based training and approaches to supporting trainee teachers to work at Masters level.

Dr Mahmoud Emira is a research assistant at the Centre for Developmental and Applied Research in Education (CeDARE) at the University of Wolverhampton. He is an associate member of the Higher Education Academy. He specializes in professional studies in education. He has taught languages at high school and university level. His main research interests are educational leadership; professional development; social inclusion; educational policy and practice; teacher education and the education of minority ethnic children.

Dr Angela Gault's (Professional Studies Lead Tutor, Secondary Initial Teacher Education) background is in secondary English teaching as a practitioner and manager, and in school improvement and continuing professional development (CPD) as a local authority consultant. Currently she is responsible for the professional studies strand of the postgraduate (PGCE) Secondary course and promotes a model of professional development based upon critical reflection and practitioner research. She is involved in the teaching and curriculum development of PGCE, GRTP and NQT modules. Angela's PhD research was in the area policy implementation and teachers' professional development.

Fay Glendenning (Principal Lecturer, Director of Secondary Education) has worked in primary and secondary schools as a teacher, advanced skills teacher, local authority consultant and teacher educator in mathematics.

Gerald Griggs (Senior Lecturer in Physical Education and Sports Studies, University of Wolverhampton) has fourteen years' experience in education, located in both primary schools and in higher education (including teacher training). He has written consistently since 2005, publishing a book focusing on physical education in the primary school and has a number of peer-reviewed papers across areas such as primary education, physical education and the sociology of sport.

Paul Gurton (Senior Lecturer in Primary Initial Teacher Education) taught for 18 years in primary schools in London, the West Midlands and Rome. He has experience of teaching in Key Stages 1 and 2. He has spent six years as a deputy and headteacher of two Warwickshire primary schools. Since his move to higher education two years ago he has taught on the undergraduate route at the University of Wolverhampton and is coordinator for primary languages. His research interests are in the areas of primary language teaching and reflective practice in trainee and experienced teachers.

Dr Debra McGregor (Reader in Developing Pedagogy and Educational Doctorate Award Leader) has been involved in teaching for over twenty years. She has worked in varied roles as student teacher, mentor, teacher educator and researcher. Her research interests are focused on the nature of learning and teaching. She has published many academic papers and written about thinking skills, teaching and learning. She has already published two books: *Developing Thinking; Developing Learning: A Thinking Skills Guide for Education* and *Practice and Perspectives: Learning in Practical Science*.

Lesley Mycroft (Senior Lecturer in Initial Teacher Education) was a primary school deputy headteacher before taking up her post in higher education in 2004. She has taught in secondary and nursery education but specializes in primary and early primary learning and assessment, special needs provision and school leadership. In her current post she has been instrumental in introducing an Early Primary pathway to qualified teacher status (BEd Hons). Lesley is in the third year of a funded project looking at student peer support approaches and reflective learning and practice, and has presented related papers on this theme at national and international conferences. On the basis of her own reflective practice she has been elected a fellow of the Higher Education Academy.

Lorraine Thomas taught modern foreign languages (MFL) in secondary schools across the West Midlands for 16 years. She was a head of department for nine years and mentored and supported many trainee teachers and newly qualified teachers (NQTs) during this time. She also taught MFL in primary schools and delivered training to primary school teachers and teaching assistants, as part of her work as a local authority primary languages coach, supporting schools to establish MFL at Key Stage 2. Lorraine also managed a school-centred initial teacher training (SCITT) secondary PGCE programme and a graduate teacher programme (GTP) and was PGCE Subject Leader for MFL for eight years. Later as a senior teacher, Lorraine managed specialist school status as Training School Manager with a range of responsibilities including ITT and professional development. Lorraine has a wide range of expertise in ITT and also delivering early professional development (EPD) and CPD programmes. Lorraine moved into higher education as Director of Postgraduate and Professional Development Studies at the University of Wolverhampton with responsibility for the MA Education and managed a very successful masters level module for NQTs. She is now Head of Secondary and Post-compulsory Education at the University of Worcester.

Sarah Powell (Senior Lecturer in Initial Teacher Training) has a wealth of teaching experience in various local authorities (Staffordshire, Dorset, Leicestershire, Bournemouth) and overseas in Indonesia. She leads on RE/PSHE modules and shares the responsibility for teaching English and professional studies to trainees following both the BEd and PGCE routes to achieving qualified teacher status (QTS). Sarah is also currently working on a project with colleagues to develop an e-version record of professional development (eRoPD) for primary teacher trainees and partnership primary schools. Sarah is passionate about teaching and her research mainly includes the use of technology to extend the use of reflective practice to aid continuing professional development in a progressive educational climate.

Julie Wilde (Senior Lecturer in Post-compulsory Education) is the route leader for the Masters in Mentoring in Education at the University of Wolverhampton. Julie has worked in secondary schools, post-compulsory education and higher education teaching sociology. She has also been involved in teaching on post-compulsory initial teacher education (ITE) programmes at the University of Warwick and now at the University of Wolverhampton. Julie is a member of the University of Wolverhampton's critical policy research cluster and is interested in the relationships between education policy, mentoring and the reflective practice of student teachers.

Foreword

The writers of this book have shared their passion for learning and teaching, along with their subject and pedagogic knowledge. They have developed their expertise through supporting generations of developing teachers at the University of Wolverhampton and in our partner schools and colleges.

This wealth of experience has informed the reflective wisdom and guidance that is collated here for you. We hope you will 'dip in' and read when you feel the need for a steer on the bumpy journey to becoming a qualified and experienced classroom practitioner.

In this book you will find an informative mix of theoretical frameworks to draw upon, reflections from real student teachers and NQTs sharing their developmental insights, and many practical suggestions about what you can do in the sort of situations you will encounter in the early years of teaching.

Finally, you are invited to take the 'longer term view' to becoming a reflective practitioner in your own career, as you pursue our common goal of enhancing young lives through the provision of the best possible learning experiences.

So, it is with great pleasure that I recommend this book to you.

Professor Caroline Gipps
Vice-Chancellor
University of Wolverhampton

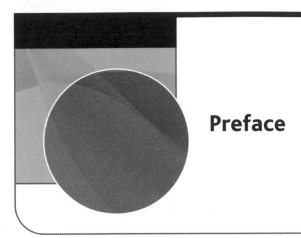

Preface

Justification for this book

With the shifting political landscape, sweeping changes in educational resourcing and a future of uncertainty and complexity, it is an appropriate time to share ways in which developing teachers might initiate and personalize their own professional learning. Reflection, reflectivity and reflexivity are all key processes that serve to underpin developmental insights and improvements in teaching practices.

Recent re-emergence and current prominence of reflection to support teacher development was promoted by the General Teaching Council (2007) and purported to lie at the heart of the profession. The Training and Development Agency for Schools (TDA) also recognizes the importance of reflection through its inclusion in the revised qualifying standards for classroom teachers of standard Q7: 'reflect on and improve their practice, and take responsibility for identifying and meeting their professional development needs' (TDA 2007: 8). There are also core standards that must be maintained throughout teachers' working lives, such as C7: 'evaluate their performance and be committed to improving their practice through appropriate professional development' (TDA 2007: 28).

Prominent theorists such as Schön, Shulman, Dewey, Kolb, Gibbs, Pollard, Rolfe, Jasper and Bolton are referred to and their ideas are applied to real examples of the dilemmas and problems that trainees and newly qualified teachers face when entering the teaching profession. From these many tools and approaches have been designed to scaffold critical review and support the development of beginning teachers' practice.

The growth of reflective practice as a process can be traced back to the development of constructivist interpretations of learning. Kolb's (1984) theory of experiential learning provides a useful backcloth for the development of reflection. He defines learning as: 'the process whereby knowledge is created through the transformation of experience' (p. 38) with reflection as a critical tenet. The learner needs an experience of 'happenings' upon which to reflect to enable the development of understandings about the new or novel occurrences. Making meaning and developing understandings from experiences enables the individual to project about possibilities in new contexts. As we cogitate on a concrete experience, reflection can develop into an expectation of 'What might happen if . . .' and a wish to test out these expectations. 'It is in this interplay between expectation and experience that learning occurs' (Kolb 1984: 42). Often minor changes in practice can have a significant change in outcome and this is where teaching is really an art form described by Brighouse and Woods (1999: 104) as: 'small interventions' that can have a 'disproportionately' positive effect on change and development.

Reflective practice is thus fundamental to teacher professional development. It is a core activity within the profession but is particularly critical in supporting and maintaining professional development in the formative years. This book particularly targets, therefore, all those engaged in initial teacher training, newly qualified teachers and those in their early professional years. It will also be of value to those professionals who support colleagues at these particular stages in their career. Recent government policies have emphasized strong links between career progression and a commitment on the part of teachers to improve pupil standards, develop their own skills and develop other teachers' expertise, as exemplified in the professional standards for teachers (TDA 2007). Coaching, mentoring, classroom-based research, networking and collaboration are all seen as essential processes contributing to what has been called the 'new professionalism'.

Allied to this, an increasing proportion of beginning teachers have been pursuing Masters degrees focusing on reflective practice. In this book, beginning teachers demonstrate the positive impact on their practice of reading, thinking and writing at Masters level. Whatever the future of initial teacher training as the new government makes plans to radically reform education and training provision (DfE 2011), future teachers will continue to benefit from the positive impact of learning through reflective practice. The redefinition of teacher professionalism demands highly skilled professionals who will make judgments and exercise professional autonomy in the classroom and make decisions based on enquiry and the use of evidence 'within a clear accountability framework' (DCSF 2008: 13). Recent developments place particular emphasis on the value of Masters study to influence the quality of learning and teaching in the most complex, challenging schools.

There is currently a range of undergraduate and postgraduate programmes for initial teacher education, postgraduate teacher education and continuing professional development for practising teachers which require participants to undertake practitioner or action research, involving reflection of various kinds, to achieve their qualifications. Reflective practice, reflective action, reflection-in-action, reflection-on-action and reflexivity can all contribute to a practitioner's professional development about, through and with praxis.

The proposed continual spread and development of employment-based initial teacher training (EBITT) programmes is likely to increase the need for resources that directly support, guide and direct in-school professional development, with a heavy reliance on reflection as a professional development (PD) tool. This book offers experiential insights and practical guidance that will inform and scaffold the capability of mentors and coaches to engage with colleagues in the process and development of reflection.

Any new professional has a number of agendas to address within themselves as a professional and these are complex and intertwined: 'subject' knowledge; 'curriculum' knowledge; 'pedagogic' knowledge; acknowledgement of educational values. At the heart of this too is the knowledge of self and how to operate within this new evolving professional context.

Defining the nature and intent of the book

This book is intended to be a companion for all beginning teachers whether on a Bachelor of Education (BEd) degree course, Postgraduate Certificate in Education (PGCE) programme, EBITT route or Teach First experience. It provides commentary and guidance directly related to the experiences that beginning teachers face and the difficulties they need to overcome. It describes and highlights how various influences and supportive frameworks can shape the nature and direction of reflective practice. Many tried and tested approaches and activities that provide scaffolding for developing professionals are included. These examples of successful practices, from a longitudinal perspective, indicate how novice professionals can be empowered through reflective processes. The writers have all supported countless teachers on their professional journey from 'intuitive practitioner' to 'knowing professional' (Atkinson and Claxton 2000). They have engaged their trainee and beginning teachers in a range of university-based and school-based activities, reflective journal writing, formative progression records and written assignments, all of which have been carefully designed to ensure that theory and practice become a harmonious whole rather than remain as opposing concepts of learning to teach. The rich and varied examples of beginning teachers' work and reflections, and the mini case studies provided, bring to life the 'theories' of reflective practice as the reader works through the book.

The book also provides a variety of resources for developing teachers to dip into. Most chapters begin with a theoretical introduction to an aspect of the development of thoughtful reflection and reflexive practice. There are also practical tasks and activities with which the reader can actively engage to further their understanding about how reflection can enhance the development of an aspect of their professional practice from creative lesson planning to assessment of their learners' progress. Each chapter discusses and explores different aspects of teacher development and is illustrated by practical examples and supplementary activities for the enthusiastic reader to engage in, pursuing reflection further. The book organization also adopts a somewhat chronological perspective, the 'chapters' echoing the developmental journey of a 'new professional' entering teaching.

The design of the chapters

Each chapter begins with an introduction and overview. The level of writing is designed to support M level thinking, but makes as few assumptions about prior learning as possible, and the book includes a glossary to support some of the more complex notions explored. The theoretical beginnings include extracts or quotations from trainees relating directly to their views, interpretations or applications of that particular aspect of reflection or practice. Each chapter includes participatory tasks for the reader to work on. There are also examples of trainees' responses to these tasks. Sometimes these will take the form of boxed case studies, where the activities have been tried and tested on various teacher preparation routes.

The text is interspersed, where appropriate, with diagrams or models emphasizing important reflective processes, opportunities or approaches within each chapter. Mini case studies are provided in the form of tables, figures or boxed examples. These may be informative or developmental, prompting readers to consider how they might feel, respond to or interpret various situations. There are sections that will offer reflective tasks, reflective quotes, illuminatory case studies and explanatory commentaries for trainees to think about or try out for themselves. The text therefore provides a mix of 'bite-size' sections that will appeal more widely to readers.

Wide subject and phase appeal

Each chapter draws on reflections from across primary, secondary and post-compulsory phases of teacher education in both work- and university-based settings. The chapters provide some theory and ideas to inform practice. The practical guidance and insightful reflections are from a variety of learning and curricular contexts including English, mathematics, science, modern foreign languages (MFL) and physical education (PE). The reflections take a variety of forms including extracts from reflective journals, action planning examples and thought-provoking quotations to engage the reader. The expertise of the authors (as indicated by the contributors' educational experiences) and 'outstanding' performance in the recent Ofsted (2010) inspections are a testament to the tried and tested approaches and techniques that will be described and drawn upon in the text.

The uniqueness of the book

This text provides a rich informative mix of theory, practical scaffolds, tools and frameworks explained through examples of 'real' practice.

Each chapter is shaped and informed by a typical question directed at the reader. Chapter 1, 'What can reflective practice mean to you?', explores differing views and dimensions of reflection that can inform the development of reflective practice. The key theorists (Dewey, Schön, Shulman, Pollard, Jasper and Bolton) and their views of reflection are introduced. The varied perspectives of reflection are considered and practical suggestions are offered to enhance the pedagogic practice of beginning teachers. Chapter 2, 'How do you become a reflective professional?' sets reflection in the context of professional development and details the professional standards. As such it links well to Masters level thinking by introducing the reader to the wider socio-political frameworks in which they are learning to teach. It also focuses on the specific needs of the new or recent entrant to the profession and how reflective practice can support this critical stage by responding to the problematic nature of teaching beyond the development of coping strategies, developing critical self-reflection and enhancing the creativity of professionals. Chapter 3, 'Who do you think you are?', links to the previous two chapters and enables trainees to interrogate their own developing identity as a teacher generally and as a teacher of a particular subject or within a particular phase. Drawing on the established work of Eraut, Furlong and Maynard, Olsen and Stenberg it also discusses how learner teachers construct their identities, encouraging them to explore the dynamic relationship between personal self and professional self. Chapter 4, 'How consciously reflective are you?', is about moving from 'unconscious' to 'conscious' reflection; it highlights how reflective practice begins to be truly valuable in professional development only at the point where it is undertaken from a position of knowledge and understanding of the broader educational picture. It explores how trainees develop from *intuitive* practitioners to *knowing* teachers and illustrates when and how they apply knowledge or ideas in their reflections in order for them to be consciously aware that professional learning has taken place. It proposes three models of reflection ('problem solving'; 'theory testing' and 'positive experience') for consideration as the readers explore their personal journey towards conscious reflection. Chapter 5, 'What kinds of challenges will you face as you start your teaching?' focuses upon how beginning teachers develop their professional identity, not in isolation but within the social context of a school or college attachment. The ideas in the chapter help trainees explore their personal narrative, review their values, and consider how they colour the ways in which they read situations and respond to them. The complex interactions that shape initial expectations and development are illustrated through case studies in physical education and English. Readers are invited to explore ways in which they can 'fit in' to new contexts and the chapter presents a model of socialization to help them do so. Chapter 6, 'Who are your partners in reflection? Identifying and mapping your complementary support systems', outlines the variety of support (sometimes unexpected) within a school community from which a beginning teacher might learn. The chapter provides illuminatory examples about the variety of ways that collaboration between professionals and within the school community can support beginner teachers. It encourages the reader to reflect on how they utilize advice given, learning over time how to 'sift' it and to prioritize targets in order to take increasing responsibility for their own learning. Chapter 7, 'How can you use reflection to develop creativity in your classroom?', explores the possibilities for developing creativity in learners through the use of learner-centred strategies. It acknowledges the need for beginning teachers to establish themselves as confident classroom practitioners before taking a more creative stance, but illustrates ways by which the two processes of effective management and creative teaching can go hand in hand. The characteristics of the 'creative teacher' and the 'creative learner' are explored and models for developing creativity proposed. Chapter 8, 'Are you a fatalist or an idealist?', is about trainees developing more reasoned objectivity underpinned by self-efficacy, defined by Larrivee (2000: 301) as 'a teacher's perceived ability to be effective'. How trainees perceive themselves and their ability to improve their practice is explored through the proposal of a 'fatalist-idealist continuum', illuminated by extracts from trainees' assignments and journals. Readers are invited to identify their own starting point along this continuum and given ideas about which way to go towards 'self-efficacy' from that point. Chapter 9, 'How can detailed reflection improve your practice? Frameworks to help make small changes with big impact', explains how, in order to attain qualification, teachers need to provide evidence of achieving appropriate standards across a range of attributes, knowledge and understanding and skills. There are a number of frameworks that beginning teachers need to pay attention to including the ways in which the Q standards for QTS are interpreted, applied and implemented to support their formative development. Overwhelmed by the number of standards to be met and performance indicators to be considered, it is easy for beginning teachers to find themselves 'going through the motions' of reflection without seeing significant improvement in their practice. This chapter provides practical frameworks for reflecting on three key themes relating to the Q and C standards, showing how reflection and action relating to what might at first seem like small things can make a big difference to practice over time. Chapter 10, 'How can you make the best use of feedback from your mentors?', explores the nature of feedback that learner teachers receive from their mentors. Feedback is one of the most emotive aspects of being a beginning teacher. This chapter considers formal, informal, formative and summative types of feedback and how trainees and NQTs have responded. It proposes a number of ways in which beginning teachers can take some control over the process, so that they are not 'victims' of feedback but are actively engaged in it as part of their professional learning. Chapter 11, 'How can you overcome constraints to enhance reflective practice?, acknowledges the constraints and barriers that often exist for beginning teachers. It draws on an analysis of the literature (Johns 2004; Craft and Paige-Smith 2008) and the reflective journals of trainees and NQTs. Suggestions are offered, with illustrations, about how these barriers may be overcome. The underlying message is that, provided you are open minded enough to take them on board, there are always strategies to support reflective learning, even against the odds. Chapter 12, 'How can e-reflection help develop your practice?', considers how e-tools support reflective learning, that in turn informs the development of reflective practice. The chapter discusses different theorists' views of trainees' developmental stages. Chapter 13, 'Reflection, reflection, reflection: I'm thinking all the time, why do I need a theory or model?', is for any reader still in doubt about the value of reflective practice. It explores how different kinds of reflection encourage varied forms of thinking, encouraging readers to develop their own, simple, models of reflection and giving examples of trainee teachers' reflections on a number of common issues and problems. The reader is left with a renewed sense of purpose about why and how to reflect. Chapter 14, 'Taking the longer view: how can reflective practice sustain continuing professional development?', provides something of a plenary to the book. Readers, so far, will have had access to a number of models of reflection, with rich examples, to ensure that they are able to be creative and critical in their thinking about how to become a teacher and how to build on early achievements in the induction year and immediately beyond. In relatively short teaching practice placements, some solutions are, by definition, 'quick fixes'. This chapter takes the reader a step further, showing how 'reflectivity' becomes 'reflexivity', and exemplifies ways in which reflection can frame 'action research'. Here problems are posed and solutions are identified, trialled and evaluated within a longer time frame, attempting to ensure that reflective practice becomes part of the fabric of professional life.

Acknowledgements

The contributors of this book would like to gratefully thank all the trainees on the Bachelor of Education (BEd); Postgraduate Certificate in Education (PGCE); Graduate Training Programme (GTP); Diploma in Teaching in the Lifelong Learning Sector (DTLLS) courses and newly qualified teachers (NQTs) who have embarked upon, and succeeded in, teacher education courses at the University of Wolverhampton.

List of Abbreviations

ACSTT	Advisory Committee on the Supply and Training of Teachers
ADHD	attention deficit hyperactivity disorder
AfL	Assessment for Learning
AST	Advanced Skills Teacher
BEd	Bachelor of Education (degree)
CPD	continuing professional development
DfEE	Department for Education and Employment
DfES	Department for Education and Skills
EAL	English as an additional language
EBITT	Employment Based Initial Teacher Training
EPD	early professional development
GTC	General Teaching Council
GTP	Graduate Training Programme
ICT	information and communications technology
IEP	individual education plan
INSET	in-service education and training
ITE	initial teacher education
ITT	initial teacher training
LSA	learning support assistant
MFL	modern foreign languages
MTL	Masters in Teaching and Learning
NACCCE	National Advisory Committee on Creative and Cultural Education
NCSL	National College for School Leadership
NCLSLS	National College for Leadership of Schools and Children's Services
NQT	newly qualified teacher

Ofsted	Office for Standards in Education/Office for Standards in Education, Children's Services and Skills (formerly Office for Standards in Education)
PCE	post-compulsory education
PD	professional development
PDP	professional development plan (also referred to as personal development portfolio)
PGCE	Postgraduate Certificate in Education
PRP	performance-related pay
PSHE	Personal, Social and Health Education
QAA	Quality Assurance Agency for Higher Education
QCA	Qualifications and Curriculum Authority
QTS	qualified teacher status
QtT	Qualifying to Teach (this term is used in relation to the standards for initial teacher training, known as the Q standards)
RQT	recently qualified teacher
SEN	special educational needs
SENCO	special educational needs coordinator
SMT/SLT	senior management team (senior leadership team)
TA	teaching assistant
TDA	Training and Development Agency for Schools
TLA	Teacher Learning Academy
TLRs	teaching and learning responsibilities
VLE	virtual learning environment

CHAPTER 1

What can reflective practice mean for you . . . and why should you engage in it?

Debra McGregor

> *Learn from yesterday, live for today, hope for tomorrow. The important thing is not to stop questioning.*
>
> Albert Einstein

There can be few better ways of elevating your life than by thinking about, and reflecting upon, how your development as a teacher will improve the education of the children and young people whose lives you will touch. Reflectively pondering and questioning what you do can improve your achievements in life. This chapter focuses on describing why you should reflect as a developing teacher and how you can reflectively consider and question different aspects of your teaching to develop into a confident and competent educator.

Reflection often begins when you pause to 'think back' after something unexpected or out of the ordinary has happened. You re-play the happenings, incident or event in your head, and, in thinking about it more, it begins to change from a sequence of chronological events into a series of questioning thoughts such as 'What happened?', 'When?' and 'How?' These initial thoughts can be purposeless and just idle musings. They become more purposeful and constructive when thinking is directed to consider questions such as: 'Why did it happen that way?' and 'How could I have behaved or done things differently?' Questions such as: 'Would action x have been better than action y at the beginning of the lesson?' or 'How could I have responded differently to the disruptive boy at the end of the lesson?' lead to thoughts about how to improve specific situations. Reflecting determindly to improve something requires effort and sustained, focused thinking centred on a particular issue or concern you might have about your development as a teacher.

Providing clear instructions or explaining ideas to others may be a talent you already possess. It may also come naturally to you to be gently supportive and encouraging of your learners. You may already have a talent for steering a learner to achieve new understanding or develop a previously unmastered skill. However, if you are to become a consistently effective teacher, developing engaging lessons on a daily basis and commanding the attention of all around you, you will need to develop a clear understanding about what you do that works well. You also need to appreciate that some things you might consider doing are unlikely to be successful, or deter you from making good professional progress. Thoughtful reflection can help you to recognize more swiftly *what is* effective practice and *what are* the key characteristics of a successful teacher.

When starting out on a teaching experience or practice, you may feel that there are some skills you already have, but recognize that others need development. You may, for example, need to think about how to address a group, or how far to go in your explanation of fractions, or even what to say to learners to help them see how they are progressing. Your academic and professional learning around issues such as these will be aided by your previous experiences, a rapid review of learners' progress during the lesson and focused contemplation after episodes of teaching. The following quotation indicates how a beginning teacher realizes, like many others:

> 66 It will be ... difficult in the classroom to take control and deal with be-
> havioural problems but hopefully I will learn from any mistakes I may make
> in the first instances and also learn from other qualified teachers as to how
> best to control bad behaviour.
> *(Patricia, one-year PGCE student, at beginning of course)* 99

Behaviour management is almost always a concern for the beginning teacher. Others include:

- knowing how to talk at an appropriate level in class;
- ensuring that lessons are both successful *and* enjoyable;
- adhering to government and accreditation expectations;
- being *liked* by learners!

To succeed in all these aspects as well as many others (for example, **formative assessment**, marking books, creating succinct plenaries) requires careful reflection about the process, delivery and development of your teaching. To teach successfully, with learners who appear to be increasingly challenging, requires the nurturing, adaptation and refinement of a range of academic understandings and a plethora of more practical professional skills.

This extract from Martyn's reflections early in his teaching practice indicates how there are many things to reflect upon when learning how to teach:

> 66 One worry I had was that they wouldn't know the answers to my questions and I would be stood at the front in a silent room! However, they were very responsive and it made the experience much more enjoyable . . . . . after the lesson . . . . my mentor pointed out that I was not to lower my voice when speaking to an individual as it prevents the rest of the class from hearing the answer. I also sometimes felt myself stumbling when talking to the whole class . . . . . . so I need to be clearer in my explanations. The second starter [beginning lesson activity] was with the same group later on in the day and I felt much more confident about delivering it after their earlier response. The pupils once again responded well, enjoyed it and they even applauded me once I had finished! I was so engrossed in ensuring my presentation was correctly set up that I forgot to stand at the front of the classroom. I feel I would have gained more authority if I had done this from the start of the lesson. The pupils became quite excitable and started shouting out the answers during the activity and although I asked them to put up their hands, some continued to shout their suggestions. From this experience, I know that I need to use management strategies to control the class, for example, not responding positively to those who were shouting out.
>
> *(Martyn, one-year maths PGCE, early in the course)* 99

Martyn's reflections indicate that he has a lot to think about, all at once! It is of course not possible to master all teaching skills at the same time, and knowing exactly what to focus on can be tricky. This chapter introduces different views of reflection that are important for beginning teachers and helps you to consider *what* the focus of reflection might be, and *how* reflection at different points can be useful. At its simplest, reflection is consciously 'looking back' at your actions and being able to make some kind of evaluation of whether your teaching was successful or not. More complex, analytical and critical reflection is that which not only recognizes what you have done, but also *how* a particular course of action (or series of actions) shaped outcomes for your learners. Most beginning teachers, like Martyn above, are able to describe what has happened in their classroom. What they find much more challenging is a level of critical reflection that enables them to identify and explain:

- what contributed to effective learning;
- what was detrimental to effective learning;
- what they could do to improve learning.

Many trainees find thinking about how to improve their practice quite a trial, because, in their early observations it is not easy to recognize what effective teachers do to control their class and make learning an engaging and enjoyable experience. It is a little like watching someone drive when you are first learning; should you observe the gear change, the clutch control or the brake pedal movement? It all looks easy, but when you try to do it there is so much to think about all at once. So it is with teaching; teasing out what is essential is not always obvious.

The nature of the reflective teacher

Most views of reflection emanate from the work of American philosopher, John Dewey (1910), who is often credited with being the originator of reflective practice. Being reflective requires active consideration about actions and their consequences. As a beginning **teacher** you might think that you must punish children who talk when you are giving out instructions. However, if you do not contemplate the implications of keeping the whole class in over a break because the interruption involved only one loud student, you will not learn from your experience quickly. Dewey (1910) recognized that the 'thinking teacher' requires three important attributes to be reflective; 'open-mindedness' to new ideas and thoughts; 'wholeheartedness' to seek out fresh approaches and fully engage with them; and 'responsibility' to be aware of the consequences of one's own actions. So, in his view, reflections to help develop these characteristics are essential to becoming a successful teacher. Patrick demonstrates the first of these characteristics:

> 66 By keeping an open mind on a given situation, I allow myself to view a problem from more than one angle . . . . . . I am prepared to try out new ideas if I believe them to be valid and am more than willing to accept feedback on the impact my approach has on an audience whether it be good or bad.
>
> *(Patrick, one-year PGCE student, at beginning of course)* 99

Beginning teachers often show a desire to be 'open minded' and are full of enthusiasm to try out new ideas. However early in their training they need to be open to suggestions about how to master the basics of teaching. From there they can move on to develop successful new approaches. This requires researching new materials or resources, discussing ideas with more experienced professionals and watching other expert teachers in action, observing what they do that is successful.

How can you ensure that activities are exciting, or that your freshly adapted resources are a triumph? This requires thinking beforehand about how best to organize their use and, afterwards, about how well they worked from both your learners' and your own point of view. This is Dewey's 'whole-heartedness'. To be a thinking teacher requires wholehearted immersion in the business of education. You will be

> The 'thinking teacher' requires three important attributes to be reflective:
> 'open-mindedness' to new ideas and thoughts, 'whole heartedness' and 'responsibility'.

constantly seeking out techniques and materials that will appeal to your learners, and thinking about tasks that will engage and motivate them. This exemplifies an attentive and conscientious approach to preparing to educate. The third of Dewey's characteristics, responsibility, demands reflection on experience. Clara, below, is taking responsibility for what happened in her classroom:

> 66 In the third week of my placement I felt confident enough to lead the whole class in a starter activity I had designed and constructed. I gave out instructions to the class and they started the activity. I was feeling very nervous about the opinion of my mentor. Whilst I was not being formally observed, I felt it important to set a good impression as he was the head of department. After about two minutes I realized that both halves of the class had been given the same set of equipment, and they should have been comparing each others' findings! How naive of me not to check the equipment before giving it to the pupils! Luckily, the activity still worked well and even more luckily, the head of department had not realized there was ever a problem. I will now be triple checking everything before it goes into the pupils' hands!
>
> *(Clara, one-year science PGCE student, three weeks into first teaching placement)* 99

Why reflect?

Extending Dewey's view of the thoughtful teacher is about considering the consequences of one's actions. Reflection is an important tool in helping you to do this, as it enables you to take a critical look back at what you did. Dewey identified two categories of teacher behaviour:

- routine action
- reflective action

To the untrained eye, schools can look as if they run like clockwork. This is not chance, but based on the accumulative effect of routine actions, for example, the way learners respond to the teacher during registration when their names are called out, the way they are expected to line up outside a classroom door, or to respond to question/answer sessions in class. As a beginning teacher you need to 'fit in' with existing routines and develop some of your own, such as the fixed stare indicating 'watch what you are doing!' or standing at the front of the class with arms folded conveying 'I am waiting for silence' or exaggerating starting a timer indicates 'I am now timing to see how long it takes you to be quiet and will waste that much of your time at the end of the lesson'. You may well pick these up from observing experienced teachers and reflecting on the triumphant consequences of their actions and consciously plan to adopt their routines. Like driving a car, once these routines are established, they require little conscious thought. Dewey (1910) contrasts these kinds of 'routine action' (doing what is guided by factors such as tradition, habit, authority and institutional expectations) with 'reflective action' (doing made up of changed actions informed by self-appraisal). As a beginning teacher you cannot take routine action for granted.

> Professional artistry is the application of 'intelligent action', experimenting in the way you respond to situations through 'reflection-in-action' and 'reflection-on-action'.

Even apparently simple tasks can go wrong unless you think through what they mean and why they exist. For you, 'routine action' will develop only from 'reflective action' as you seek constantly to improve ways of working.

Developing Dewey's ideas further, Schön (1983, 1987) highlights how professionals often face situations that are unique, but apply their knowledge and previous experiences to inform how they act. He defines this active, somewhat experimental process as **professional artistry.** He suggests that practitioners who respond or act in such a professional, competent way in uncertain situations are 'knowing-in-action' (1987: 25) and can reveal different sorts of knowledge that emerge through their 'intelligent action' (1987: 25). In your teaching practice, for example, you might have given the learners a writing task, but while you are setting up the technology to use a video clip to stimulate discussion, you notice the increase in quiet whispering. You know that if the noise reaches a certain level the discussion will not go well. To maintain quiet control of the group you could do with extending the task or re-engaging the quick learners in a subsequent activity. Anticipating this need, being prepared for it and responding to it is great teaching artistry. Another time, towards the end of the lesson, the tasks have been completed and there are still 10 minutes before the bell. Professional artistry would facilitate the engagement of the learners to reflect on the lesson, summarize what they have learned; you as the teacher pull it all together, connect the outcomes to the learning objectives and **success criteria**, and still have them thinking about what they have learned as they leave the room. So where does this 'professional artistry' come from?

Dewey suggested that professionals might experiment in the way they respond to situations by using both 'reflection-in-action' and 'reflection-on-action'. The former involves thinking about action while actually doing it, and may result in change during the teaching process. Schön (1983) argues that this could be a form of action research (discussed further in Chapter 14), changing or adapting your practice to deal with a particular demand or situation. He indicates that this kind of practice is freed from established theory and able to inform the personal theory that you might construct from your experience. As a beginning teacher you will think about what you are doing during the lesson, and think back to what happened after the lesson. However you will also benefit from contemplating what could happen in lessons and how you will prepare for learning before delivering a lesson. This we could call reflection-before-action. Pollard (2008) sees reflection that informs the development of teaching as a cyclical process that should be scaffolded by various frameworks (discussed in Chapter 9) and mediated through collaboration and discussion with colleagues. He extends these ideas by emphasizing the rigorous nature of reflective teaching, moving beyond 'common sense' to gather evidence, research literature and obtain critiques from colleagues. The monitoring, evaluating and revising of one's own practice should therefore arise through evidence-based enquiry, a premise that informs the structure of many trainee development programmes. Seven key characteristics of reflective practice (adapted from Pollard 2008: 14) include:

1 having an active focus on the aims and consequences of your teaching;
2 taking a cyclical approach to regularly monitoring, evaluating and revisiting your practice;
3 using evidence to make judgments about success and how to progress;
4 retaining open-mindedness, responsibility and wholeheartedness;
5 basing developing pedagogy on insights from research as well as judgments from evaluating own practice;
6 engaging with colleagues through collaboration and dialogue to improve professional learning and personal fulfillment;
7 redeveloping practice by creatively integrating external frameworks and models of practice.

The aim of reflective practice is thus to support a shift from routine actions rooted in commonsense thinking to reflective action emerging from professional thinking (Pollard 2008: 26) drawing from external evidence-based sources. All seven key points are addressed throughout the chapters in this book.

Reflective task 1.1

A number of different views have been briefly outlined above. Think about any recent experience you have had teaching or instructing someone to do something new (helping them to learn a new sporting skill or using a different technique on a computer):

1 Did you think through how to help before doing anything, or pause mid-action, or mull over later how you were explaining, demonstrating or encouraging the learner?
2 Could you align this contemplation to reflection-before-action; reflection-in-action; reflection-on-action?
3 If you were to do this again would you do it the same or differently next time? How? Why?

What should you be reflective about?

There are many different things to consider and think about when you are developing as a teacher. Figure 1.1 suggests how many different facets of a teacher's work can shape and influence their development. This model (developed from Shulman's 1987 and 1998 work and Higgins and Leat 2001) indicates the various dimensions that beginning teachers should pay attention to. It could be very useful to consider each of these features as part of the toolkit that arms you with helpful tactics, strategies, frameworks and general guidance about what to pay attention to on your reflective journey to becoming an effective teacher. You could view them as key components of the legend on the road map to becoming a qualified teacher.

Reflecting on subject knowledge

This is a key prerequisite for teaching. You need to know and understand the subject content that you are going to teach. If you do not 'know your stuff' you will not have a clear idea about what your students should learn. Before teaching any lesson, it is important that you understand the substantive or important subject knowledge in your area of curriculum. You need to know the content as well as how it is constructed. For example, in science there are three main subject areas: biology, chemistry and physics, but there is also an underpinning view that 'how science works' (the nature and historical development in science) should be nurtured through the three different disciplines. In MFL you need to be able to

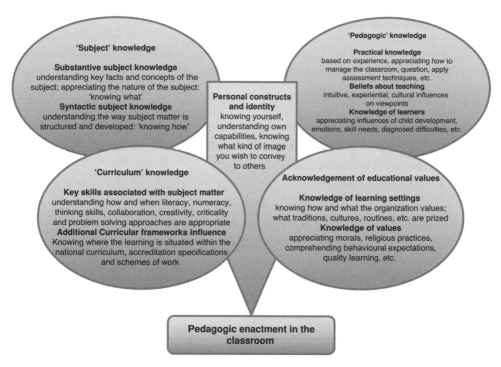

Figure 1.1 Simple schematic adaptation of Shulman's model of teacher development
Source: Shulman 1987, 1998; Higgins and Leat 2001; McGregor 2007

understand, and communicate accurately in, the target language, but you must also understand how the language works (what the grammatical patterns are) in order to prepare your pupils to become independent learners.

Thus subject knowledge is about knowing the key facts and appreciating and understanding how they are connected together; this could be summarized as 'knowing what'. As a developing educator you should also recognize how the subject matter should be organized, for example if you are a PE teacher you will recognize that you cannot teach children how to play rugby or netball if they have not yet learned the basic skills of passing the ball. There is a need to pay attention to, and develop competency in, one area before progressing to the next. This is an example of syntactic subject knowledge, understanding the way that subject matter can be organized and developed. This could be referred to as 'knowing how'. Before you begin teaching it is important that you reflect on the extent to which your understanding of 'knowing what' and 'knowing how' is appropriate. Most teacher preparation courses provide a knowledge and skills audit, so that would-be trainees can reflect on 'what do I know currently?' and 'what do I need to know before I start?'

Curriculum knowledge

As well as acquiring subject knowledge, learners also develop other skills and understanding related to the subject. It is important for you to see how, for example, literacy, numeracy, thinking skills, collaborative skills, creativity, criticality and problem-solving approaches fit into subject teaching. Skills and knowledge are integral to any subject area. In history, for example, students might be required to analyse key factors influencing the development of World War Two; or they might need to synthesize arguments about the contrasting nature of Buddhism and Judaism in religious education (RE). In art they may need to generate alternative presentations of a slogan, or abstract interpretations of an object. Such skills are not confined to older learners; in mathematics even young children learn to develop different ways of solving a problem, or in English they might need to report the same event from two contrasting viewpoints. It is important to recognize how skills may be key to the learning of substantive or syntactic subject knowledge. This could be thought of as 'knowing-what-else'. Curriculum knowledge is also about knowing how and where the subject fits in to the whole curriculum and how it is assessed and accredited at different stages of education.

Pedagogic knowledge

Pedagogic knowledge, or knowing how to teach, is multi-faceted:

- *Practical teaching knowledge* is used to ensure effective learning through the application of practical strategies that include classroom and behaviour management, organization, questioning techniques and formative assessment techniques.
- *Beliefs about teaching* (intuitive and experiential understandings of *what works*) may also influence your thinking and practice. Perhaps you think that mixed ability is good when a lesson is focused on skill development, such as team building in PE, and **setting** is appropriate to have all students learning together in a high ability MFL class.
- *Understanding of learners* and their unique capabilities (appreciating influences of child development, emotions, skill needs, diagnosed difficulties, talents or gifts) may influence how you design the learning tasks or organize the classroom.

This could be viewed as 'knowing what works'.

Acknowledgement of educational values

- *Influence of learning settings* can shape the way you teach. The school culture that includes the routines, practices and performances that have become an automatic and accepted way of working might constrain or develop your practice. Sixty-minute lessons, or regular field trips, or fixed commentary boxes on reports, or the ICT network support can shape how you perform as a professional.

- *Acknowledgement of an individual's values* (individual standards, morals, religious practices, home cultures) can influence how and what things happen. A headteacher's view of handwriting or wall displays, or the fact that you are working in a religious school, can influence what you say and how you conduct your lessons.

These could be described as 'knowing what else matters'.

Personal constructs and identity

It is important for you to understand that how you view yourself as a teacher (and a person) will have a bearing on the way you perform in the classroom. How you communicate with others (authoritatively or submissively, enthusiastically or very matter-of-fact) can convey your beliefs and how you think you should or could act in any professional situation. Equally you need to be aware of how you *wish* to be portrayed to your learners, colleagues and peers. This is discussed much further in Chapters 3 and 5 in particular.

Pedagogic enactment

This is about how you teach. The level of confidence that you have when you first enact your role as a teacher will be greatly influenced by:

- how well you are mentally prepared;
- how carefully you have thought about what you will have the students do and what you will say;
- how you will question your learners.

Your performance or enactment as a teacher will express your understandings (about your subject, its nature and sequence) and beliefs (about how your students learn) and the influences of the institution (daily routines, weekly practices and integral values). All these factors (and more) will impact on you as a teacher and how you present yourself. As you develop professionally and you recognize something is not working too well, you may find it useful to take each of the aspects described above and reflect on them in turn, identifying where you need to focus further to facilitate your development.

With the different facets of becoming a teacher in mind (Shulman's model, Figure 1.1) read Case Studies 1.1 to 1.3 and consider the questions that follow.

Case Study 1.1   Clive the mathematician

Clive is a quietly competent mathematician teaching a group of Year 9 students. In attempting to teach about angles and how to measure them, he had produced some brilliant animations (on an interactive whiteboard) of swirling right-angled objects, and engaging activities where the students measured the angles of objects around the classroom. His demeanour, however, was somewhat timid and he allowed the students to choose where they sat and who they (loudly) conversed with. He asked probing questions and his presentation of ideas about how angles could be measured and calculated was crystal clear. This trainee illustrated strengths in his understanding of mathematics as a subject and could communicate to willing listeners how to describe and measure different kinds of angles. The tasks he designed for his learners were engaging, differentiated and challenging to the more able. Yet the behaviour of his classes could erode his confidence and perhaps even deter him from pursuing teaching. His reflection needed to be carefully directed so that he could identify where his strengths lay and where he needed to focus the next steps in development.

Reflective task 1.2

1 What do you think are Clive's strengths and weaknesses?
2 What aspect of his development would you encourage him to reflect upon next?

Case Study 1.2   Mimi the scientist

Mimi is a highly qualified scientist who has previously worked in industry. She was teaching secondary students about diet. She was knowledgeable about the key aspects of a healthy diet and the essential contribution of vitamins and minerals to food we eat. She had devised an interesting practical activity involving testing foods for the nutrients they contained. She organized 'testing' stations around the laboratory so that the different groups would work at various, well spaced, points around the perimeter of the classroom. The apparatus was neatly laid out for collection by a representative from each group to avoid collisions in the haste to grab equipment and do some science. She provided a carefully explained set of instructions, demonstrated techniques and requested 'hands up' to check all understood the method to be used. Some students did not appear to understand exactly what to do so she also directed reflective questions at those who appeared not to be paying careful attention with a request to 'repeat what you have to do in the experiment'. She had a pre-prepared worksheet upon which the students could quickly record their results and draw their conclusions. Despite all these props for the practical, the lesson was not successful.

Reflective task 1.3

1 What aspects of Mimi's teaching or preparation may have led to an unsuccessful lesson?
2 What would you suggest she reflectively focus upon?

Case Study 1.3   Nigel the physical education trainee

Nigel was an athletic, energetic and enthusiastic trainee. He was teaching Year 8 how to throw the shot. Before the lesson he laid out markers for the students to use as launching points and he impaled javelins at either end of the throwing area, and knotted a tape from one to the other, to denote the height the shot should reach. His learning objectives were shared with the class through a bulleted list on a portable whiteboard. At the start of the lesson he asked the students about the success criteria for throwing the shot, ensuring safety and helping a peer improve their performance. He had the students working in pairs, alternately operating as athlete and coach. They took it in turns to practise a throw and make peer observations to suggest to each other how their performance was good and also how it could be enhanced. Their initial throws were carried out on their knees to ensure they understood the importance of 'clean palm', 'dirty neck', 'high elbow' and 'none putting arm as guide for direction of throw' before they could progress to a full standing throw. At the end of the hour lesson each student had improved in their techniques in putting the shot.

Reflective task 1.4

1 What strengths did this trainee clearly show?
2 What should Nigel focus on to improve his lesson?

Deepening your reflection so that it becomes more meaningful

Reflection-on-action

This is probably the most straightforward kind of reflection. It involves considering an experience and thinking about how to improve it next time. On a long car journey, for example, you may have opted for the most direct route, but it takes twice as long as the more circuitous motorway. Reflection-on-action will inform the route you take next time. If you wish for a shorter time in the car the motorway is better. However, if the cost of fuel is paramount the direct route may be more desirable. Similarly with teaching, after reflecting on an experience with a class you may make decisions about how to change things next time. This is Fiona's reflection after teaching her third lesson:

> " At the end of the lesson I felt like I could write an entire essay just on what I had learnt from that hour! These are some of the most salient points:
>
> 1 Never, ever give out equipment until you want them to do something with it! Especially true for a lower ability set, the cups I gave out for the activity were too much of a distraction!
> 2 Always double check who in your class will struggle with which tasks. I gave out role play cards and was very embarrassed to learn I had given a complicated role to a pupil who could not read! I was also upset to realize I had asked the newest member of the class to hand out the books; this pupil was also Polish and did not speak much English. These were particularly disappointing things to do as I had spent lots of time researching the needs of my classes in extensive detail, but I now know that class so much better.
> 3 I need to work on the tone and pitch of my voice. While the teacher fed back that I varied my voice well, it did become high and squeaky sometimes and my nerves probably came across to the pupils.
> 4 Always wait for silence. I insisted on it several times and tried my best to wait for silence but I am aware I did not always wait for absolute silence before progressing. In hindsight, this was probably because I was aware of the timing of the lesson and that it had taken longer than I anticipated getting the initial part of the lesson started. I appreciate that it is an important part of my classroom management to follow through with what I say so I will definitely be practising that from my first lesson back after half term.
> 5 Praise. I was pleased with my questioning technique and felt as though the pupils were confident in answering my questions; however I did not thank them for their answers nor praise them when they were correct. Again, I am sure this was because of my awareness of timing and I will ensure from now on that I include the word PRAISE on my lesson plan so that I am reminded when I look at it to use some more 'well dones'.
>
> *(Fiona, one-year PGCE trainee, three lessons after start of teaching)* "

Reflective task 1.5

Having read Fiona's reflections on her lesson, can you identify where she needs to focus next?

The following is a key reflection from Greta, again three weeks into her teaching practice on a one-year PGCE course:

> 66 I recently read that pupils only spend 12% of their time in lessons (Capel et al. 2009) which surprised me and made me realize how important it is to make use of every moment in a lesson to maximize learning. Teacher assessment of learning is crucial and pupils are always being reminded of their target grades, how to improve and are pushed to achieve their highest potential. I have observed lots of lessons where teachers use formative assessment to monitor the progress of their class. One strategy I liked was the use of mini-whiteboards on which pupils write down their answers and hold them up – which I intend to use in some of my lessons.
>
> *(Greta, four weeks into her PGCE teaching experience)* 99

Reflective task 1.6

1 What else are you likely to learn by watching other teachers?
2 How is the reflection of their actions different to reflection on your own actions?

These are Mark's reflections after watching two different teachers, one in English and the other in science:

> 66 A teacher in English has shown me how to structure an instruction, repeat it and then explain it in another way. This is so he can use a whole 'catch all' approach to get his class going on what to do next. Another member of staff always uses pupil language to describe tasks to be done like 'add a splash of iodine to the food mixture' or 'this is a mortar and pestle – also known as a grinder'.
>
> *(Mark, one-year PGCE science, second week in classroom)* 99

Reflective task 1.7

1 What do you think are the benefits of watching other more experienced teachers teach at the beginning of your practice?
2 Can you identify which features of teaching Mark is most focused on early in his development?
3 How do you anticipate these might change as he becomes more experienced?

Reflection-in-action

This type of reflection is a little more sophisticated and will require more on-the-spot responsive thinking. On a car journey the road ahead is blocked because of an accident, but you have to reach your destination in five minutes' time. You must make an in-the-moment decision about whether to wait or try an alternative road. You need experience of the local road network to make an informed judgment. Similarly, in the classroom, some experience is needed to flexibly review an in-the-moment happening to decide if a different course of action is appropriate. This is Saheed's view of reflection-in-action:

> As someone who was expecting to find reflection difficult, I am pleasantly surprised by how much I am learning from it. I am now gaining in confidence about reflecting-in-action; something I had to do when my starter activity was going wrong and I needed to re-issue instructions to the class. Reflection-on-action, of which I have done a great deal, has helped me analyse the lessons as I taught them. This made me think about them all the way through. I am now beginning to understand why becoming a reflective practitioner will be so useful as a teacher, I will constantly be evolving in my teaching style and learning from every single lesson I teach.
> *(Saheed, one-year PGCE, third week in placement)*

Reflective task 1.8

1 To what extent is reflection serving to help you currently?
2 How do you see it supporting your professional development in the future?
3 Can all the features in Shulman's model be addressed through reflection-in-action?

Reflecting-before-action

Using reflection to inform planning is a useful strategy for considering the alternative ways you could prepare and teach a lesson, just as preparing for a long car journey, preparatory information can be provided by looking at a map, exploring alternative routes via the internet, asking other drivers which way they would go, or speaking to advisors from an automobile association. However, the planning and decision making about when to fill up with fuel, when and where to stop for a break and how much food and drink you should carry is ultimately your decision as the driver of the car. Just like the planning for a lesson, you can invest more or less time in the preparation of a car journey. Taking time to consider possible outcomes based on certain actions can be time well spent. A long car journey that is undertaken during severe weather conditions will require more in-depth thought to thoroughly prepare for anticipated eventualities. Similarly dealing with a challenging class can feel like entering a storm, and needs careful thinking through. Preparation requires looking back on experiences to project forward and plan as carefully as possible. Consider this comment from Pritpal:

> 66 Since I began observing in an active school many things have changed in my understanding, chiefly among which is that I now have an understanding of what goes on in a school on a day-to-day basis. Previously, aside from the teaching and monitoring, the life and work of a teacher was a mystery to me. I had no idea what they did between classes and how much prep they did before a lesson, thinking that many would just make it up on the fly. Some do, but that's because they have been teaching a while. You sing the songs for long enough you can forget the song sheet. It would also seem that the professional role seems to step beyond that of instructor. A teacher seems to be simultaneously an instructor, guide, carer, confidante and informer all in one.
>
> *(Pritpal, PGCE trainee, three weeks into his first placement)* 99

Reflective task 1.9

1 How does Pritpal apply reflection-on-action?
2 Which features of Shulman's model of development do you think are more likely to be developed by reflection-on-action?
3 How does Pritpal's view connect with other theorists about reflection?

This is Paul's reflective view of teaching after a few weeks in school:

> ❝ I have come to realize during my brief time teaching that shouting and aggressive language is something that is definitely required but should be used sparingly. Punishments and disciplining are not required to be at high decibels and with a frown. For some pupils the drama, commotion and attention are exactly the response that they hoped to provoke. For others such a response may be so upsetting that they are unable to concentrate on their work through embarrassment, anger or disappointment. ❞

He later adds:

> ❝ The fact remains that there is no need to have a negative emotional response to a child's behaviour. Although it is difficult not to feel aggravated by insolent behaviour, keeping calm is the exact same self-control you as a teacher expect from your pupils when asking for silence and they want to chat. It is for this reason that disciplining children through a fair and consistent behaviour policy, in a calm and pleasant manner, without causing a scene or drawing whole-class attention to the pupil concerned, is the most effective method to establish mutual respect from all involved.
> *(Paul, one-year PGCE, after two weeks in placement)* ❞

Reflective task 1.10

1 What kinds of reflection is Paul bringing to bear here?
2 How far can you judge which features of the Shulman model he is addressing?

Summary

This chapter has introduced some key ideas about reflection that are taken further in many subsequent chapters. The central thread of discussion here is about how reflection can inform the development of practice. Well-known theorists and their associated ideas have been introduced. Dewey's (1910) view of routine actions and reflective actions has been considered and contrasted with Schön's view (1983) of reflection as a continuous process supporting development of professional practice. His view of reflection-in-action (while doing something) and reflection-on-action (after doing something) are applied to beginning teachers' situations. Shulman's (1987) distinct multi-faceted perspective on the nature of teacher development is utilized to help learning teachers to focus their attention in different directions and consider where progression might be best steered. Pollard (2002) builds on the views of these eminent scholars and considers further the more dynamic nature of reflection-in-action, to explore how the dilemmas and challenges beginning teachers face influence effectiveness in the classroom. Readers have been invited to reflect on the differing nature of the key theorists and their views' of reflection.

Conclusion

As you progress through other chapters in this book, or dip into them, you will find frequent references to 'pedagogic', 'subject' and 'curriculum' knowledge and to 'personal constructs' or 'teacher identity'. This chapter serves as an introduction to these concepts so that as they recur in your reflections you will feel increasingly comfortable with them.

Key learning points

- There is a range of views about reflection.
- Reflection can clearly inform and support development of practice.
- Reflection-on-practice can include consideration of established routines and practices and how these might be improved or changed as needs demand.
- Reflection-in-practice can be conceived as action research.
- Reflection can arise before practice.
- Different perspectives of reflection can be woven together to suggest how the pedagogic craft of praxis (the application of theory to inform practice) of beginning teachers can be supported so that their actions are informed through reflective reasoning.
- It is vital to understand that reflection is a strategy for learning about teaching.
- It is important to appreciate how reflection can focus on different aspects of teacher development.
- Beginning teachers need to consider how prominent views of reflection (Dewey, Schön, Shulman and Pollard) can illuminate different aspects of their developing practice.

CHAPTER 2

How do you become a reflective professional?

Lorraine Thomas and Gerald Griggs

Every day you may make progress. Every step may be fruitful. Yet there will stretch out before you an ever-lengthening, ever-ascending, ever-improving path. You know you will never get to the end of the journey. But this, far from discouraging, only adds to the joy and glory of the climb.

Winston Churchill

Introduction

You will already be aware, from Chapter 1, of the journey you are undertaking both as a beginning teacher and a beginning **reflective practitioner**, and you have been introduced to what it means to 'reflect', what to reflect on, and how to do it. This chapter begins with a brief overview of the reflective practice movement against the background of accountability in education. In order to see your role as a beginning teacher in the wider context of your teaching career, you need to have some understanding of the socio-political landscape into which you are entering. This is because there may be tensions between what you would *like* to do in the classroom and what you are *required* to do. You will also gain insight into some of the issues being faced by the colleagues in school who will support, coach and mentor you through your professional development. It then introduces the professional standards that will lie at the heart of your training and career development. With a specific focus on the core strands of learning to teach, this chapter will guide you through ways of using reflective strategies so that you do not fall into the trap of seeing reflection merely as a coping tool (What can I do to survive in this situation? How do I get them through this test?). Important as these questions might seem, reflection must also be a tool for developing your teaching to ensure that your pupils learn and thrive under your guidance, developing a passion for learning and the capacity to become independent learners. This chapter will draw on the narratives of some trainee teachers going through the process of developing more creative, pupil-centred approaches to their teaching. It will also focus on assessment for learning, providing you with examples of critical reflection that enhance classroom practice and, ultimately, your career development. You will be offered opportunities to reflect on these in different ways depending on your current stage of development. This first extract, from Sara, indicates *how* she wishes to teach, but cannot.

> ❝ I so wanted to get them excited by the language, by the rich vocabulary they could be using. 'Clothes' is just not the most exciting topic for 16-year-olds, is it? So I thought, if I took pages from the La Redoute catalogue, and got them to find the French for 'strappy top' and 'knee-high boots', etc. They could learn a lot that was really relevant and we could have some fun. My learning objective was that pupils would be able to talk about what they would wear to a party, or to a pop festival. But my mentor just said: 'No, none of that is in the GCSE defined content. All they need to do is describe what they are wearing – skirt, trousers, shoes and so on. They need to practise that a lot to get the best marks they can in the oral.' I knew the lesson would be really boring and it was.
>
> *(Sara, PGCE MFL trainee, in her final teaching practice, with a Year 11 class)* ❞

Reflective task 2.1   What drives our curriculum?

1 Can you relate to Sara's situation? Can you describe a similar experience?
2 What prompted the response from Sara's mentor?
3 How do you think Sara felt?
4 How do you think the pupils felt in being prepared to describe what they were wearing in French?
5 How do you think they would have responded?
6 What might have been their response to the lesson that Sara had planned?

It will be very surprising indeed if you get through the first two or three years of teaching without feeling the tension between the need to ensure that your pupils achieve well in national tests and public examinations and the desire to provide creative and exciting learning experiences. You will need to find a balance between that aspect of teaching that you associate with managing an externally imposed curriculum, national assessment regimes and learners' behaviour, often referred to as **technical rationality**, and that aspect of your teaching that you associate with managing your learners' ideas and imagination, and the infinite and unpredictable complexities of social interaction, often referred to as professional artistry. We begin with a brief outline of the origin of these tensions, and go on to explore how reflective practice can help you balance them as you develop your own teacher identity. Later chapters (notably 3, 5 and 7) develop this theme further.

Accountability, responsibility and professionalism: the growth of reflective practice

It is not an accident of fate that teaching professionals in places as far afield as Australia and New Zealand, North America and Europe have embraced the philosophy of reflective practice. In the latter part of the twentieth century, there was a marked shift in the balance of power in education. Until then, governments had on the whole left the decision making about education in the hands of the professionals. In the 1980s the old economic order changed; there was a sudden rise in oil prices, and the collapse of the traditional manufacturing base of many countries. The development of new technologies made it possible to relocate manufacturing to countries where labour costs were cheaper. These factors, plus the increasing deregulation of economies and financial markets, all contributed to undermining 'the power of Western governments to deliver prosperity, security and opportunity to their citizens within "walled" economies' (Mahony and Hextall 2000). As a result, governments and the public have become increasingly aware of the high cost of public sector services such as health and education, and there has been a universal demand for 'value for money' from these services, leading to the introduction of a range of strategies to measure the accountability of professionals. In education, including teacher education, these have variously included:

- the introduction of a national curriculum with programmes of study and expected attainment levels at key stages spelled out;
- measures of school effectiveness, such as national test results, public examination grades and truancy rates, published so that government, local authorities, school governors and parents can make judgements about the quality of education;
- more rigorous external inspections;
- a requirement for regular and frequent self-evaluation of educational institutions;
- **performance management** and performance-related pay for teachers;
- individual and organizational self-evaluation, target-setting and monitoring;
- national standards for initial teacher training (the **Q standards**);
- the promotion of teaching as a career, beginning with NQT induction and continuing with a requirement to meet lifelong professional standards and to undertake CPD;

- the promotion of the school, as opposed to the university, as the significant training environment for new teachers.

The above were encapsulated in the term 'new professionalism', which first appeared in policy documentation in the Green Paper *Teachers: Meeting the Challenge of Change*. The objective was to create a modernized teaching profession in which learners would be able to access a 'world-class education service' (DfEE 1998: 12).

Much controversy has surrounded these developments. Put simply, they have been seen by proponents of the school improvement movement (Fullan 1993; Hargreaves 1994) as a much-needed reform of a system not delivering 'value for money' and by others as interference from external agencies imposing a 'top-down' model of school improvement (Zeichner 1994). The pros and cons of school-based training have been well researched since the 1990s and much has been written to support teachers in their role as mentors to trainee teachers. In a review of the international literature on mentoring beginning teachers, Hobson et al. (2009a) have identified some of the benefits of mentoring for trainee teachers as:

- reduced feelings of isolation;
- increased confidence and self-esteem;
- professional growth;
- improved self-reflection and problem-solving capacities.

However, the fact remains that for some beginning teachers these advantages are not fully realized. Examples of this include: insufficient challenge to trainee teachers (Hobson et al. 2009a), with encouragement to engage in 'low risk' activities (Malderez and Wedell 2007); 'trial and error' approaches (Edwards 1997) with insufficient emphasis on **pedagogy** (Lee Chi-ken and Feng 2007); and lack of social and psychological support that can contribute to withdrawal (Hobson et al. 2009b). Hobson et al. (2009a: 214) report that increased and unmanageable workloads make it difficult for mentors to accommodate their trainees' needs. Reflective practice can help the beginning teacher overcome some of these difficulties (see in particular Chapter 5).

In more general terms, the reflective practice movement can be viewed as being favoured by those who do not wish to see the 'professional artistry' of teaching consumed by more **instrumentalist** interpretations of education: 'on the surface this international movement . . . that has developed under the banner of reflection can be seen as a reaction against a view of teachers as technicians who merely carry out what others, removed from the classroom, want them to do' (Zeichner 1994: 10). Sara's reflections on her mentor's rejection of her lesson plan illustrate the tensions that can exist in such a climate; the mentor feels accountable to her learners, their parents, the school and possibly even the government, and sees her responsibility as getting the best examination results possible. Sara sees her responsibility in terms of providing a lively, relevant and engaging learning experience for her pupils. Hers is not an isolated problem. Brindley and Riga (2009) found that when trainees came to apply the 'theory' learned in university to practice in school, they came up against a number of tensions, one of which is like Sara's: 'the dilemmas trainees face is in seeking to unite two quite different and sometimes apparently opposing declared purposes for assessment – support for effective learning and judgement of student standards' (Brindley and Riga 2009: 73). Initiatives to move away from what Hall and Thomson (2005: 8) have called the 'sterility and joylessness of the standards curriculum' provide the possibility for more **creative approaches** to learning and teaching (see Chapter 8), although Hall and Thomson (2005: 18) fear that 'while the cultural turn nods in the direction of these improvements, of personalised learning and broader curricula, the vision . . . . is still likely to be focused on teachers' and pupils' conformity to a centrally determined agenda'.

Reflective task 2.2   Balancing accountability with creativity

1 Do you think that the positions of Sara and her mentor are irreconcilable?
2 To what extent do you think it is possible to deliver accountability (good test and examination outcomes for learners) and creative, engaging lessons that engender a passion for learning?

Effective teacher behaviours embodied in standards

A contributory factor to teachers having to face public scrutiny is the fact that, apart from the obvious need for subject knowledge and some basics in school procedures, what teachers know and what they do remains a mystery to the untrained eye. Zeichner (1994: 10) refers to what he calls the 'invisibility' of teacher knowledge, suggesting that because little account is taken of the expertise that exists within the teaching profession, it becomes easy to impose professional development externally. Despite, or perhaps because of, having been to school, the public has little conception of the skills

As the current model of teacher development relies heavily on mentoring and coaching by fellow practitioners, it is vital that teachers can articulate the myriad skills they have, communicating them to others, and not simply taking them for granted.

and knowledge of the teacher. For one thing, the relative shortness of the school day, and even the school year, belies the long working hours that are invested in planning, assessment and evaluation that lie beneath the surface of an effective lesson. For another, good teaching looks easy! Only the tip of the iceberg is visible to the pupils engaged in the lesson. Perhaps this is how it should be; the point is for learners to enjoy their classroom experiences and not feel burdened by how many hours their teacher spent preparing their lessons. However, as the current model of teacher development relies heavily on mentoring and coaching by fellow practitioners, it is vital that teachers can articulate the myriad skills they have, communicating them to others, and not simply taking them for granted. One way of doing this is through reflective practice, as it recognizes 'the wealth of expertise that resides in the practices of good teachers' (Zeichner 1994: 10). Ironically, increased accountability has also led to greater visibility in the form of the professional standards (TDA 2007). These put in the public domain a description of the characteristics and behaviours of effective teachers at key stages (described in Figure 2.1) of their career development, and teachers must provide evidence of having met them. At present in England there are five progressive levels of standards.

The standards comprise three common core strands at each of these five levels: professional attributes, professional knowledge and understanding and professional skills (see Table 2.1). A deep understanding of these core strands, and the specific standards that relate to your stage of career progression, is essential as you progress in your career. While the model ties performance management in with pay, and is therefore linked to accountability, the standards clearly relate to principled, committed and effective teaching practice.

Reflective task 2.3   Using Shulman's model with the teaching standards

1 Look again at McGregor's adaptation of Shulman's model of teacher development (Chapter 1, Figure 1). Study the **Q** or **C standards** towards which you are currently working. Can you place the standards into one or more of the headings: subject knowledge; personal development; pedagogic knowledge; curriculum knowledge; acknowledgement of educational values?
2 Which fit easily? Where is there overlap? Why do you think this is?
3 Are there any standards that are not easy to place in Shulman's model? Why is this?
4 Which standards lend themselves to 'professional artistry' and which are more **technicist** in nature?
5 Do you see the model as relevant to a teacher's initial training, early career, or whole professional life? Explain your reasons.

Primary and secondary teacher standards

- Professional attributes
- Professional knowledge and understanding
- Professional skills

Trainees/pre-service teachers

Qualified Teacher Status (Q) Standards
Standards to be met by the end of the initial training period.

Induction year and beyond

Core (C) Standards
Teachers should meet the core standards (C) at the end of the induction period and continue to meet them throughout their teaching career. They include consolidation in new contexts and supporting the professional development of others, for example through collaboration, mentoring and coaching.

Teachers on the upper pay scale

Post-Threshold (P) Standards
Teachers should continue to meet the C standards and in addition meet the P standards, making a distinctive contribution to raising standards by acting as an effective role model for teaching and learning.

Excellent teachers

Excellent (E) Standards
Teachers should continue to meet the C and P standards and in addition meet the E standards by taking a leading role in raising standards through support for the professional development of others. This means having extensive and deep knowledge and understanding of subject knowledge and pedagogy, drawn from classroom-based research, reading and reflection.

Advanced Skills teachers

Advanced (A) Standards
Teachers should continue to meet the C, P and E standards and in addition meet the A standards by demonstrating models of excellent, innovative teaching and engaging in professional development activities across a range of workplaces, drawing on the experience gained elsewhere to improve their own practice and that of others in school.

Figure 2.1   Professional standards for teachers (TDA 2007)

Table 2.1 The core strands of the professional standards

Core strand	Key features
Professional attributes	High expectations of self, colleagues and learners; commitment to the development and well-being of all learners; positive attitudes, values and behaviour; commitment to improving practice through reflection, evaluation, innovation and collaboration with others; being open to the value of coaching and mentoring.
Professional knowledge and understanding	Continuing development of subject and pedagogic knowledge in order to be an effective classroom practitioner meeting the requirements of teachers' statutory frameworks.
Professional skills	Collaborative working practices; clear frameworks for classroom discipline; safe and purposeful learning environments; clear frameworks for teaching, learning and assessment through planning; engagement of learners of all abilities so that they make appropriate progress; innovative practices in teaching and assessment, including appropriate use of ICT and e-learning and out of school contexts.

It is worth pointing out here, if indeed you need to be reminded, that the current model is not always a comfortable one. As one of our mentors commented recently: 'there is nowhere to hide in this profession!' Dymoke and Harrison (2008: 221) have pointed out that performance management "will mean that teachers are subject to ongoing scrutiny throughout much of their professional lives".

Reflective task 2.4   How do you feel about being a 'new professional'?

Reflect on the questions in Table 2.2, selecting those appropriate to your current stage of development.

Table 2.2 Being a 'new professional'

If you are beginning your teacher training	If you are at least half way through your teacher training	If you are a newly or recently qualified teacher
How do you feel about being subject to 'ongoing scrutiny' during your career? What form do you think this will take during your initial training? What do you need to know and do in order to prepare yourself for providing evidence of meeting the standards?	What does it feel like to be monitored, assessed and scrutinized? To what extent do you feel in control of the evidence that is supporting your progression towards the Q standards and what contributes to this? Which standards seem hardest to evidence? Why?	In what ways has the 'scrutiny' of your practice changed since you were awarded QTS? How do you feel about this? What are the key differences between the way you evidence the C standards and how you evidenced the Q standards? Which standards are currently the most challenging, and why?

So what should you reflect about?

Although not explicit in the wording of the standards, reflective practice is central to many of them. We recommend that, as you reflect, you keep in mind the professional standards to which you are working in order to give meaning and focus to your thoughts. Over 20 years ago Valli (in Calderhead and Gates 1993: 9) warned of the dangers of reflection for its own sake, commenting that 'racial tension as a school issue can become no more or less worthy of reflection than field trips or homework assignments'. Moon (1999: 57) laments the fact that insufficient attention is paid to the relationship between reflective practice and classroom learning. Bleach, writing directly to NQTs, (2000: 138–9) makes the important observation that:

> "The Standards should not be regarded as embodying benchmarks that you pass or fail like an MOT car test, they should lead you to look beyond 'competence,' in a technical sense, to aim for gradations of performance that

> *recognise the development of more sophisticated patterns of, and perspectives on, professional behaviour."*

In order to 'look *beyond* "competence"' you will need to analyse and interpret the standards to discover what really lies at the heart of each one. As you begin this process, it is worth noting that since the mid-1990s there have been significant shifts away from the technical rational approaches engendered by accountability regimes. The press for an evidence-based profession has led to many government-sponsored research and classroom-based inquiry initiatives (Foreman-Peck and Murray 2008), and the moves to a Masters level profession will require a deeper approach to understanding learning and teaching. The Q standards themselves, more than their precursors, embody key aspects of professional artistry across all the core strands. It is to the development of professional artistry that we now turn, using the core dimension of professional skills to examine ways in which beginning teachers have addressed their own dilemmas similar to that of Sara and used reflection to develop their skills 'beyond competence' in order to tackle key aspects of teaching and learning. See also Chapter 8, and the concept of 'beyond realism'.

From professional skills to professional artistry

Make no mistake; professional artistry, like the artistry required to play Mozart's violin concerto or paint the Mona Lisa, is not acquired overnight. Creative thinking and an open mind, not to mention risk taking, are required (see Chapter 7). Case Studies 2.1 and 2.2 draw from beginning teachers' reflections as they strive to apply what they have learned in theory to classroom practice. In applying these case studies to your own professional learning, you will need first to reflect on your current stage of development and ensure that you take a progressive approach to your own development. That is not to say that there is one smooth, linear path that we all follow in a uniform way, but there are widely accepted steps in the learning process that you should find helpful to consider.

Case Study 2.1 Learning and assessment: the dilemma of 'teaching to the test'.

Robert was a PGCE trainee in MFL on a final teaching practice that began in January and ended in May. During the final few weeks of the placement he was required to undertake a classroom-based enquiry with one focus class, on whether pupil-centred approaches to developing listening skills could improve the listening outcomes for pupils. Thus his work involved the application of his subject, curriculum and pedagogic knowledge to the planning and teaching of a sequence of lessons, and a critically reflective evaluation:

> ❝ From my own informal observations I noticed that the pupils were much more confident about tackling the end-of-unit listening test than they were in January; in short, they appeared to have a higher sense of 'self-efficacy' (Graham 2003) or a belief in their abilities to succeed. This might be because the pupils all experienced a degree of success in the listening activities prior to the assessment, which gave them more confidence to tackle the listening assessment in a positive manner; however, it may also be due to the fact that I was successful in creating a more relaxed classroom environment and in equipping my pupils with cognitive and meta-cognitive strategies to become more effective listeners. Over the course of the sequence of lessons, I also witnessed not only an improvement in learner self-efficacy but also a remarkable improvement in behaviour. The improvements that I saw in behaviour and attitude were perhaps due to improved planning and attention to detail on my part. However, my better planning was informed by what I learnt from Chambers (2007), who points out the importance of contextualizing listening activities and giving pupils a reason to listen. In the first lesson, for example, I discovered that the pupils actually enjoyed predicting content and that it made them eager to listen during the subsequent listening task. I also found out that many of the pupils with special educational needs (SEN) in the group benefited from the extra pre-listening and post-listening work as this provided extra scaffolding and structure, which, as Wire (2005) points out, are particularly important for Autistic Spectrum Disorder (ADS) pupils. ❞

Although Robert was very pleased with the way his lessons had gone, there was a mismatch between the skills and competence that pupils had developed during the sequence of lessons and the outcomes of the formal end-of-unit assessment. He reflects that:

> ❝ This discrepancy illustrates the fact that **summative assessment** is of limited use as it gives a picture of a pupil's capabilities at only one specific point in time. It also highlights how important it is not to focus too much on the grading aspect of assessment at the expense of its learning function and the giving of useful advice (Black and Wiliam 2001); many of my pupils were disappointed by their end-of-unit assessment results even though they had no reason to be because they had achieved well during the sequence of lessons [because they verbally answered questions well and participated fully in the learning activities]. ❞

Table 2.3 Robert

1 What aspects of curriculum and pedagogic knowledge are evident in Robert's reflections?
2 What evidence is there that Robert's reflections improved his teaching and enhanced his pupils' learning?

If you are beginning your teacher training	*If you are at least half way through your teacher training*	*If you are a newly or recently qualified teacher*
3 In your initial observations of teaching, and your first encounters with pupils, perhaps through supporting their learning in groups, note some examples of what Robert calls the 'learning function' of assessment. What factors have contributed to learning, and why?	Think about a lesson that you have taught recently. What did pupils learn? Reflect on their skills as well as knowledge. What contributed to this learning? What evidence do you have that learning took place?	What tensions exist for you between assessment as a means of giving a summative grade and assessment as a tool to inform learning (formative)? Give an example. How can you resolve this tension in your planning and teaching?

Reflective task 2.5 Balancing formative and summative assessment

Refer to Case Study 2.1 and reflect on the questions in Table 2.3, selecting those appropriate to your current stage of development. As you work through this and the following two case studies, the reflective questions should guide you in what you need to be considering at your own current stage of development.

Case Study 2.2 Collaborative professional learning to investigate pupils' misconceptions in science

David had learned as part of his PGCE science course that we all develop individualized views of how the world works as we grow up. Pupils bring to their science lessons a range of alternative perspectives (of the curricular concepts) that often need re-developing in order for them to acquire the correct factual understanding.

David was about to teach magnetism to a Year 8 class, and his research led him to appreciate that students confuse electrical force and magnetic force in physics. Discovering that very little research has actually been undertaken in the area of pupils' misconceptions in magnetism, David undertook what reading he could, then discussed issues with members of the department before planning a series of lessons informed by **social constructivist** theories of learning. Following his evaluation of the sequence, David produced a report for the department and invited their feedback. His work generated much interest, despite the prevailing climate of accountability.

> 66 I had involved many staff throughout the project. My chosen group was normally taught by two teachers. The head of science had shown an interest, there was a physics specialist with whom I consulted, and there was of course my mentor; all of these had some input. At the end of the review, I produced a written report for all staff, spoke to them individually and invited their responses.
>
> Their responses were positive, revealing that it had introduced new ideas to them all, most said it had highlighted misconceptions that they had not been aware of, and several stated that it would affect how they taught the topic in future. One teacher, who had not taught the topic to his Year 8 group at the time of reading the report, even asked to use my **scheme of work**. Some felt it was a good idea to introduce gravity when looking at the Earth's magnetic field as it was something they had never done previously, although a note of caution was raised in that introducing gravity into the topic may in some way actually fuel a misconception where one had not previously existed. In this respect several staff thought that they would only introduce gravity if they felt a connection already existed, or introduce it as an extension task for more able pupils. 99

Reflective task 2.6   Learners' errors and misconceptions

Refer to Case Study 2.2 and reflect on the questions in Table 2.4, selecting those appropriate to your current stage of development.

Table 2.4   David

1	What aspects of curriculum and pedagogic knowledge are evident in David's teaching and reflections about learning?	

2	What evidence is there that David's reflections improved his teaching and enhanced his pupils' learning?	

	If you are beginning your teacher training	*If you are at least half way through your teacher training*	*If you are a newly or recently qualified teacher*
3	Discuss with your peers (for example in your university teaching group, or with other trainee teachers in school) what you all feel to be the common errors, misconceptions or alternative understandings in a subject that you teach. Check this list with an experienced teacher and invite comment. What information does this give you about how you could approach your teaching with any given class?	Before planning a scheme of work or sequence of lessons, consider the collective knowledge and experience of others, both peers and experienced colleagues. How do they, or would they, address pupils' misconceptions or alternative understandings in this topic? What can you learn from the 'mistakes' they have made in making assumptions about learners' prior knowledge and understanding?	What has your own teaching experience taught you so far about learners' common errors and misconceptions in topics/subjects you have taught so far? There are many different ways to assess how successful you are in helping your students learn, list the different approaches and their strengths and weaknesses. Are there any areas where your own subject knowledge, and/or your pedagogic knowledge, needs strengthening? Who can help you to do this, and how?

Case Study 2.3   From teaching to learning

Raj was in her final term of a BEd primary course. This is her reflective response to re-reading feedback from lesson observations of her lessons:

 After carefully examining my lesson observations, I recognized that the feedback I was given indicated I tended to have a very teacher-led approach. Although I had outlined in my plan that I would provide sufficient opportunities for pupils to work collaboratively, I did not exploit this technique in practice. It was pointed out to me, that letting pupils mind map new vocabulary with their peers, gives them more autonomy over their learning.

The **constructivist** approach places the pupil at the centre of the learning process whereby learners are encouraged to 'find their own way through the tasks, developing and creating their own knowledge' (Kinchin 2007: 35). As a result, I modified my lesson plans in order to promote more independent and collaborative learning. This led to students brain-storming key items of vocabulary in groups. This helped me see how to adapt the concept of 'thinking time' during the categorization of activities. This 'thinking time' allowed students to share and reflect on their answers with their peers, was an additional method of learning collaboratively and allowed me to formatively 'listen-in' on their discussions. It was clear to see that through application of this theory, pupils were much more engaged with their learning. They enjoyed working together and were enthusiastic during whole-class feedback. Formative assessment allowed me to monitor how well pupils were coping. Pupils responded with greater items of vocabulary when they were working with their peers. The less able pupils significantly benefited from the more able pupils. They worked collaboratively, sharing knowledge with one another, which enabled them to achieve the best results possible. Personally, this is an area which I need to develop. I must plan effective opportunities which place the pupil at the centre of the learning process, enabling them to come up with their independent learning strategies. This pupil-centred approach encourages the pupil to find their own way through their learning. Thus it is imperative that I find the correct balance between teacher-led and pupil-led activities. I need to ensure that pupils have freedom to work independently but that I also provide sufficient scaffolding within the lesson, equipping pupils with the appropriate tools to work autonomously.

(Raj, primary BEd, year 3, part way through final teaching practice) 🙰

Reflective task 2.7 The transition from 'teaching' to 'learning'

Refer to Case Study 2.3 and reflect on the questions in Table 2.5, selecting those appropriate to your current stage of development.

Table 2.5   Raj

1	What aspects of curriculum and pedagogic knowledge are in evidence in Raj's teaching and reflections?	
2	What evidence is there that Raj's reflections improved her teaching and enhanced her pupils' learning?	

	If you are beginning your teacher training	*If you are at least half way through your teacher training*	*If you are a newly or recently qualified teacher*
3	Trainee teachers are, rightly, concerned most about their 'performance' in the classroom. At the start of your teaching, you need to ensure that you have classroom presence: confident body language, a strong voice. You will need a detailed lesson plan and well-organised resources. You should also know your pupils' names, understand the school's policies on **sanctions** and **rewards**, and have some basic classroom management strategies at your disposal. Before you start to teach, reflect on the extent to which all this is in place.	At some point in your training, you will be ready to move from anxiety about your teaching to concerns about pupils' learning. Raj has clearly reached this stage. What evidence is there of this? What evidence do you have of your own readiness to reflect more on how your pupils are learning? How does your planning reflect this? What subject, curriculum and pedagogic knowledge are you using to enhance your pupils' learning?	If you have moved to a new school after your training, you will to some extent, have needed to go through the processes again of establishing your classroom presence in a new context. At what point has this become (on the whole) effective, and what evidence do you have of this? To what extent are you able to focus on aspects of your pupils' learning more than on your own performance? How are you doing this? How do the 'theories' you acquired in training continue to inform your practice?

Summary

In this chapter we have drawn your attention, with a very brief introduction, to the socio-political climate in which reflective practice has become established in teacher education. The so-called 'new professionalism' will have a lasting impact on your training and career development as you are required to meet initial and ongoing national professional standards throughout your working life. Many beginning teachers, both trainees and NQTs, struggle with the tensions that come from the desire to teach creative and exciting lessons in schools that are often focused on exam results and other key performance indicators. Here, two case studies have been presented to explore these tensions. The first shows how collaborative working practices can involve a whole subject department in a deeper understanding of aspects of pedagogy, and the second explores how one trainee reflected on the problems that can arise from summative assessment practices.

In recommending reflective practice as one of the most important tools you will have as you build your expertise, we also caution against allowing reflection to 'take on a life of its own' (Valli in Calderhead and Gates 1993: 9). By this she means that some things are really worth reflecting about and others less so; there is no automatic correlation between reflection and enhanced classroom practice. While the level of your reflections will vary according to the stage of your professional development and the context about which you are reflecting, the two constant criteria in deciding how you reflect and what you reflect about should be:

- Does this reflection *improve* my teaching?
- Does it *enhance* my pupils' learning?

The final case study illustrates how one trainee used reflection to develop one aspect of her work as she strived to develop her teaching within a social constructivist framework. All three beginning teachers in these case studies use deep, informed reflection which augurs well for the future learning of their students and for their later career progression.

Conclusion

In conclusion, as you move through the other chapters in this book, discovering many different facets of reflection, and finding those that suit you best, we urge you to bear in mind that as a teacher you are charged with helping every child to achieve their full potential, and to keep in mind the key message of this chapter, that what you reflect on should support that important goal.

Key learning points

- The standards reflect a model of professional accountability but also of professional excellence.
- Teachers often face tensions between the 'professional artistry' of their role and the more technicist aspects associated with student attainment as a key indicator of school performance.
- Reflective practice as you begin teaching will enhance your ability to deepen and broaden your knowledge and understanding of the core strands of the professional standards throughout your teaching career.
- Choosing what to reflect on is important; the purpose should always be linked to improving teaching and learning.

CHAPTER 3

Who do you think you are .... and who do you think you will be as a teacher?

Mary Dunne

The uniqueness of every teacher's approach to teaching, shaped by personal teacher identity, is what makes every classroom 'look' different.

(Walkington 2005: 5)

Introduction

Despite the apparent homogeneity of a national curriculum, standardized assessment regimes and statutory professional standards for teachers, every classroom is different, because every teacher is unique. It is widely recognized (for example Korthagen and Vasalos 2005; Beauchamp and Thomas 2009; Stenberg 2010) that an individual's personal experiences shape their values and attitudes, which in turn influence how they see themselves as teachers and what kind of teacher they are. In any staffroom you will meet men and women from different social and cultural backgrounds, each with a different emotional makeup and with different personal and professional aspirations. Olsen (2008: 24) has called these 'embedded understandings' that 'shape how teachers interpret, evaluate and continuously collaborate in the construction of their own early development'. In so doing, they are developing what we call **teacher identity**. While notions about how teacher identity is shaped and developed, and even the term itself, are complex and multi-dimensional (Beauchamp and Thomas, 2009), the model in Figure 3.1 may be useful in helping you to understand what might influence your teacher identity. From it we can see that we are influenced by both personal and professional experiences. Thus 'teacher identity' can be defined as the relationship

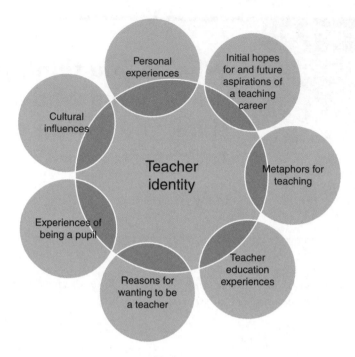

Figure 3.1 Possible influences on teacher identity

between our personal self and our professional self. Stenberg (2010: 332) refers to these two aspects as:

- self-identity: who am I?
- professional identity: who am I as a teacher?

Because our experiences continue throughout life, the potential to modify both our personal and our professional identity is ever present. Each teaching experience, from your first teaching practice to your induction year and into your **early professional development** (EPD), each interaction with learners, tutors, mentors and peers, has the potential to shape your teacher identity. This potential will be realized only if you see your teacher identity as dynamic and not fixed. You need to be able to reflect on who you are and why. In Chapter 5 you will explore and reflect on the relationship between the professional contexts in which you work and your attitudes, values and beliefs, and how these interact to shape your professional attributes as a teacher. Whether you are just thinking about applying for a teacher training course, in training or in the early years of your career, this chapter has two main purposes:

- to support you in understanding some of the possible influences on your teacher identity;

- to encourage you to interrogate your beliefs and assumptions and to be more critically responsive to a range of contexts; to respond in a dynamic way to professional experiences and develop your teacher identity appropriately.

The role of reflection in exploring and shaping teacher identity provides 'valued ways for people to probe their teaching existence so that they understand their position within their practice' (Beauchamp and Thomas 2009:182). The ideas you have about teaching at the start may be turned upside down as you gain experience in different contexts, but reflection on your professional self in relation to your personal self will enhance and enrich your teacher identity.

Influences on teacher identity

The personal self that beginning teachers bring to their early training is drawn from a wide range of influences, some of which might never have been consciously examined but just subconsciously absorbed. These influences form what Weber and Mitchell call 'a cast of fictionalised characters ... that takes on larger than life proportions' (1995: 14). The following aspects of the model in Figure 3.1 are considered:

- **metaphors** for teaching;
- cultural influences;
- experiences of being a learner;
- initial hopes for and future aspirations of a teaching career;
- teacher education experiences.

The case studies exploring the development of teachers' early identity will provide some illuminatory examples which, along with the reflective tasks provided, will help you to understand and develop your own identity as a teacher.

> The ideas you have about teaching at the start may be turned upside down as you gain experience in different contexts, but reflection on your professional self in relation to your personal self will shape and enrich your teacher identity.

Metaphors for teaching

It makes a great deal of difference to our practice ... if we think of teaching as gardening, coaching or cooking. It makes a difference if we think of children as clay to mold or as players on a team or as travelers on a journey.

(Weber and Mitchell 1995: 20)

The metaphors identified in the above quotation capture significantly different views of teaching, and subsequently learning. The degree to which you find yourself drawn to one view rather than another could reveal important clues about the values, attitudes and beliefs that you bring to the profession. For instance, the view that pupils are clay to be moulded implies learners who are passive. In this view, teaching is perceived as something that is 'done to' the learners. The teacher, only, holds the vision of the learning outcomes, although the 'clay' might behave in unpredictable ways! If, however, you are drawn more to the idea of a learner as a fellow traveller on a journey, then teaching and learning may appear to be a more shared, exploratory process in which the learner as well as the teacher can share in leading the way.

Metaphors, or images of teaching, can be useful in categorizing and realizing how we see ourselves as teachers at different points in time, although the images we apply to our role are likely to change as our 'teacher identity' changes in response to circumstances, and as we mature professionally and reflect upon how we are teaching and why we teach in this way. Studies by Cooper and Olsen (1996) and Reynolds (1996) described in Day et al. (2006: 607), identify 'the "multiple selves" of teachers which are ... continually reconstructed through the historical, cultural, sociological and psychological influences which all shape the meaning of being a teacher'. Cooper and Olsen also refer to the tensions that teachers experience between how they conceive of teaching (drawing on their previous childhood histories and memories) and the contexts in which they find themselves while learning to be teachers. This process they describe as 'creating their world while also being shaped by it' (Day et al. 2006: 607). In this sense, the metaphor may be a useful tool for describing your concept of being a teacher at any given point.

Reflective task 3.1   Using metaphors to define teacher identity

This task may be easier to do in pairs or small groups.

1 What metaphor captures your current idea of what a teacher is?
2 If you already have experience, were your ideas and metaphors different at the outset? How have they changed, and why?

Cultural influences

Cultural influences will include your family background and life experiences, including how you were educated, an aspect dealt with separately in this chapter.

How you view concepts such as 'equal opportunity' and how easily you relate to people from different cultures and background to your own, will largely depend upon your previous encounters, and these are multi-faceted and personal to you. In this section the focus is on your perception of what a teacher is as it may have been internalized from the cultural models surrounding you: from the literature you have read, from films, television images and from the wider media portrayals of teachers.

You draw on experiences of being taught by a wide range of educators (not just in school, but perhaps also through sport or theatrical coaching, leisure pursuits and other outside interests) and even working in an educational context alongside others who have made strong impressions on you. You have also been influenced by public perceptions of teachers and teaching. Depending on other influences in your life that have shaped who you are, you will interpret these influences in different ways, as Case Study 3.1 illustrates.

Case Study 3.1   Trainee teachers' responses to a portrayal of a teacher in a film

In an early training session, a group of teachers was asked to reflect on the character of Mr Keating (Robin Williams' character in the movie *Dead Poets' Society*) when he is hoisted triumphantly onto his pupils' shoulders after he 'takes on the system' at a highly prestigious, conservative American private school. He challenges the learning-by-rote and brain-washing practised by the establishment with an injunction that his pupils should 'seize the day' and make their lives extraordinary. However his maverick approaches are implicated in one boy's suicide. When asked to provide adjectives for his character, the beginning teachers offered a rich array of descriptions from 'charismatic', 'engaging' and 'inspirational' to 'dangerous', 'egotistical' and 'self-obsessed'. There was admiration from some beginning teachers for a character who appears to be advocating self-expression, non-conformity and personal exploration. However, some also recognized that in confronting the status quo so vehemently, he [Mr Keating] was in danger of imposing his own discourse on his pupils and making it difficult for any of them to oppose him. This demonstrates the extent of their insight into the very complex issues explored in the film, where the values of the individual teacher are in conflict with the values of the institution.

This theme is explored further in Chapter 5.

Experiences of being a learner

The reflective journals written by our trainee teachers reveal similar findings to those of wider research on teacher identity, for example, wanting to become a teacher is influenced by experiences of being in school and being engaged in community activities (Walkington 2005: 57). Earlier, Calderhead 1991, in Eraut, 1994: 71 found that teachers 'rely heavily on the images of practice that are acquired from past and current experiences in schools'. Furthermore, he claimed that these images can be accepted without reflection: 'taken and implemented uncritically'. Thus in its broadest sense, our teacher identity is how we define what education is for, based on our own experience of it; if you felt inspired by enthusiastic teachers, you may set out from a position of 'love of subject'; if your learning was very formal, you may consider the 'transmission of knowledge' as the way forward.

Consider the contrasting examples below, extracted from trainee teachers' initial reflections on their teacher identity. Each reveals something of the attitudes and beliefs of the author.

> **Jane:**
> 'My role is to make sure that the naughty ones don't disrupt other pupils.'
> 'My job is to teach them the facts.'
> 'Children need to understand the penal code and what is expected of them.'
>
> **Claire:**
> 'I want to find creative and exciting ways of actively engaging pupils in their own learning.'
> 'I want them to enjoy school and to share my passion for learning.'
> 'I think it is my role to encourage independent thought and exploration.'

Jane brought to her training her own educational experience in a context where pupils sat in rows and they were all well behaved. She explained later that the prospect of badly behaved pupils terrified her; thus her statements are heavily bound up in notions of 'control', suggesting instrumentalist, **behaviourist** views of learning that are rooted in the idea that children are empty vessels to be filled and need to be 'trained', with an emphasis on punishment for transgressions, into socially acceptable ways of behaving. Unless she questions her initial conceptions and is helped to develop them, Jane is likely to remain fixed in what Leavy et al. (2007) call a 'self-referential' approach with the focus remaining on herself as teacher rather than on students as learners. Without guided reflection, she is therefore unlikely to move towards **constructivist** and **social-constructivist** approaches where students become active participants and collaborators in their own learning with the teacher as the guide providing challenge and support. These approaches are implied in Claire's conception of her role (see above). She is focused on the learners as agents of their own learning.

> **Reflective task 3.2** Shaping teacher identity from your experience as a pupil
>
> 1 Think of your most effective teacher. Make a list of their characteristics. What did they do that made them effective? An effective teacher is one who ensures that pupils learn what they need to learn and that the appropriate learning outcomes are achieved.
> 2 Consider whether this was the same teacher as your favourite teacher. A favourite teacher is one that you most enjoy teaching you.
> 3 If not, what were the differences between them and what made this person your favourite?
> 4 Next consider your most memorable teacher. A memorable teacher is one you remember best, which might be for positive or negative reasons. What made them memorable?
> 5 Finally, are any of these the teacher you are aspiring to be? Which of their characteristics would you like to emulate? If your most memorable teacher is such for negative reasons, try to list the characteristics you wish to forestall.

Initial hopes for teaching

Perhaps through some of the influences identified above, teachers at the start of their training often have very clear ideas about what kind of teacher they want to be. As they progress through training, experiencing different teaching environments, and move into their first school as a qualified teacher, their teacher identity adaptively changes. This is sometimes a painful experience, but can be much less traumatic if you understand that it is a normal process in your development as a teacher; each new environment will enrich and (re)shape or (re)form your teacher identity.

The following three extracts are taken from the personal statements of beginning teachers' application forms, outlining their personal philosophies of teaching:

> 66 I want to be the kind of teacher whom children will not be afraid to approach, the kind that they can ask questions of, where they know that if they don't 'get it' the first time, or the second, or the third, they can still ask me and I will still be explaining patiently.
>
> *(Janet, primary employment-based route)*
>
> I want to open my pupils' eyes to the mysteries of science. I want them to see that there is a kind of wonder in the world but that everything can have a logical explanation.
>
> *(Abdul, one-year secondary science PGCE)*

> I want to inspire pupils and instill a self-belief in them to aid them in achieving the best they possibly can.
>
> *(Charlene, secondary drama employment-based route)* 99

These candidates have started to demonstrate the qualities that they value: qualities of trustworthiness, patience, **self-efficacy**, approachability, enthusiasm and inspirational guidance. Possibly because of anxieties about how to 'control' pupil behaviour, beginning teachers often express a desire to be popular with pupils:

> 66 At the start of my first placement, I thought it was really important that pupils liked me.
>
> *(Rebecca, one-year English PGCE, end of training year)* 99

This kind of sentiment highlights aspects of beginning teacher identity concerned with being a successful teacher who is not disliked or held in fear. These feelings are not untypical and have been recognized by Furlong and Maynard, (1995), as characteristic feelings of 'early idealism' as beginning teachers adapt and adopt strategies to ensure 'personal survival'.

Although they often have high aspirations regarding their role, beginning teachers can see teaching in simplistic terms:

> 66 I can't believe my naivety now. Before I started this course I really thought that teaching was just about standing up in front of a group of children and sharing my knowledge. I thought that if I just explained everything clearly enough they would learn what I wanted them to learn.
>
> *(Terry, secondary English, employment-based route, end of training year)* 99

An almost universal theme articulated by beginning teachers is their wish 'to make a difference' as was expressed by David writing in his initial reflections. However, what he begins to realize is how complex this notion is:

> 66 ... since I wrote the pre-course chapter of this journal, my thoughts and knowledge have evolved, and I have also come to realize that to become a good teacher the challenges ahead are going to be a lot harder than I originally thought. Since I started working within my school, I have come to realize that notwithstanding the guidance in university sessions, teaching methods and approaches are a lot harder to apply in practice. This has led me to conclude that the nature of teaching is varied, challenging, and every action that I will undertake will have an effect on my pupils. These actions must be individual to the circumstances in which they are undertaken.
>
> *(David, one-year primary PGCE, end of first placement)* 99

Through reflection, David is already showing evidence that he is revisiting his early assumptions and is beginning to consider the complexity of what he will need to master if he is to be effective.

Reflective task 3.3a   Who do you think you are currently?

Do you, or did you, like the beginning teachers above, have an over-simplified view of the role of the teacher, or perhaps an inflated view of the difference you could make? Is concern about behaviour casting a shadow over your hopes and expectations about being a teacher? Select from Table 3.1 the column that best suits your situation and consider the questions. They are intended to help you to reflect on your teacher identity.

Table 3.1   Reflecting on your teacher identity

	If you are beginning your teacher training	*If you are at least half way through your teacher training*	*If you are a newly or recently qualified teacher*
1	What attracts you to be a teacher? What skills and personal attributes do you think you will bring?	Think back to how you perceived yourself as a teacher before you began to teach. How different are your current perceptions, and why?	In what ways has becoming qualified changed how you perceive yourself as a teacher? Why do you think this is?
2	What do you expect the greatest challenges to be? What do you think you will find easiest?	Compare and contrast what you thought would be your greatest challenges with the challenges you are actually facing. What have been your greatest achievements to date?	What challenges do you currently face? In what ways are these the same as and different from the challenges of teacher training? What have been your greatest achievements since qualifying?
3	What sort of teacher do you want to be and why?	What sort of teacher are you becoming? How does this compare with your initial expectations? How would you describe the teacher you are aspiring to be at the moment?	What are your aspirations as a teacher now?

Future aspirations for teaching

Although at times it will feel as if your vision for the future will barely extend beyond how you will plan next week's lessons, teachers do begin to develop a sense of their future career aspirations surprisingly early, as the following trainees illustrate:

> 66 I can't see myself as a head of department; there is so much administration. I gave up an office job to be more 'hands-on' and don't want to be back dealing with endless paperwork. I wouldn't mind having some departmental responsibility though, like being in charge of the sixth form, or developing an ICT strategy.
>
> *(Sarah, one-year PGCE MFL, at end of training)*
>
> I have discovered that I have a real interest in pupils with learning difficulties and would welcome opportunities for professional development in special needs education.
>
> *(James, three-year primary BEd, writing in his career entry and development profile)*
>
> My love of Spanish, that I thought was so strong at university, has been overtaken by a passion for teaching in challenging schools; I am discovering that it isn't really about how much Spanish they learn. What matters is how well I can enhance their self-esteem, teach them to respect me and each other, and develop independent learning skills, and ultimately have a fulfilling life.
>
> *(Sophie, one-year PGCE MFL, part way through final teaching practice)*
>
> I can't believe what an interesting life my mentor has. As an AST he is so busy, but he loves everything he does, and he knows so much about teaching and learning! I would love to think I could do what he does in a few years' time.
>
> *(Raj, one-year science PGCE, end of training year)* 99

Reflective task 3.3b   What are your future aspirations?

As your initial training ends, you will be encouraged to think about what you hope to achieve during your induction year; how you will meet and maintain the core professional standards and what opportunities for development you would like the school to provide. These same issues are also part of your continuing professional development.

1 Consider the statements above, and speculate about what kind of teacher each person is. What style do you think they might adopt in the classroom? To what

extent are you thinking about your future teacher identity in terms like these? If you are, what are your current thoughts, and what does this tell you about your professional self?

2 If you have the opportunity, compare and contrast your responses with those of your peers. Discuss the extent to which context has shaped the varying responses.

Teacher education experiences

This whole book is about how reflection on your and others' experiences in training and beyond shapes the teacher you are and will become. In Case Study 3.3 we use a simple illustration of how one trainee, through reflection on teaching styles, shifted her view of what 'good' teaching is:

Case Study 3.3   Geraldine: reflecting on the meaning of 'good' teaching

When she was asked at interview about her 'best' teacher, Geraldine described her as a 'wonderful' advanced level teacher who 'seemed to know everything about everything . . . she was a fount of knowledge to us and we just lapped up every word'. She described how they took detailed notes and were able to reproduce these in their examinations. As a beginning teacher who had already had some teaching experience in a challenging context, when asked whether she had reproduced those approaches in her own practice, she immediately said: 'Oh no – I couldn't use those approaches with those children. They needed lots of different activities, lots of small, structured steps, lots of opportunities to think for themselves.' In the middle of explaining this, she suddenly stopped and referred back to her own experience as an advanced level student saying: 'Actually, now I think about it like that, more interactive teaching would have been good for me, too. All I learned was how to regurgitate what we'd been told. That's probably why I struggled in my first year at university.'

Reflective task 3.4   How has your teacher education influenced your teacher identity?

This task is enriched by group discussion where possible.

1 Look back to your application for teacher training and/or early written reflections on your role. What has changed in your thinking, following at least one school-based experience?
2 Try to articulate these changes in professional language.

New contexts and your teacher indentity

Every new context in which you find yourself (new school, new class, new experiences with individual pupils and colleagues) will shape your teacher identity and determine the sort of teacher you wish to become. However, that is not to say that you are a hapless victim in this process! Through reflection, you will be able to use these experiences to your advantage, just so long as:

- you continue to reflect on the kind of teacher you want to be;
- you are critically reflective about your professional experiences and recognize how you can use them to shape your professional self.

Beijaard et al. (2004) explored the extent to which teacher identity is context dependent. They investigated whether teachers saw identity as developmental rather than static and unchanging. In reviewing and summarizing over twenty studies that focused on teachers' professional identities, they found that although the concept of identity has different meanings in the literature, what they have in common is the idea that 'identity is not a fixed attribute of a person, but a relational phenomenon' (Beijaard 2004: 108). That is to say, different contexts enable us to develop different skills, and this in turn helps us to develop a 'fluid' teacher identity. Many of the teachers interviewed in the studies saw their professional identity as an 'ongoing process ... a process of interpreting oneself as a certain

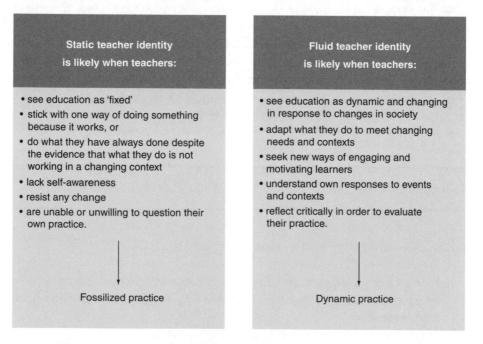

Static teacher identity is likely when teachers:	Fluid teacher identity is likely when teachers:
• see education as 'fixed' • stick with one way of doing something because it works, or • do what they have always done despite the evidence that what they do is not working in a changing context • lack self-awareness • resist any change • are unable or unwilling to question their own practice.	• see education as dynamic and changing in response to changes in society • adapt what they do to meet changing needs and contexts • seek new ways of engaging and motivating learners • understand own responses to events and contexts • reflect critically in order to evaluate their practice.
↓	↓
Fossilized practice	Dynamic practice

Figure 3.2   Fluid and static teacher identities

kind of person and being recognized as such in a given context' (Gee 2001, in Beijaard et al. 2004: 108). Thus our identity remains static only when we fail to learn from our experiences. Figure 3.2 demonstrates the difference between 'fluid' and 'static' teacher identities. Learning from experience requires reflection on our experiences. In their review of the literature on teacher identity, Beauchamp and Thomas (2009:183) have also concluded that reflection is a 'powerful way for students and practising teachers to delve deeply into their teaching identities'.

Interrogating your beliefs and assumptions

You will have started your teacher training with a more or less clear idea about what teaching is like and what sort of teacher you want to be. The reflective scaffolds in Figures 3.3 and 3.4 may help you to interrogate your current

When	Why	Tracking a teacher for a day
Either in the first few days of being in school as part of your training, or during a school visit in preparation for a course application or interview.	To look beneath the surface of what is obvious about the teacher role to find out as much as possible about what a teacher does.	**Tracking a teacher for a day** Check whether your teacher training programme requires you to undertake something similar. If so, it is advisable to follow the brief they provide. 1 **Seek out information.** Find out about the current legislation in respect of teachers' roles. What are teachers expected to do contractually? 2 **Experience the classroom.** With the support of your mentor or other contact in school, identify a teacher whom you can track for a day, from their arrival in school until leaving at the end of the day. Write down what they do with approximate times alongside. 3 **Take in the bigger picture.** Arrange to spend 10 minutes with this teacher to discuss what they do in addition to what you have observed and to establish to what extent this day is typical.

Reflection

Make notes on, and/or discuss in groups, the following:
- What surprised, or even shocked, you about this experience?
- How does what you have learned compare with your initial conceptions of the teacher role?
- What modifications to your own teacher identity (for example, how you define what sort of a teacher you want to be) will you now make?

Figure 3.3   Interrogating your assumptions about the teacher role

When	Why	
Either in the first few days of being in school as part of your training, or during a school visit in preparation for a course application or interview.	To look beneath the surface of what is obvious about the learner role to find out as much as possible about the nature of learning.	**Doing a pupil trail** Check whether your teacher training programme requires you to undertake something similar. If so, it is advisable to follow the brief they provide. 1 **Acquire the knowledge.** With the support of your mentor or other teacher, identify a pupil whom you can observe for a full day. Do not let the pupil know that they are specifically the centre of your attention, as this is likely to influence their behaviour. Find out what they will be learning, if possible by accessing the learning outcomes and studying the scheme of work and/or curriculum documents relating to the lesson. You can do this afterwards if it is not possible to do it before. 2 **Live the experience.** Follow 'your' pupil for a day, excluding breaks and lunch time. Write down what they do with approximate times alongside. 3 **Explore the bigger picture.** Arrange to spend five minutes with this pupil to discuss this day in relation to the school week.

Reflection
Make notes on, and/or discuss in groups, the following:
- How consistent was your pupil's behaviour, attitude and response throughout the day? What do you think could have influenced this?
- What surprised, or even shocked, you about this experience?
- How does what you have learned compare with your initial assumptions about learners and learning?
- What modifications to your own teacher identity (for example, how you define what sort of a teacher you want to be) will you now make?

Figure 3.4 Interrogating your assumptions about learners

beliefs and assumptions in order to ensure that your teacher identity remains fluid.

Summary

Your teacher identity is derived from a number of influences:

- the life experiences that have shaped your personal values, attitudes and beliefs, for example your personal **ideology** about the purposes of education, how you view the concept of 'equality' or 'multiculturalism';

- your developing pedagogic, curriculum and subject knowledge as experienced during your teacher training;
- your interaction with school contexts during and beyond your initial training;
- your developing reflective practice.

As you shape and reshape your teacher identity, you will need to internalize and demonstrate what is meant by 'an effective teacher' and, desirably, 'an outstanding teacher'.

Conclusion

The Greek philosopher, Socrates, highlighted the importance of having 'intellectual humility', that is, a sensitivity to what you know and what you do not know. This means being aware of your biases, prejudices, self-deceptive tendencies and the limitations of your viewpoint (Elder 2010).

This is a crucial aspect of forming professional identity and, whatever stage of your professional development you are at, you might wish to consider the following questions (adapted from Elder 2010):

- What do I really know about myself as a beginning teacher?
- To what extent do my prejudices or biases influence my thinking?
- To what extent have I been indoctrinated into beliefs that may be false?
- How do beliefs that I have accepted uncritically keep me from seeing things as they are?
- Do I behave in accordance with what I say I believe, or do I tend to say one thing and do another?
- Am I willing to change my position when the evidence leads to a more reasonable position?
- To what extent do I uncritically accept what I am told by my government, the media, my peers?
- Do I think through issues on my own, or do I merely accept the views of others?

Teachers who are applying this critically reflective gaze will be able to articulate the changes in their thinking and practice over time. In twenty years' time, their experiences will have shaped their identity; they will not be the teacher with one year's experience repeated twenty times!

Key learning points

In order to develop a fluid teacher identity that provides a 'best fit' between your personal self and your professional self, you will need constantly to reflect upon:

- the role of the teacher in society;
- why you want to teach and what kind of a teacher you want to be;
- the extent to which your practice reflects the expectations and definitions of the professional role as expressed in the professional standards (TDA 2008);
- the ways in which your personal and professional values (and associated actions) underpin your professional identity and your professional decision making.

How consciously reflective are you?

Lesley Cartwright

It is not enough to have a good mind. The main thing is to use it well.

Rene Descartes

Introduction

This chapter is designed to help you to make reflection a conscious activity. Three different but related approaches to reflection are described. You should be able to recognize, select and apply these different strategies at different points in your development in order to become empowered as professional learners with a belief in your ability to succeed in what sometimes feels like very challenging tasks; in other words, to develop what we call self-efficacy.

Reflection can arise at different times and in varied locations. It can be a formal process, for example:

- a reflective journal or diary;
- a piece of academic writing for an assignment;
- a written lesson evaluation;
- written reviews of progress prior to mentor meetings.

It can also be an informal process, for example:

- a discussion with a peer;
- engagement in training activities in university, school or other setting;
- how you think and feel in given situations (reflection-in-action);
- how you think and feel after the event (reflection-on-action);

There are two principles that underpin reflection in this chapter. The first is that meaningful reflection is a balance between the rational (logical thought) and the affective (how you feel) and the second is that reflection at its most effective comes only with growing professional knowledge based on the acquisition of theory and its critical application to practice. Where reflection leads to conscious self-efficacy, it draws critically on professional knowledge and understanding. It is often formed out of professional dialogue (both verbal and written) underpinned by critically applied theory. This kind of higher order thinking is the bedrock of professional development in the twenty-first century, as the drive for a Masters (M) level profession illustrates. Reflecting with theories about education in mind consolidates key skills in high level critical thinking, thus facilitating progression to M level work.

The reflective process: what do you know?

As we have seen in Chapter 1, much attention has been given since the early 1990s or so to definitions of reflective practice. Teacher educators in Britain and overseas have been exercised by such questions as 'can reflective practice be taught?' (Russell 2005) and 'how can reflection be supported?' (Martin 2005). To be able to answer these questions we need to explore the process of reflection, consider the stages that beginning teachers move through in order to develop effective reflection.

But first, a word of caution: there is much research and literature around professional reflection but no agreed single conception of the reflective process and how it is acquired. However, many writers since Dewey (1933) and Schön (1983) have helped to shape our own thinking about how reflective practice is acquired and used. Brookfield (1995) identified four 'lenses' through which reflective practitioners can view their practice: their personal biography, the eyes of the learner, the eyes of colleagues and from the perspective of theory. This is a very useful starting point. It is often our personal biography that gives form to our *unconscious* reflection. That is to say, at the unconscious, intuitive level our reflections are based on what we know about classrooms from our own schooling. Some writers, for example Eraut (2000), refer to this as **tacit knowledge.**

LaBoskey (1993: 24) has labelled what we are calling here 'unconscious' reflectors 'common sense thinkers'. Common sense, because that is what they rely on: their own knowledge from being a pupil. For LaBoskey, common sense thinkers are comfortable with the 'trial and error' model of learning, and thus take a short-term view of their professional development, because it is about getting things right for now. Their metaphor for teaching is that of 'transmitter of knowledge'. Moving to a level of *conscious* reflection requires us to understand where our unconscious reflection might be leading us, for example: 'What is my intuitive response to this, and why am I feeling or acting this way?' From there we need to pick up other lenses through which to view our professional practice and to answer such questions as:

1 What does my teaching feel like to my students/pupils? (seeing through the eyes of learners)
2 How should I respond to the professional feedback provided by others on my practice? (seeing through the eyes of colleagues)
3 How should I learn from my observations of experienced practitioners? and
4 What part does an understanding of theory about teaching and learning play in my reflective processes? (reviewing professional activity from the perspective of theory)

LaBoskey (1993: 25) defined those able to do this as 'pedagogical thinkers', facilitating learning. Taking a longer term view of how to solve problems and remaining open to learning, they recognize there are no simple answers and the conclusions they reach are likely to be tentative. They see teaching as a moral activity and are strategic and imaginative in their thinking, which is grounded in knowledge of themselves, their students and their subject.

The widely held view of the teacher as a 'theory-guided decision-maker' (Clarke 1986, in Korthagen and Vasalos, 2005: 50) has led to models of reflection based on Kolb's learning cycle (Kolb and Fry 1984, in Korthagen and Vasalos 2005: 50). Kolb's model is concerned with concrete experiences and a rational response to them through a cyclical process (see Chapter 13 for more detail). An oversimplification of Kolb's model can lead to its use in providing quick fixes for classroom problems. For example, when beginning teachers struggle with disruptive behaviour in the classroom, mentors often try to provide a 'quick fix' solution along the lines of 'you could try separating those two boys/writing their names on the board/keeping them in at break'. This puts into the learning cycle an idea, or concept, to be tested next time, and can lead the teacher and the mentor to believe that they are engaging in reflective practice, whereas in reality they may not be addressing the longer term issue, the problem of disengaged learners who are resorting to disruptive behaviour.

Reflective task 4.1   Analysing how you reflect

Think back to a lesson when pupil behaviour interrupted learning. Make a list of possible reasons for this.

1 Now jot down any questions you have about your own practice as a teacher, and compare your list with the one below. At an unconscious level of reflection, you may be looking for reasons, such as:
   • it's the last lesson of the day

- their previous lesson was disrupted
- they don't like this topic
- they've just had PE
- it was raining at break so they haven't let off any steam.

At a conscious level, however, you will use your professional knowledge to probe more deeply, going beyond the (sometimes legitimate) reasons like those listed above, to explore questions such as those listed in Table 4.1.

2 Finally, consider the extent to which, in reflecting on this simple situation, you were doing more than simply relying on an intuitive, or unconscious, response. For example, did you draw on:
- Shulman's model of teacher development: subject, curriculum and/or pedagogic knowledge? (see Chapter 1)
- knowledge of the routines and practices, beliefs and values in the school? (see Chapter 5)
- the professional standards to which you are working? (see Chapter 2)

Table 4.1 Key questions to promote deeper reflection

Sociological *Relates to human social behaviour within the context of an organization, such as a school, or within society as a whole*	1 Do I understand and draw upon the values and ethos of the school and its expectations around behaviour and learning? 2 What messages about behaviour and learning do I convey as a teacher through my own demeanour as a teacher (verbal and non-verbal communication)? 3 Do I understand and take account of the interaction between pupils in my classroom?
Psychological *Relates to the emotional or behavioural aspects of an individual or group*	1 What do I understand about how these pupils learn? 2 What do I know about their prior learning and levels of attainment? 3 Do I understand how to challenge learners, so that the level of task I ask them to do will facilitate their progression?
Pedagogical *Relates to the practice of teaching and how this influences learning*	1 How appropriate was the activity to the learning outcome? 2 How well did I model the activity? 3 How well did I explain the activity?

How do you feel?

The complexities of the situations in which teachers find themselves demand a professional knowledge base, as indicated above, from which to evaluate contexts

Figure 4.1 The ALACT model of reflection

Source: After Korthagan and Vasalos 2005: 49

and events. There are various ways in which professional knowledge has the potential to improve the reflective process and enhance beginning teachers' self-efficacy. Alongside the development of your professional knowledge as a tool for conscious reflection, you also need to consider the affective aspects of learning to teach.

More recent models of reflection have taken account of the developing awareness of the less rational aspects of teacher behaviour. One such is the Action-Looking back-Creating Alternate methods-Trying out alternate ideas (ALACT) model (Korthagen and Kessels 1999) of five stages (see Figure 4.1). At phase 2 of the cycle (looking back on the action), this model seeks 'a balanced focus on thinking, feeling, wanting and acting' (Korthagen and Vasalos 2005: 50) by encouraging key reflective questions (Table 4.2).

> Reflection is a balance between the rational and the affective: how you think and how you feel.

Questions relating to specific events are drawn from the above, for example, 'how do you think pupils felt when you asked that question?' Thus the ALACT model seeks to structure the reflective process in a way that allows for feelings to be explored. It demands a degree of empathy, from the teacher towards the pupils and from the mentor towards the teacher, so that as Brookfield suggested (1995) we see our actions through the eyes of others (our pupils, our colleagues). Taking the model a stage further, Korthagen and Vasalos (2005) have identified 'core qualities' of a teacher that can be evidenced at the deepest level of reflection, or 'core reflection'. These include courage, creativity, sensitivity, decisiveness

Table 4.2 Key questions to focus on the rational (thinking) and affective (feeling) aspects of reflection

From teacher's perspective	From learner's perspective
What were you hoping to achieve?	What do you think the pupils hoped for?
How were you hoping to achieve your lesson outcomes?	What do you think the pupils' experience of the lesson was?
What did you do?	What did the pupils do?
What were you thinking (as the lesson progressed)?	What do you think the pupils were thinking?
How did you feel about the lesson?	How do you think the pupils felt about the lesson?

Source: Korthagen and Vasalos 2005: 50

and spontaneity and 'are indeed essential qualities for teachers, qualities seldom appearing on the official lists of basic competencies' (Korthagen and Vasalos 2005: 56).

The approaches described in this chapter should engage you in developing an awareness of your core beliefs and qualities, and the role these play in shaping your professional life and associated activities. This will mean a preparedness to recognize and respond to your own feelings, and to have empathy for colleagues and learners.

Developing deeper reflective processes

Many beginning teachers find it difficult to move on from the initial approach to evaluation of their teaching that remains at a tick-box level, with such comments as 'pupils quieter today' to support the perception that this was a 'good' lesson. Being aware of levels of reflection is a helpful starting point in moving forward; just as being able to pinpoint the level of attainment of your pupils, and understanding what they need to do to get to the next level, helps you to plan lessons for effective learning and progression, so an understanding of your own progression as a developing professional can help you to develop conscious reflective practice! Thus, the approaches to reflection proposed will require you to identify your stage of development at both a literal and a cognitive level.

As members of a Masters level profession, teachers are required to make informed and critical judgments about their professional actions, and use these to improve their practice both individually and collectively. Some beginning teachers falter at this point, believing that there is some mystique attached to the notion of criticality. There isn't. Figure 4.2 sets out some of the key teacher behaviours

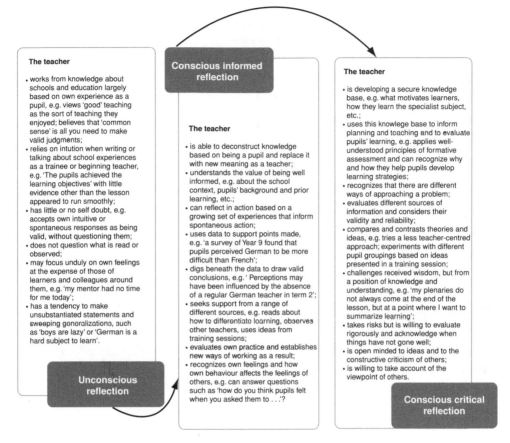

The teacher

- works from knowledge about schools and education largely based on own experience as a pupil, e.g. views 'good' teaching as the sort of teaching they enjoyed; believes that 'common sense' is all you need to make valid judgments;
- relies on intution when writing or talking about school experiences as a trainee or beginning teacher, e.g. 'The pupils achieved the learning objectives' with little evidence other than the lesson appeared to run smoothly;
- has little or no self doubt, e.g. accepts own intuitive or spontaneous responses as being valid, without questioning them;
- does not question what is read or observed;
- may focus unduly on own feelings at the expense of those of learners and colleagues around them, e.g. 'my mentor had no time for me today';
- has a tendency to make unsubstantiated statements and sweeping generalizations, such as 'boys are lazy' or 'German is a hard subject to learn'.

Unconscious reflection

Conscious informed reflection

The teacher

- is able to deconstruct knowledge based on being a pupil and replace it with new meaning as a teacher;
- understands the value of being well informed, e.g. about the school context, pupils' background and prior learning, etc.;
- can reflect in action based on a growing set of experiences that inform spontaneous action;
- uses data to support points made, e.g. 'a survey of Year 9 found that pupils perceived German to be more difficult than French';
- digs beneath the data to draw valid conclusions, e.g. ' Perceptions may have been influenced by the absence of a regular German teacher in term 2';
- seeks support from a range of different sources, e.g. reads about how to differentiate learning, observes other teachers, uses ideas from training sessions;
- evaluates own practice and establishes new ways of working as a result;
- recognizes own feelings and how own behaviour affects the feelings of others, e.g. can answer questions such as 'how do you think pupils felt when you asked them to . . .'?

The teacher

- is developing a secure knowledge base, e.g. what motivates learners, how they learn the specialist subject, etc.;
- uses this knowlege base to inform planning and teaching and to evaluate pupils' learning, e.g. applies well-understood principles of formative assessment and can recognize why and how they help pupils develop learning strategies;
- recognizes that there are different ways of approaching a problem;
- evaluates different sources of information and considers their validity and reliability;
- compares and contrasts theories and ideas, e.g. tries a less teacher-centred approach; experiments with different pupil groupings based on ideas presented in a training session;
- challenges received wisdom, but from a position of knowledge and understanding, e.g. 'my plenaries do not always come at the end of the lesson, but at a point where I want to summarize learning';
- takes risks but is willing to evaluate rigorously and acknowledge when things have not gone well;
- is open minded to ideas and to the constructive criticism of others;
- is willing to take account of the viewpoint of others.

Conscious critical reflection

Figure 4.2 Developing conscious critical reflection

at different levels of reflection, and Figure 4.3 provides examples of reflective questions. From this you should be able to see what you need to do next to develop your reflective skills. Wright's description of levels of reflective writing (2008: 80) clearly shows how theory informs deeper reflection (Table 4.3). Bear in mind that your personality and your core values will influence your potential for criticality. Moon (2008) has identified professionals who have what she calls 'academic assertiveness'. That is not to say that they know everything, or can speak or write confidently on subjects. On the contrary, they are aware of what they do not know, are open-minded, proactive in seeking knowledge and understanding, and in doing so are willing to take account of the viewpoint of others. They challenge the views and behaviours of others but equally, they seek to be challenged themselves, showing an ability to cope with, and recover from, sometimes getting things wrong (Moon 2008: 79). In contrast to the trainee described by Richert

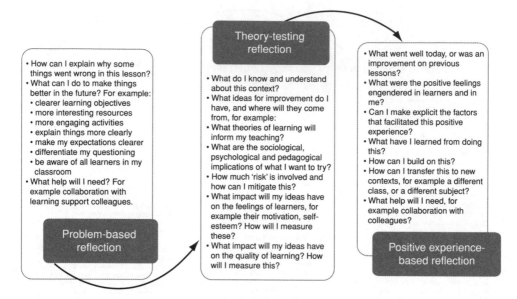

Figure 4.3 Alternative approaches to reflection: a suggested framework

(1992) above, Moon is describing teachers who are prepared to feel uncomfortable from time to time, seeing the longer-term benefits of taking a longer-term view as well seeking 'quick fixes' in their classroom. Developing a degree of 'academic assertiveness' will help you not only to become consciously reflective but also set you on a path that will help secure your Masters level accreditation, support your career progression and become an advocate of reflection.

Table 4.3 Stages of reflective writing

Level of writing	Components of writing at that level
Level 1	Diary description: an account of what happened in the classroom
Level 2	Diary description + analytical commentary: an attempt to answer the question 'why did that happen?'
Level 3	Diary description + analytical commentary + application of appropriate reading and theory. Illustrating how to use the literature on professional knowledge and understanding to support reflection, develop pedagogy and inform professional learning. Attempting to answer questions 'why did that happen?' + 'what is known about it?' + 'How can I use what is known to develop my professional practice?'

Source: After Wright 2008: 80

Reflective task 4.2   How are you reflecting now?

1 Think back to a recent activity you have undertaken either in school or in a training session. This could be a lesson observation, a class group task, feedback from your mentor or other teacher about a lesson you have taught, or an assignment you have written and/or feedback you have received.
2 Jot down the following:
   • how you felt about this at the time; for example, if you were receiving feedback about your teaching and work, were you pleased/proud/ anxious/indignant . . . ?
   • why you felt like this;
   • how you responded to these feelings, and what impact you think your response, if an active one, may have had on others.
3 Think carefully about and write down:
   • what knowledge and understanding you gained from this activity. You could categorize this as sociological, psychological or pedagogical knowledge, and consider where these overlap, and how they relate to Shulman's model of teacher development (Chapter 1) and the professional standards (Chapter 2)
   • what you learned about yourself;
   • what professional learning has emerged from this activity, for example something that you will implement or do better in the future.
4 Now read the performance descriptors of levels of reflection in Figure 4.2. You may also find it helpful to use these descriptors to identify, perhaps in group discussion, the levels of reflection shown in the case studies in this chapter.
   • Do you see yourself as an unconscious or a conscious reflector?
   • To what extent is your reflection informed and rational (based on knowledge and understanding) and to what extent are your reflections shaped by affective influences (how you feel)?
5 What is the next stage for you in developing your reflectivity?

Alternative approaches to reflection

Reflection can be stimulated in different ways as outlined in Figure 4.3. The first is generally recognized as **problem-based reflection**, and can be traced back to Dewey (1933); reflection is stimulated by a difficult situation to be remedied or the presentation of a problem to be solved. Thus many models of reflection will require you to answer, or ask yourself, such questions as: 'How can reluctant learners be engaged in the lesson?' or 'How are the most able learners challenged in this mixed ability class?' However, there has in recent years been an interesting shift towards the use of more positive experiences as a stimulus for reflection and learning. Janssen et al. (2008) propose using reflection on positive experiences, inspired by 'solution-based therapy', developed in the 1980s. This psychologically informed approach focuses not on the causes of patients' problems but on their strengths and qualities, using these to establish goals for improvement. They refer to Seligman's 'positive psychology' (Seligman and Csikszentmihalyi 2000) emphasizing that 'treatment is not fixing what is broken; it is nurturing the best' (Janssen et al. 2008: 116). They see the Korthagen and Vasalos (2005) 'core reflection' model of teacher reflection, while stimulated by the existence of difficulties and problems, as moving away from problem-based reflection in two important respects: first, it focuses on solutions and the setting of goals rather than on problems; and second, it demands the active use of personal qualities to achieve these goals (Janssen et al. 2008: 117). Janssen et al. (2008) compared trainee teachers' reflections on two positive and two negative experiences, and found that:

1 reflecting on positive teaching experiences leads to more innovative resolutions for future teaching than reflection on negative experiences;
2 there was greater motivation to try out more innovative teaching based on positive experiences;
3 positive reflection engendered positive emotions.

Janssen et al. (2008) acknowledge that positive experiences are likely to be based on some innovative teaching, even if this is done intuitively initially. For example, a teacher may already have a 'gut feeling' (tacit knowledge or common-sense understanding) about the value of learner-centred approaches. If, after using these in the classroom, the lesson evaluation is positive, then 'All the student teacher has to do is make this knowledge explicit' (p. 123). Difficulties arise where tacit knowledge is absent. 'The teacher realizes that something was not working well but does not know how to remedy the situation, and as a consequence finds it much harder to formulate an innovative resolution' (p. 123). In this situation, the beginning teacher is more likely to seek 'safer' options, which often means reverting to the 'you could try . . . ' model that focuses more on short-term behaviour management than longer term pedagogic solutions.

Reflecting on how you feel, and highlighting the positive aspects of your feelings, may be a first step in building the confidence needed to step outside of your comfort zone and experiment with teaching and learning. The first 'feel good' moments may not be related to direct classroom experience, as the following illustrates:

> 66 There have been incidences where colleagues have asked me for their advice as well. For example there is one teacher who is originally from Mauritius and therefore a native speaker of French . . . and teaches beginners' German.

> One day she asked me – as a native speaker of German – for some advice about correct pronunciation and meanings of a few German words. Her argument was that, if pupils were taught the dialectal pronunciation of the capital of Germany that would be a good thing, since Berlin was the most important city in Germany. She was surprised when I told her that the Berlin dialect was perceived as low class and was different from the 'high German' taught in schools.
>
> *(Janine, one-year secondary PGCE MFL, after six weeks in school)*

This may seem like a small point at first glance; however it was important enough for the trainee to include in her reflective journal. The reason for this becomes apparent in the last lines of this particular entry:

> After her lesson she came to me again and thanked me for my support. I felt very good that I could help this colleague as that showed that she accepted me as a member of staff in the department.
>
> *(Janine, one-year secondary PGCE MFL, after six weeks in school)*

This trainee was able to reflect on a positive emotion, that of feeling a sense of belonging, that ultimately contributed to her being able to grow and learn during her placement.

Case Study 4.1a   Reflecting on a positive teaching experience

Sarah had established herself well in terms of behaviour management and overall class control, but was facing the problem, highlighted by her mentor and university tutor, that she was too teacher-centred. In order to gain and maintain control of her classes, she was, in her mentor's words, 'doing all the work', so that her students were engaged in very little independent learning activity:

> The national curriculum states that good teaching creates opportunities for learners to develop as self-managers, creative thinkers and independent learners. Thinking about my lessons, I did not always do this effectively. Pupils were not thinking for themselves or being independent, they were being spoon-fed. Conversations with my university tutor made me realize how much I was controlling the students in my classroom. I was not sure how to move forward, until I lost my voice! As I couldn't speak, students had to follow a series of clues and they had to find out what they had to do on their own. We started to use non-verbal communication skills and pupils responded to this really well. One of the most important learning moments

> I have experienced is that as long as you facilitate the lesson, you do not have to be in control for the full period of time.
>
> *(Sarah, one-year MFL PGCE trainee, half way through her first school attachment)* **99**

Still at an early stage of her development at the time of writing in Case Study 4.1a, Sarah is using tacit knowledge and understanding that are gradually becoming explicit as she articulates and builds on her successes in order to solve problems. However, some weeks later, after a series of university-based training sessions linked to directed reading activities, the same trainee was using much more **explicit knowledge** to reflect on her teaching:

Case Study 4.2b   Further reflection on a positive experience

 My learning moment came from a university-based session in which we were introduced to inductive and deductive approaches to learning. It appeared to me that I had always approached grammar topics deductively, in that pupils in my class were given a rule or a guiding principle, and then moved away from it, in a logical fashion, to apply it to a specific problem or context. This approach enabled me to explain topics in a straightforward way, but in retrospect, pupils were not doing the work for themselves; therefore a 'reactive rather than interactive' role was promoted for pupils (Coyle 2002: 157). I've learnt that by using an inductive approach, the teaching of grammar can be linked to developing pupils' personal, learning and thinking skills (PLTS), which encourage learners to work out rules or principles independently from a communicative context, as 'communicative competence and linguistic competence should not be seen as separate entities' (Miller 2002: 159). This approach appears much more engaging and allows room for developing creativity in the classroom. I observed a Year 8 French lesson, in my second placement, where this approach was applied, with extremely successful outcomes. Pupils had to identify adjectives in a text, and then produce a rule in a written poem about why endings on adjectives sometimes change. Pupils seemed to have much more fun using this approach and were provided with increased autonomy over their work.

(Sarah, MFL PGCE trainee, half way through her second school attachment) **99**

Such an approach to reflection draws on what we will call here 'theory-testing reflection'. Here, the beginning teacher is taking ideas, suggestions and theories and conducting their own little experiments in the classroom. At its most basic level, theory-testing reflection is a response to the 'you could try. . . .' situation, which may or may not be helpful in improving practice, but is reflection at the micro level and is unlikely to lead to long term solutions. At its best, theory-testing reflection seeks deep knowledge and understanding at the macro level, applies theories and ideas drawn from literature as well as from the views of other, more experienced colleagues, and seeks innovative approaches to support more sustained development and future goals. Frank summarizes this well; by the end of his first teaching placement he had moved from concerns about how to teach to a deep interest in how his pupils were learning:

66 It is as much about the children and how they want to learn as it is about the teacher and how they want to teach. The two are intrinsically linked and can't work independently of one another.
(Frank, one-year MFL PGCE, at end of first teaching practice) 99

Summary

We all reflect at an unconscious level about many aspects of our life. This is often reflection at a micro level as it is concerned with how day-by-day happenings impact on us. However, reflection in a professional context requires us to move to a level of reflection in which we are conscious of, and responsive to, the wider context in which we are working: macro-level reflection.

Conclusion: from unconscious to conscious reflection

To guide you in thinking about which approach you might use for reflection, you can consider which questions in Figure 4.3 might be most applicable at any given point. While such questions provide a broad framework for reflection, there is a danger in seeing reflection simply as responding to an externally imposed structure. Moon (1999: 172) warns that 'recipes' for reflection, where a quick response can be given, often fail to challenge the professional learner and may not actually engender reflection at all. It is not the intention here to oversimplify the process of reflection, but to stimulate your thinking and to encourage you to use a range of reflective strategies that are appropriate at different points in your training and early career.

Key learning points

The approaches to reflection put forward in this chapter are designed to help you to become consciously reflective by encouraging you to:

- be aware of your core values and beliefs and your feelings about learning to teach;
- recognize your strengths and build on these;
- understand what your priorities are rather than try to address everything at once;
- articulate the tacit knowledge you have so that it enters your consciousness and can be built upon;
- consider different ways of reflecting and be able to select the most appropriate for your current situation;
- engage in the critical application of theory to your practice.

CHAPTER

5

How does your teacher identity fit in with the culture of teaching and the organization?

Angela Gault

Through learning we re-create ourselves. Through learning we become able to do something we were never able to do.

(Senge 2007: 13)

Your early professional development can be likened to a journey. This chapter considers the journey as it progresses through the professional landscapes and climates of your various school or college learning contexts. For simplicity, the term 'school' is used throughout although you may be working in a college. You are equipped with guides in the form of colleagues, and various maps in the guise of policy documents, curriculum plans, and assessment descriptors to help inform your direction for development. Milestones along the way will mark your achievements towards meeting the various Q and C standards (TDA 2007). You will accrue professional knowledge and hone professional skills during your professional working life (see Chapter 2). However, the process of developing your teacher identity requires something even more fundamental from you. It is important to appreciate that your journey is not only physical but also emotional and psychological. This is because as you learn how to be a professional your identity will evolve. In order to 'fit in' and become a teacher you will meet some essential personal and professional demands, entitled professional attributes (see Appendix 1 Q1 and Q2).

This chapter explores how you can develop your professional attributes by negotiating the terrain and climate of your learning contexts. It is important that you appreciate the significance of the social 'landscapes' and 'climates' within your schools and understand how to 'read' the various roles, interests and power dynamics at work. This journey into developing your professional identity reaches into the heart of why you want to teach and what kind of teacher you want to become.

What are professional attributes?

The term 'professional attributes' is used to identify one of the three core strands of the professional standards (TDA 2007, see Chapter 2) but can also be seen as a generic term for all aspects of professional behaviour associated with our values and attitudes, such as 'commitment' and 'high expectations'. Some of these professional attributes can be quite difficult to 'evidence'. For example, how do you show that you have high expectations of children?

> 66 Pupils know I expect them to do well because I tell them they should get all of the answers right.
> *(Amy, one-year science PGCE, two weeks into her first teaching practice)* 99

However, this standard reaches far deeper than expecting learners to do well on tests. For example, it may be quite easy for the learners to get all of the answers right because the questions the teacher set were not demanding enough in the first place. What you teach, why and how, all reveal aspects of your teacher expectations, and these expectations are conveyed to learners.

Becoming and being a teacher is not just an academic exercise, it is an emotional undertaking (Hargreaves 1998; Hobson and Malderez 2005) which takes place within particular learning situations (Lave and Wenger 1991). In order to begin thinking about, and understanding, what is meant by 'professional attributes', it is useful to reflect on what it 'feels' like to behave as a teacher in typical teacher situations.

'Being' a teacher in the classroom

> 66 The first time I stood in front of a class was so scary. I had prepared everything I could in advance so I thought I was OK, but once the class was there I felt a weight pressing on my throat, my mouth went dry and my heart was thumping.
> *(Mahmoud, GTP music, after his first lesson)* 99

Think about how it felt when you stood up in front of a class for the first time to teach a lesson. Suddenly all eyes are on you. The responsibility is yours. You have your lesson plan but now is the time to bring it to life. In order to succeed you have to adopt the persona of a teacher. This begins with the messages you give to pupils through your choice of attire. It also involves your body language, how and where you position yourself in relation to the pupils, and your voice, how you speak as well as what you say and when. You begin to feel what it is like to take on a very specific role or identity, and this is likely to be a very new experience for you.

Lynne describes how 'talking like a teacher' helped her to establish her authority with pupils and convey her professional values:

> 66 I am happy now with my use of professional language. I have discovered that by using such language as soon as I entered the classroom, I experienced less resistance from pupils than I expected. I realize that it is important to continue using professional language at all times so that authority is maintained within the classroom.
>
> *(Lynne, three-year BEd primary on her first teaching practice)* 99

How you speak to pupils conveys messages and expectations. Professional language:

- is formal and authoritative in tone;
- models standard English;
- avoids personal and negative comments;
- is positive and focuses on learning.

Reflective task 5.1   Using professional language in the classroom

1 What might the impact be upon pupil self-esteem and the learning environment in each paired example in Table 5.1?
2 Does anything here resonate with your own practice? What effective practices can you embed? What changes do you need to make?

You may adopt the role of teacher with ease, or it may take some time. You may find it easy with some classes; less so with others. Nevertheless, how you feel, act and speak as a teacher will reveal your fundamental values and beliefs about what it means to be a teacher. This is more than acting: it is 'being'. Your

Table 5.1 Examples of contrasting teacher talk

Shurrup you noisy lot!	Five seconds to finish off your point and then we'll come back together as a class to share ideas.
Stop messing about!	Let's see how you are getting on with this . . .
When are you guys going to learn?	This is quite difficult but I know you can do it. How about if . . .
You are being stupid now.	I'll ask you again in a moment – so be ready to help us out.

actions and words become an embodiment of your professional attributes. If you really believe that your pupils can achieve their potential, or even beyond it, because you can't be sure what that potential really might be, then this will be evident from your interactions with them. Likewise, if your new school or department is one where teachers have low expectations, then they will have shown it, and their pupils will know, indicated by the comment: 'I don't know why you're bothering. We're the thick class!' (Darren, 15-year-old student, to his new teacher).

Reflective task 5.2   Responding to pupils in the classroom

1 How would you deal with this kind of comment?
2 Look at the professional attributes standards (Appendix 1). Your response would make visible your professional attributes, demonstrating your fundamental beliefs about the purposes of education. Do you have any real examples that evidence your professional attributes in this way?

'Being' a teacher with colleagues

Your pupils are very important but they are not your only 'audience'. Becoming a teacher involves crucial interactions with other professionals. At first these will be teacher colleagues and teaching assistants. As your experience grows, and certainly after your induction year, you could be dealing directly with professionals such as speech therapists, social workers and community health workers. Here, however, we are concerned with your initial encounters, as a trainee or NQT, with those close colleagues who will be supporting you.

❝ I was really looking forward to meeting my mentor but kind of nervous as well. I hoped I could talk to him easily because I had to rely on him to guide me through the next ten weeks.
(Sarah, one-year science PGCE, on meeting her first mentor) ❞

Think about how you felt when you met your new teacher colleagues for the first time. It would be quite typical in this situation for you to have felt unsure. You may have found it difficult to join in their professional, or work-related, conversations. This is not just because you don't know *them* very well, although this is part of it, but you don't really understand what/who they are talking about on a professional level. You do not yet belong to their 'group culture' and you are not tuned into their professional attributes or values, their language and the specific characteristics of their work place. If you are thinking at this point that you have never had difficulties in joining in such conversations then either your teacher colleagues were extremely accommodating to you, or your 'reading' of the situation may not have been entirely reliable.

❝ Well, she challenged something the Assistant Head said in the staff room and we nearly fell off our chairs.
(school mentor about her new trainee, two days into teaching practice) ❞

Reflective task 5.3   Creating a first impression

1 What impression of herself did this beginning teacher create in the eyes of her new colleagues?
2 What impression was she perhaps trying to make?
3 Where did she go wrong?

'Being' a teacher in the school

Your feelings towards the type of school you are placed in and the way you respond to people and situations can influence your conduct as a beginning teacher. Consider the reflections of Paul and Jenny below:

❝ My new school is in quite an affluent area. I looked up their results and the 5 A* – C GCSE results were above the national average. I thought it would have an academic ethos and the pupils would be keen to learn. I was wrong. Lots of pupils are unwilling to contribute. They don't appreciate

anything you do for them. My mentor told me that that although the pupils' GCSE results appeared to be good, in fact many of the pupils here are underachieving. Pupil engagement and motivation became key challenges for me. I wish I had begun my placement with a more open mind.
(Paul, PGCE mathematics trainee, two weeks into second teaching practice)

I was dreading my placement school. Everyone said it was rough. When I got there, I was amazed. The teachers were great, everyone was so friendly and supportive and OK some of the kids were challenging but I really loved being there. It was like an oasis of calm – once you got inside those locked gates that is.
(Jenny, GTP ICT trainee reflecting on second school placement) 〞

If you are a subject teacher then you will also have to fit into your department and this will have its own particular ethos or culture. Ball and Goodson (1985) write about the 'separateness and ideologically distinct social and institutional roles' of subject specialists. Each departmental ethos may, or may not, mirror or even complement the philosophy of the whole school (or yours). This can create tensions for beginning teachers who are trying to fit into their school department. Similar conflicts can arise if you are working across phases, where for example there might be different approaches for different year groups (or key stages).

Joining the teacher culture and making relationships

If you want to be a teacher then you need to find a way into the general teacher culture and into your subject culture. Relationships with your colleagues are essential to you. They will support you teaching your classes and working alongside them will help you become part of a team, school and wider professional culture. Belonging to a team or department involves sharing beliefs and behaviours (see Case Study 5.1).

Case Study 5.1   Adapting to different school cultures

Phil was a PGCE secondary trainee who, as part of his training, spent a week in a primary school between his two secondary placements. He wrote:

❝ At Primary School, the pupils led their lessons to some extent. The discussion sessions allowed them to think about a topic, be creative and express their opinions . . . These activities then helped the teacher decide how to direct the lesson. This was an aspect of

> differentiation I had not considered before. These approaches gave the pupils responsibility for their learning and were really refreshing to observe. I intend to run discussion sessions in my next placement. **99**

However, several weeks later, Phil wrote:

> **66** The teaching style in my school is extremely teacher-led, with the pupils trying to learn what the teacher is telling them in the way that the teacher is telling them. I feel very nervous about implementing the approaches I have planned as they will 'go against the grain' in my secondary school. **99**

Phil came up against what Hargreaves calls 'cultures of teaching' (1995: 85), in finding the views of his department colleagues to be different from his own. Other studies have explored the relationship between professional communities and new members of the community. Lave and Wenger (1991) describe how relationships between people working toward the same goals create members of a 'community of practice'. Novice members of such communities begin as 'peripheral participants' and develop their expertise (and become more central) by working alongside more expert others. The newcomers appropriate professional practice (including necessary knowledge and technical skills) through involvement in the school community (considered further in Chapter 6).

Hodges (1998: 280) stresses the importance of wanting to belong to the group and how this desire will influence 'the quality of participation' and therefore the quality of belonging. Sacks (2005: 15) further explains that teachers 'construct their own ideas of "how to be", "how to act" and "how to understand" their work' and that this process is one that is constantly negotiated with others.

Thus we can see learning to become a teacher as a socio-cultural process and, drawing on Vygotsky (1978), at the heart of this process is professional language or 'teacher discourse'. Teachers use discourse both to describe their work and to learn through their work (Jurasaite-Harbison and Rex 2010: 268). These conversations (and non-verbal communications) arise within educational structures, such as schools and subject departments, and can range from formal meetings to casual conversations.

In addition, teachers learn by 'thinking as teachers' and 'being teachers' in a variety of teacher situations or contexts. This point links back to the significance and nature of teacher cultures or **communities of practice**. In order to learn you need to find ways of belonging, and this will require you to 'read' social situations and critically reflect upon them in order to participate effectively. As ten Dam and Blom (2006: 658, emphasis added) have pointed out, 'Participation is thus both a learning objective and a means of learning. Learning through participation as described above, however, demands *"reflection"*.'

Typical difficulties facing beginning teachers

Praxis shock

The first experience of beginning teaching has been described as a potential '**praxis** shock' (Veenman 1984; Kelchtermans and Ballet 2002a; Smagorinsky et al. 2004). This particular challenge arises when beginning teachers try to adopt a professional identity and purpose in an unfamiliar, perhaps conflicting, context. In other words the reality of being a teacher does not match what was expected. In order to be able to recognize this 'praxis shock', and the feelings of vulnerability and uncertainty that can accompany it, you will need a good understanding of yourself and your values.

Knowing yourself

What kind of person are you? Do you have a strong sense of belief in yourself and your judgements? Do you lack confidence? Are you instinctive? Are you sensitive to those around you? Do you like to talk? Are you a good listener? What are your values? How far do you reflect on events and situations in order to learn from them? Are you an idealist or a fatalist? (see Chapter 8). These more personal, or affective, aspects of yourself, which are often called your inter- and intrapersonal skills, will impact directly upon your capacity to learn how to be a teacher in your school.

As highlighted in Chapter 3, your identity and your aspirations will have been shaped by your previous life and educational experiences, also known as your narrative or biographical perspective (Carter and Doyle 1996; Goodson 1996). However, although you will have been influenced by your own teachers and educational experiences, you are entering new territory, and as a teacher, not a learner.

Using critical reflection

Your main allies on this professional learning journey are the personal and developing professional qualities within yourself (your professional attributes), your colleagues and most importantly your capacity to learn within different contexts. Your principle learning tool is that of critical reflection and it is most effectively employed in collaboration with others within different learning situations (Brookfield 1995; Larrivee 2000; Moon 2006). Through critical reflection you will deepen your understanding and appreciation of the milieu of situations, behaviours and discourse which is school life. Critical reflection enables you to solve problems. It prepares you for what is round the next corner.

So what do you reflect about and what makes reflection 'critical'? Reflection begins when you re-wind the story of an incident or event in your head and it starts to change from a sequence of events in chronological order into a sequence of questions with possible answers. You move from the 'who, what and when', to the 'why and how'. Why did this happen as it did? How could I have behaved differently? Why would action x have been a better choice than action y? When you add other perspectives and possible interpretations from your colleagues and your reading into the mix, and thereby reach even deeper understandings and possible strategies for practice, then you are reflecting critically. As a result you will be learning and developing your professional identity.

> "Reflection is recognized as a key means by which teachers can become more in tune with their sense of self and with a deep understanding of how this self fits into a larger context which involves others; in other words, reflection is a factor in the shaping of identity."
>
> *(Beauchamp and Thomas 2009: 182)*

For reflective practice to be meaningful, and thereby lead to professional learning, it needs to link into theory. It should be triggered by, and impact upon, practice.

Learning to be a teacher in a professional context

You may be on a teaching placement or you may have been appointed to a teaching post. You are excited and possibly apprehensive and you are about to begin the process of fitting into this new context. You bring with you your teaching knowledge and skills but also your personal values and professional attributes. Even if you know the school, perhaps having worked there as a teaching assistant or as an ex-student, you will be seeing it through different eyes and people will also see you differently.

University tutors' experiences of working with beginning teachers, together with relevant research (Hodkinson and Hodkinson 1997; Findlay 2006; Malm 2009), confirm that your ability to 'read' your terrain or school context and to appreciate how your colleagues are also reading and shaping this context, are vital to your success.

Teacher culture is made visible by the ways colleagues behave and interact. Therefore it is wise to watch and listen.

Case Studies 5.2 and 5.3 are two examples of beginning teachers who faced challenges in contrasting placement schools. Questions for reflection and a discussion of issues follow each example. Then there is a theoretical consideration of potential strategies or approaches that may help you to get the most from your placement.

Case Study 5.2   Creating a first impression

Hannah

Hannah arrived at her school in the spring term when the school was undergoing a period of major readjustment following the arrival of a new headteacher. Staff were unsettled. Hannah bounced in very loudly, full of enthusiasm and energy. When she disappeared at lunch time on day one to go off site, as she had on her first placement, her new colleagues wondered where she was. When they found out she went for a walk to find somewhere for a smoke, they were not impressed.

Hannah was very keen to make her mark. During day two she observed the subject leader's lesson and at the end of it, when the subject leader asked for students to leave their exercise books on the table on the way out, Hannah remarked, 'You needn't do it like that,' and proceeded to implement the method she had learned on her first placement. Hannah thought she was being helpful, showing initiative and modelling a 'better' approach. The subject leader took a different view.

Reflective task 5.4   Thinking about Hannah's situation

Why did things start to go wrong for Hannah?

1 Put yourself in the subject leader's shoes. How might you have felt about Hannah's intervention?
2 What did Hannah want to achieve? Can you think of an alternative approach that she may have taken?
3 Which professional attributes was she clearly failing to meet?

Reflecting on Hannah's situation

So what went wrong for Hannah? You may think it obvious, but it was not obvious to her. You may think that Hannah's ideas and motives were sound but that she went about things in the wrong way. Hannah was not sensitive to her new context and the ways her new colleagues behaved. She did not understand her 'place' as a newcomer. Hannah did not experience any initial 'praxis shock' (Kelchtermans and Ballet 2002a). That experience came later, when it was much harder to make the necessary adjustments and rebuild relationships.

Hannah assumed that it was appropriate to leave the premises to have a smoke because this had been accepted on her first placement. She knew that her second school was very different in terms of the catchment area and examination results, but had not considered how the staff culture may also be very different. Hannah did not appreciate that she needed to spend time getting to know her colleagues in order to find out about the department culture and expectations. As Van Maanen (1988: 3) explains, 'culture is not itself visible'. Instead, teacher culture is made visible by the ways colleagues behave and interact. Therefore it is wise to watch and listen before acting or reacting.

Hannah was a confident person who felt comfortable with the teacher identity she had established on her first placement. However she did not expect her new school colleagues to have different values and expectations. In fact theirs was a very different community of practice (Lave and Wenger 1991). Hannah did not spend any time trying to 'read' this new social landscape. She did not begin to 'fit in' and therefore she struggled to establish her teacher identity in her new school.

> "[S]uccessful socialisation is contingent not only on the individuals located at the heart of the process, but equally on the explicitly promoted school ethos, as well as the tacitly agreed rules, norms and values guiding pupils and staff in their day-to-day behaviour towards each other."
>
> (Jones 2005: 517)

In addition, Hannah did not appreciate her place and status in a senior teacher's classroom. For example, had she said to the subject leader that in her previous school she had been encouraged to collect the books in a particular way and asked whether it would be an appropriate method, then the conversation may have developed into a comparison of different schools and students and how one method may be appropriate in one school (perhaps where pupils are likely to leave without handing work in) but not be as necessary in another.

Unfortunately this incident, together with several others, served to sour the relationship between the trainee and her colleagues. Hannah was placed in the category of 'trainees who think they know everything'.

What we can learn from Hannah?

A key factor underpinning Hannah's difficulty was her inability or unwillingness to critically reflect. Her case could support McIntyre's (1993) view that beginning teachers do not have sufficient experience to engage in reflective practice. Instead they need to engage in 'practical theorizing' whereby they 'learn in their practice from other people's ideas, both those of experienced practitioners and those of educational researchers and scholars' (Hagger and McIntyre 2006: 58, in Hagger et al. 2008:162).

However, this 'apprenticeship' model is a very limited view of the capacity of most trainee teachers. Practical theorizing gave Hannah practices that worked for her on her first placement but these behaviours did not transfer successfully into her new school. The difficulties she faced could only be resolved fully through critical reflection. It was not enough simply to remodel herself on her new colleagues' behaviour. In order to gain QTS Hannah had to reach a deeper understanding of her new position and realign her professional values in order to acquire a teacher identity that was acceptable in her new context.

Reflecting on theory and strategic approaches

Roberts and Graham (2008), drew from the work of Lacey (1977) and Zeichner and Tabachnick (1985), to identify a sequence of three social strategies that may be useful for beginning teachers to help them 'fit in' to their schools and make progress in their professional learning. The first is relevant here, and it is called 'promoting conformity'. This strategy involves compliance with the demands of the learning context.

In order to 'comply', beginning teachers need to use their social skills to 'read' the school and subject culture while building relationships with colleagues. Induction into school and subject cultures involves adaptation to and adoption of the language and practices of the group (Vygotsky 1978; ten Dam and Blom 2006). As we have seen, Hannah did none of these things. It is helpful to recall Lave and Wenger's ideas about 'community of practice' and how only through quality participation can beginning teachers develop their identities and professional practice (Hodges 1998). It is also worth reflecting on Hagger et al.'s (2008) finding that an acceptance of context and a willingness to 'make things work' are necessary approaches to learning effectively in new settings.

Reflective task 5.5   How well do you 'fit in'?

Study Table 5.2. How do you feel currently about your school, and at what stage do these feelings place you? To what extent are you doing what Roberts and Graham suggest that successful teachers do at this stage? What else could you do?

Table 5.2   Examples of contrasting teacher talk

1	What kinds of schools have you worked in to date? How did you learn about your new schools?		
	If you are beginning your teacher training	*If you are at least half way through your teacher training*	*If you are a newly or recently qualified teacher*
2	To what extent is the 'culture' of your first school congruent with your expectations, values and ideas about teaching?	What 'culture clashes' have you experienced to date in your placement schools, and how have you dealt with these?	How did apply for your first teaching post? Did you select the school? On what basis? How comfortable are you that your values are congruent with those of the organization?
3	How easy or difficult is 'fitting In' proving to be? What reasons would you give for this?	Have you found it easier to 'fit in' in some schools than in others? Why/not?	In what ways is being a qualified teacher easier, and in what ways is it more difficult, in respect of 'fitting in' to the school culture?
4	To what extent will you need to 'conform' to the culture of your school? How will you do this?	What is to be gained by conforming to organizational culture? What are the disadvantages?	In what ways have expectations, values and ideas about teaching have changed since your first experience of a school as a professional?

Strategic approaches in practice

So far we have considered a case in which a beginning teacher did not acknowledge, let alone adjust to, the specific natures of her school context and failed therefore to build positive relationships with her colleagues. In Case Study 5.3 the beginning teacher has taken those initial steps of fitting into a new learning community and then finds himself not being given the support needed to progress.

> **Case Study 5.3   Using reflection to fill gaps in mentoring support**
> **Ravin**
>
> 66 I was thrown into the proverbial deep end and allowed to sink or swim. Thankfully, I swam and very quickly found myself being left alone with a class whilst my mentor, 'got on with something else'. This meant I was not learning as much as I should. By the third week of my placement, I found myself becoming increasingly frustrated with my mentor. However, I found it difficult to assert myself for fear of rocking the boat or, my mentor becoming increasingly critical and perhaps even suggesting that I fail. I find myself with increasing frequency, having to bite my tongue and accept things that normally, I would not.
>
> I started to question my mentor's motives. Is she seizing the chance to get other work done? Or, does she believe this is how I will learn, as she claims? I believe the former is more likely.
>
> I do not feel that I can trust my mentor or her advice, as I do not feel that she has had my best interests at heart. Instead, I have been using the advice and feedback of another teacher in the department. It seems as if all of my constructive criticism has come from her and any issues that I have had, she has dealt with them for me. In a way, she has become my unofficial mentor. 99

Reflecting on Ravin's situation

Unfortunately Ravin's mentor adopted a 'sink or swim' approach to training, which was not what Ravin was expecting but it can happen (Hobson and Malderez 2005: 122). Ravin's capacity for reflection and analysis is strong. His initial reading of the situation was that the mentor left him to get on with it because she was busy, and because he was managing. When he did express some concerns about his ability to manage a class, the mentor still felt that she could leave him alone with them. Clearly this confirmed Ravin's growing doubts about her commitment to his training, and therefore to him.

Ravin wanted mentor support to help him progress. He had clear expectations of his mentor and she was not meeting them. The ensuing conflict between his expectations and reality created anxiety and frustration for him: he was experiencing 'praxis shock' (Kelchtermans and Ballet 2002a). Ravin had obviously considered the options open to him. He was only too aware of the significance of status and power relations, learning to 'bite his tongue'. This is not an uncommon syndrome, as Roberts and Graham (2008: 1402) have pointed out: 'trainees, as powerless newcomers, have an overriding need for security and inclusion in the school community. They do this by fitting in and avoiding confrontations with powerful staff, of whom the mentor is seen as most crucial to their survival.'

Ravin continued to manage his classes alone but was frustrated that he was not learning how to develop as a teacher and participate fully as a member of the department (Lave and Wenger 1991; Sachs 2005). His response was to take control in the only way available to him, by adopting another member of staff as an unofficial mentor.

Learning from Ravin's experiences

Clearly 'fitting in' is not a one-way process. Ravin was eager to belong and learn but his mentor did not fulfil her expected role. Thankfully Ravin exhibited an essential teacher characteristic, that of resilience (Castro et al. 2010). Ravin also sought help, and adopted a willing colleague to be his unofficial mentor.

'Promoting conformity' (Roberts and Graham 2008) or complying in order to 'fit in', has been discussed earlier in connection with Hannah. Drawing from Lacey (1977), Roberts and Graham present two further strategies which are relevant here: 'passive self maintenance' and 'strategic redefinition'. These are presented below as stages in learning to 'fit in' and may resonate with your own experience:

Strategic redefinition features in Hagger et al.'s (2008) discussion of how successful beginning teachers operate on school placement.

Ravin read his situation and realized that to a certain extent he had to accept it, so he engaged in 'passive self maintenance' for a while. He accepted what he could not change. However, his understanding of his situation led him to appreciate that he could affect some advantage, namely by adopting another mentor. Ravin achieves 'strategic redefinition' and begins to appreciate that even from a position of perceived powerlessness he was able to exercise some control over his professional development.

Beginning teachers have high expectations of the schools in which they are placed. Sometimes these expectations are unrealistic, and need to be revised; even the most willing and supportive mentor can be pulled in different directions in a busy week. Sometimes, even realistic expectations are not realized. Nearly qualified teachers, even with an entitlement to mentoring in their induction year, often find a large gap between the support they had while training and once qualified. Tools for reflection, designed to improve your practice and help you make progress, are to be found throughout this book and will help to mitigate these problems.

Reflective task 5.6a   Using reflective tools to augment school support

1 From the list in Figure 5.1, based on the findings of Hobson et al. (2009a) in relation to possible shortfalls in mentoring support, identify one area where school support, for whatever reason, may not be meeting your expectations.
2 On the action plan sheet (Appendix 4) note what this area is and at least one target for improvement. Think about how other frameworks for reflection in this book might help you.

Figure 5.1   Augmenting mentor support

For example, feedback on a lesson observation may reveal that you need to improve your questioning skills. You are not being sufficiently 'challenged' in school to be creative in the way you question pupils. You set yourself a target of using more creative ways of questioning one class you are teaching. What support does this book provide to help you?

Professional socialization

What you are doing, as you engage in the processes above, is what is often called 'professional socialization'; you are learning to fit in and engage with the organization rather than remaining on the outside as a victim of its imperfections.

From the field of Health, the Hinshaw-Davis model of socialization for trainee nurses can provide a useful comparison with the strategies outlined above in Table 5.2 (see Figure 5.2). This model goes as far as 'acceptance'. The Roberts

Table 5.3 Promoting conformity in a new school setting

	What successful beginning teachers do	How they feel
Stage 1 Promoting conformity	• Plenty of observing and listening – people and situations • Keep notes as there is too much to remember, e.g. names and information • Show enthusiasm and a willingness to be involved	• Enthusiastic and perhaps apprehensive • A desire to 'fit in' and be seen as a teacher • Concern that there is so much to find out and remember • A desire to be successful and avoid mistakes
Stage 2 Passive self-maintenance	• 'Read' accurately the situation in which they find themselves. • Recognize the need to comply with this situation and determine to do so • Use conscious tactics to maintain compliance	• Dissatisfaction at need to conform • Tensions stemming from perceived differences in values and attitudes • Disappointment at perceived unsatisfactory relationship with mentor and/or other colleagues
Stage 3 Strategic redefinition	• 'Look and listen' to achieve compliance • Develop strategies to change how they are perceived by colleagues • Proactively seek opportunities to shape and advance their professional development	• Sensitive to their personal and professional selves but also the needs of others • Confident in their own developing pedagogical and subject knowledge • Increasingly part of the 'community of practice' • Comfortable about, or at least reconciled to, the need to be professionally proactive

Source: After Roberts and Graham 2008: 1402

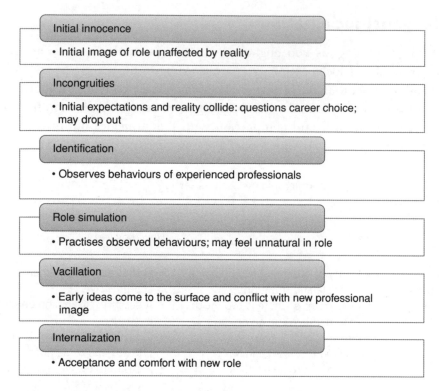

Figure 5.2 A model of professional socialization

Source: Adapted from the Hinshaw-Davis model of socialization in Chitty 2005: 204

and Graham teacher model extends the final stages of the Hinshaw-Davis model by presenting ways in which conflicts or challenges can be resolved not through acceptance but through opportunism, or proactive behaviour, on the part of the beginning teacher. By engaging in reflective practice to address the challenges you face, you will be moving into the final stages of professional socialization in your current context, and furthermore you will be developing key skills to make the socialization into new environments easier to manage. The reflective questions in Figure 5.3 should help you further to consider the kinds of questions you could be asking in order to get the most from your placement. It sets Moon's (1999: 180) schema of reflective thinking alongside a process of teacher socialization which is informed by Lacey (1977), Roberts and Graham (2008), and the Hinshaw-Davis model (1976, in Chitty 2005).

Sequence for reflection →

Socialization strategies		Emerging awareness	Developing and clarifying new learning	Integrating new learning	Enhancing, anticipating or imagining the nature of improved practice
Induction	Orientation Role expectations	What information do I need? Where do I get information from? What is expected of me?	What are the significant background factors here? What have I learnt so far that will help me fit in?	What do I already know that will help me to continue to learn in this context?	How do I need to behave in order to learn here? What do I need to be able to do?
Fitting in/ compliance	Building relationships with significant others	Who are my colleagues? What are their roles and responsibilities? What do they expect of me?	How do my colleagues relate to each other? What can each teach me? Who will be most important to my learning? Who can show me how?	How have I learnt from colleagues in the past? How best can I work with these colleagues in order to learn from and with them?	They are helping me to learn/ improve – how can I reciprocate? How can I try new ideas and involve them too?
Self-preservation	Identification of tensions/ conflicts/ vacillation	Are there any difficulties, tensions or conflicts eg. concerning policy or procedures/ between colleagues/between myself and my colleagues? Can I describe these tensions? How do I feel about this?	What is the nature of these conflicts/tensions? What do I think is causing them? How can I understand this better – what can I read/who can I talk to ?	How is this situation different from what I have experienced in the past? How is this situation affecting how I am learning and what I am learning? How is it impacting upon my position here? What are the implications for my learning?	How can I continue to learn within this situation? How should I act in order to not be adversely affected by this situation? How should I act in order to benefit from this situation? To what extent is this possible?
Strategic repositioning	Internalization and resolution	Am I able to get the most from this placement? To what extent am I meeting requirements? What are the opportunities and barriers here?	To what extent am I meeting expectations? What do I need to learn? How can I exceed expectations?	How can I continue to build on the developments I have already made? To what extent am I applying my learning with ease i.e. it is becoming second nature? What is still hard to reconcile and how am I dealing with it?	What does my reading tell me about alternative possibilities? Is it possible to change the situation to my benefit and if so how? Is it possible to take advantage of situations in order to develop my learning and if so, how? How might this experience help me in the future?

Figure 5.3 Socialization matrix for beginning teachers

Source: Developed from Moon's schema of reflective activity; Roberts & Graham's socialization strategies and the Hinshaw-Davis Model of Socialisation

---

Reflective task 5.6b

1 Using the socialization matrix as a guide, identify the questions you need to answer in order to succeed in your action plan.
2 Identify sources of help from within this book to support your learning and finalize your action plan (Appendix 4).

Summary

This chapter has presented critical reflection as central to the process of acquiring a professional identity within different professional learning cultures and thereby developing as a teacher.

Your teacher education course, specifically the placement experience, can be seen as a process designed to socialize you into the accepted behaviours and **norms** of being a teacher. Phelan (2001: 584) presents this as 'an integrating rather than a radicalizing role'. A key argument in this chapter is that the best teacher education supports integration, but also should provide a basis for future radicalization. That is to say, you need to know how to conform, but you should also learn how to become an innovative teacher who can contribute to changes in teaching. It is clear that adopting a teacher identity and having a sense of belonging to a teacher culture are necessary for you to develop professionally. Your acquisition of professional attributes becomes an outward display of your inner values and beliefs about learning and teaching. As stated in the introduction to this chapter, your journey towards becoming a teacher is both cognitive and affective.

Conclusion

Ideally your learning context is an environment, or community of practice, (Lave and Wenger 1991) that will support your professional development. As you progress professionally you will use critical reflection to move your knowledge, understanding and performance towards that of your more experienced colleagues. Teacher socialization, however, can cause the progress to falter. Real situations are sometimes less than ideal training contexts, and beginning teachers need to be critically reflective and active agents in their learning. From a position of 'fitting in' or 'integration', you are able to move into full participation in your professional learning. If the circumstances are not 'ideal' or 'supportive', you will have to find a 'best fit' position from which to look for ways to change situations or take advantage of any professional development opportunities that arise (Lacey 1977). The uncertainties and problems faced on placement can appear to be negative experiences. However, it is important to take a longer term view and see them as opportunities to learn. Helsing confirms the importance of uncertainty, even confusion, in the developmental process as 'a reflective practitioner can recognize these feelings as opportunities for growth, learning, and increased success' (2007: 1323).

In the long run 'a smooth ride' in which you do not learn to be proactive and independent may not be good preparation for a teaching career in a fast-changing world and it is not a good training ground for independence, leadership and innovative practice.

Key learning points

1 Learning how to become a teacher:
   • is an emotional and psychological undertaking;
   • involves acquiring a new professional identity;
   • involves developing professional attributes or qualities;
   • involves critical reflection.
2 Professional attributes reflect your values which are revealed by such things as your appearance, body language, voice and actions.
3 Professional attributes are an expression of your teacher identity.
4 Learning how to be a teacher is a social activity. You must learn how to belong to a teacher culture and every learning setting is different.
5 You may experience praxis shock – a clash between your ideals and the realities of school life.
6 Critical reflection will help you to make sense of yourself, other people and situations so that you can reach deeper understandings and find possible solutions to future challenges.
7 Critical reflection will help you to move from the periphery to participate in the centre of professional life.
8 There is a hierarchy of socialization that can help you to learn how to belong and develop your teacher identity:
   • learn how to fit in by watching, listening and sensitively participating;
   • build relationships;
   • recognize problems or tensions;
   • re-position yourself to take advantage of, or even create opportunities.
9 Your initial goal is to integrate and develop a 'working' teacher identity. However, eventually you may use your 'insider' understanding to make innovations and help to transform education.
10 An unproblematic placement may seem desirable but it is highly unusual. Reflective practice tools help you to supplement and augment any perceived 'gaps' in support and solve problems.

Identifying and mapping your complementary support systems: who are your partners in reflection?

Dot Heslop and Linda Devlin

Individual commitment is a group effort – that is what makes a team work, a company work, a society work, a civilization work.

Vince Lombard (American football coach)

Introduction

Learning to teach, and reflection on your teaching, are clearly not solitary activities. This chapter explores some of the possibilities for learning with others. In your professional training you will encounter may sources of support as well as the more documented, formal support from tutors and mentors. You will observe good role models of how to be as a teacher, and you will learn what sort of behaviours you wish to avoid. You will receive emotional support to sustain you, moral support to encourage you, and guidance on how to respond in given situations. You have already seen, in Chapter 5, how every person with whom you interact has their own personality and value system, and, like you, is required to 'fit in' with the norms and values of the institution. A key message of this chapter, therefore, is that your reflections with and about other people should be open-minded and responsive, taking account of the affective and the cognitive aspects of your professional relationships. As the chapter progresses, the following questions are addressed:

- What kinds of support exist within organizations, and who can offer it?
- How can you be proactive in seeking complementary support?
- What reflective skills will best support you in your encounters with a wide range of professionals?

What kinds of support exist within organizations?

In Chapter 5 we saw how sometimes formal support systems can fail to meet beginning teachers' expectations or needs, and that few school experiences are unproblematic by the nature of things. In this chapter we provide ideas about how you can be proactive in identifying appropriate personal networks to supplement and complement formal support.

Consider first Andrew's then Katie's reflective comments below, about their experience of teaching PE and science in secondary school:

> 66 Building good relationships with various staff members helps endlessly when in need of advice, gaining relevant and good specific feedback to teaching, and assistance when needed in controlling pupil behaviour. Everything is interlinked through building a good working relationship with members of the department and school.
>
> *(Andrew, one-year PE PGCE, middle of final practice)* 99

As a non-specialist in dance, but with the courage to teach it to Years 7 and 8, Andrew needed both educative ('this is what you could do') and supportive ('you'll be great at this, but I'm here to help') input. Although not his mentor, the dance specialist had very specific expertise that Andrew lacked. He observed her teach, jointly reflected on the dynamics of his classes, clarified learning objectives and discussed teaching ideas. Initially they co-planned some lessons, but Andrew became increasingly autonomous as his confidence grew. An unexpected positive outcome was the motivational effect this had on the pupils, who benefited from the collaboration between expert and enthusiastic novice. Katie's source of support came from a different source:

> 66 In science teaching there is always a need to take advice when working in the labs. Bill the lab technician is always really helpful advising how to improve methods by altering apparatus or chemicals. He has so much experience and has seen when things don't go so well. It has been very worthwhile talking with him at the planning stage to make sure that I can learn from this and the pupils can have a better experience in the classroom.
>
> *(Katie, one-year science PGCE, start of final practice)* 99

Bill had seen many teachers undertaking practical experiments with many different classes. Furthermore, he was always around when trainee teachers were taking their first tentative steps in demonstrating and engaging learners in practical science. His extensive experience was invaluable in helping Katie to know what she could hope to achieve with different classes and at different stages of her practice.

Contrast the above with Phil's statement below:

> 66 When my mentor asked me to see the professional tutor to discuss my final report, I felt nervous. She was a deputy head who commanded a lot of respect in the school, and was always busy. Why was she making time for me? She allayed my fears straight away with a warm smile. She had read my profile, and she knew the Q standards inside out. We discussed my strengths, what I hoped to develop next, and how I planned to write my career entry profile. She surprised me by knowing that I had made real progress with my challenging Year 9 class, and asked me what I thought the pupils had learned during this process. She asked how I would build on this in my NQT year and wanted to know how much I understood about the C standards I would be working on next. I left her office feeling proud of what I had achieved, but not complacent. I was left in no doubt about what I still had to do to become worthy of the profession!
>
> *(Phil, one-year MFL PGCE, end of final placement)* 99

These case studies illustrate different types of support from which beginning teachers benefit. The non-managerial role of the dance specialist provided a challenging, but non-judgmental environment in which Andrew moved out of his comfort zone to extend his skills in teaching and learning a new activity area. In reflecting on necessary preparations for their teaching journey, Andrew and Katie nurtured relationships with more expert professionals in their learning community (Stoll et al. 2003). This could be described as a way of fulfilling the reflective practitioner's need for time to 'break from the technical rational models of learning to concrete problem solving' (Schön, 1991: 24). In other words, perhaps intuitively, they recognized that informal support provided within their institution would help with areas where they lacked confidence. Phil's meeting with the professional tutor had a managerial function, with an emphasis on the quality of his work in the context of the wider professional community. Yet there is evidence of 'nurturing' in that his successes were celebrated alongside the setting of targets for further development. A key message from the above is that whether support is formal (a designated mentor or tutor with responsibility for evaluating your performance and making judgments against professional standards) or semi-formal (working alongside other professionals who have high expectations of your behaviour and learning) or informal (offering help and information without the constraints of assessment or judgment) it can fall into any of the purposes identified in Table 6.1 (p. 94). Katie's support was informal, but it provided an opportunity for structured learning. Andrew built up a strong personal

Table 6.1 The types and functions of professional support

Kadushin 1976	**Educational** The development of individuals in order that they maximize potential and contribute to organizational success	**Supportive** The maintenance of personal well-being, harmonious working relationships and collaborative practices	**Administrative** The promotion and maintenance of good standards of work
Proctor 1988	**Formative** Constructive feedback to support development	**Restorative** Listening and supporting but also challenging to achieve potential	**Normative** Operating within organizational norms and codes of practice
Hawkins 1989	**Developmental** Developing the skills, understanding and capacities	**Resourcing** Recognizing and addressing the emotional impact of working in stressful situations	**Qualitative** Recognizing and addressing human failings, blind spots and vulnerability
Purpose	To support the development of relevant understanding and skills To provide a regular space for beginning teachers to reflect upon the content and process of their work	To validate and support the beginning teacher both as a person and as a professional To ensure that as a person and as a professional the beginning teacher is not left to carry difficulties and anxieties alone	To ensure that individuals plan and utilize their personal and professional resources effectively To assure individual and organizational quality To take disciplinary or corrective action if necessary

Provision of			
Expert role models	A listening ear to problems and tensions	A statement of expectations at macro level (for example professional standards) and micro level (for example organizational policy statements)	
Structured learning			
Clarification of the skills and knowledge required in the specific setting	Feedback on content and process of work		
	A celebration of successes	Quality assurance mechanisms, monitoring systems and processes	
Feedback on all aspects of work to support professional development	Monitoring of potential weaknesses		
Expectation that individuals will reach their full potential, with opportunities to do so.	Rigorous, open discussion when problems arise	Opportunities for the beginning teacher to be proactive rather than reactive	

Source: Adapted from Hawkins and Shohet 2006: 58–9

relationship with the dance teacher, but she gave him rigorous feedback on his teaching, and Phil's formal meeting, at which national standards were discussed, had a very personal and supportive 'feel'.

From the examples considered and the summary in Table 6.1 you can see that support can come from a range of formal, semi-formal and informal situations and relationships. For many beginning teachers support is provided by those immediately available colleagues working closely with you on a day-to-day basis. Although it is difficult to capture the full range of potential in this area, there are some obvious possibilities, including your mentor, your colleague in the department or year group, another NQT, senior staff, support staff working in the classroom and other colleagues who may briefly have a significant role to play. Modern languages teachers check their subject knowledge with the foreign language assistant in school, and design and technology trainees hone their skills on unfamiliar tools and equipment alongside the technical staff in the department.

As a beginning teacher it is important that you recognize the wide range of learning supports in your setting. However the formal support from a mentor, tutor line manager or coach will remain a central feature of your professional learning. Hawkins and Shohet (2006: 58) refer to three types of 'supervision' in supporting new professionals put forward by Kadushin (1976). These are defined as *educative, supportive*, and *normative.* They also highlight a similar model (Proctor 1988) defining these types as *formative, restorative* and *normative*, and add their own using the terms *developmental, resourcing* and *qualitative.* These terms are variously used in the supervision and induction of health care professionals, counsellors and social workers and since their development they have been increasingly applied to educational settings (Hawkins and Shohet 2006). Whatever terminology is used, each recognizes:

- the complexities of professional knowledge and applying it in practice;
- the emotional stresses and strains of professional life;
- the entitlement of the 'client' (in the case of teaching, the learners) to a high quality service, and therefore the need for rigorous quality assurance.

Professional networks should therefore provide help and support in acquiring theoretical subject and pedagogic knowledge and applying it to the development of teaching skills. Hawkins and Shohet (2006: 59) have suggested foci for each of the categories listed, and these have been adapted for the purposes of the beginning teacher in Table 6.1.

Not all the possibilities for complementary support lie within the four walls of your school or college. There are also some valuable links to be made outside of the immediate working environment, for example, many local authorities release

NQTs (like John in the example below) on a regular basis to attend newly qualified teacher networks, or share NQT training with a neighbouring school. Many subject associations may also offer reduced membership rates to beginning teachers with local and virtual support networks offering face-to-face events and forums. Many schools engage in network activity among groups of schools which serve a myriad of purposes. If you are still in training then the support networks established with your peers and other colleagues are invaluable, especially if they can be cross-phase and/or subject.

Who can support you?

Consider how interaction with a range of different people in a school setting can sometimes provide surprising opportunities for professional learning:

> 66 Regular meetings each term with other NQTs have helped me realize several things. For example, we used an 'iceberg' model to explain why the students (and staff) did not behave as expected. This showed us that the visible part of people is not all there is. There are a lot of things underneath that you can't see that make up that person.
>
> *(John, primary NQT)* 99

By reflecting on this image, John was able to use it to help him deal with a specific situation:

> 66 This idea came at a point when there was a lot of tension amongst the staff in the year group, people not getting on very well. It helped to see people differently and to be encouraged to think about how to approach them. That helped a lot as we are usually more concerned with the work that needs to be done rather than the person that is doing it. 99

In addition to the opportunity to work with colleagues closely in the formal sessions, John also recognized the high level of significance of the informal outcomes of the programmed events. He explained:

> 66 I go to the NQT meetings with Yvonne in reception. We don't have much chance to talk when we are there as we mainly talk to colleagues from other schools. It is the car journey on the way back that has turned out to be our most valuable time. We always talk about where things are going to apply in school and where it is not quite so relevant. This really helps me to see where I can use some of the ideas. 99

At this point it might be prudent to pause in order to reflect on the nature of the 'informal chat'. Pentland's (2007) view is that there is 'no such thing as idle chat'. It is simply an activity that provides time for tacit communication and unconscious bonding. While it is important that you as a beginning teacher appreciate the value of this informal learning, there can be pitfalls.

Professional behaviour requires discretion; the wise person makes it a rule not to engage in gossip or to use unprofessional language. For example, the trainee who was overheard in the staff room telling her boyfriend on her mobile phone that she had 'just had feedback from the mentor from Hell' was asked to leave the school. Note Tom's reflections:

> **❝** I managed to build good professional relationships with the staff at the school including those not in the PE department. I had regular contact with year group head teachers, LSAs (learning support assistants), maintenance, admin staff and dinner ladies.
>
> *(Tom, GTP PE Trainee, several months into teaching experience)* **❞**

Forming a good working relationship with everyone whose path you cross in life is clearly useful; in professional terms any organization where colleagues 'get on' together is more likely to be forward looking and dynamic as a result of collaborative learning and support. However, there are lines to be drawn in terms of professional values and practice.

Reflective task 6.1   Building professional values into professional relationships

This task is most useful if completed in discussion groups.

1 Consider the statements of trainee teachers below.
2 What do you perceive to be the possible pitfalls of the networks formed?
3 What advice would you give to each trainee about how they develop relationships with non-teaching staff?
4 What might be the advantages of such networks?

Will: The caretaker knew all about those boys. He gave me really good advice about how to deal with them.

Jas: The dinner lady had children in the school herself, so she was a good source of inside information.

Marie: The school secretary was on the phone to parents all the time, and really understood them. Talking to her helped me understand the children much better.

Tobias et al. (2009) emphasize the importance of acknowledging that relationships with students and their families must be based on mutual respect, trust and, where necessary, confidentiality. Forming good working relationships with non-teaching colleagues is very important, but their *experience* of pupils is not the same as having *professional knowledge.* Their research (Tobias et al. 2009) into ethics and moral reasoning in teacher education reported that trainees saw 'talking about students' personal issues in a staffroom', as disrespectful to the student. Yet casual conversations, if conducted professionally, can be enormously helpful:

> 66 In the staffroom, I mentioned the problems I was having with a boy in my Year 9 class and the teaching assistant told me about his problems at home and suggested I had a chat with his form tutor. He was great at suggesting some strategies. This made it so much easier to help him, and it helped me keep a sense of proportion about his behaviour.
>
> *(Tom, GTP PE Trainee, several months into teaching experience)* 99

When seeking support, you need to ask the question: 'What are the benefits of this partnership? Are there any negatives?' This is not easy at first, but as your knowledge and experience grow, you will be able to recognize what is useful, and why, in your professional networking. Consider Navdeep's case study (6.1) to explore the potential benefits from finding alternative reflective partners. Note the positives that can come from this, but also be aware of the potential negatives.

Case Study 6.1   Navdeep's reflections

Navdeep experienced conflict with her mentor, whose feedback was frequently negative, with no opportunity to discuss or respond. This relationship was controlled by the dominantly managerial/normative style mentor, where he maintained the power. Navdeep, previously a confident and creative trainee, began to doubt her ability and reduced her imaginative and innovative approaches to teaching PE. This clash of values and **ethos** created an extremely challenging and potentially damaging environment.

A two-way process of mutual support developed with an NQT in the department. There were many positive elements to this partnership, including the mutual boosting of morale and sharing and development of resources. Their discussions, ideas and reflection on their teaching and learning ensured progression. Sharing lesson materials enabled both young teachers to explore different teaching styles and alternative approaches. This restorative/supportive partnership seemed to be working, but its effect was to 'cut off' the mentor, who was aware that the trainee and NQT had 'joined forces'! Thus they did not identify any problems or ask for further support, but adopted a stance that 'you just have to get on with it'.

Good intentions and positive support can mask problems that need addressing and prevent solutions from being found. Better to find a cure than to keep on taking the tablets!

Reflective task 6.2 'Mapping' your support systems

1 Get a large piece of A3 paper or bigger and place your name, a symbol, or a picture that depicts yourself in the centre. Under this, add a question or problem to which you would like answers.
2 Begin a 'spider diagram', adding the types of support you need, along with names as you acquire them.
3 Consider what may be the disadvantages as well as the advantages of these encounters. Are you, for example, masking problems that need addressing rather than finding actual solutions?

This diagrammatic map is a good starting point for beginning to think about taking control of what you want to learn, and with whom.

What reflective skills will best support my learning with others?

As has been made clear in other chapters, knowledge and experience will lead to learning only where there is reflection in and on action. Making effective use of professional networking requires conscious reflection (see Chapter 4). Different people will offer different viewpoints, and there will be variations in their interpretation of events (see Chapter 3).

> For you to get the most from the network of support available to you, you need to develop your reflective skills in order to be able to sift advice and select what seems to be the best solution in your situation.

This can be helpful, provided that you are able to reflect critically, unpacking and processing the ideas of others and selecting which are useful to you. For example, some beginning teachers see different ideas presented to them as 'confusing'; they are hoping for a single 'magic bullet' to solve their problems. Others see them as 'enriching' because they have learned how to reflect and filter until they have come to a tentative solution. You will feel, at various times, guided, prompted, directed, nudged and pushed into action, and until you learn to manage this it can feel uncomfortable. For you to get the most from the network of support available to you, you need to develop your reflective skills in order to be

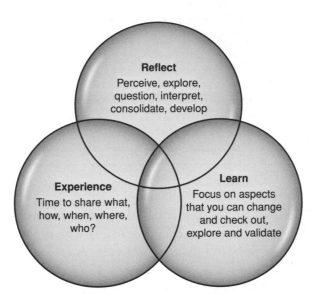

Figure 6.1   Useful foci for reflective talk

able to sift advice and select what seems to be the best solution in your situation. The remainder of this chapter encourages reflection on how to make the most of collaborative learning through:

- the power of talk (understanding each other);
- empathy with others (understanding others' situation);
- self-reflection (understanding your own needs);
- critical incidents (recognizing and exploiting opportunities to learn).

The power of talk

The power of dialogue and reflective practice is recognized as a tool for organizational problem solving (Schön 1983; Senge 1990; Isaacs 1999) and semi-formal support is one way in which this dialogue can be facilitated. The benefits of reflecting with others, in pairs and groups, can be used to develop awareness of the wide range of issues utilizing one or more support opportunities. Professionals in training or working sessions often pool their ideas in group activities, using language to reflectively explore and consider issues expressed in Figure 6.1.

Within a group, there may be different ways of interpreting and conceptualizing happenings, events or actions, as the activity in Reflective task 6.3 illustrates

---

Reflective task 6.3   What do you mean, what do I mean?

1 Find a willing partner.
2 Independently record what the words in Figure 6.2 mean to you and write an example of how you have applied them in the past.
3 Share your responses. Are they identical?
4 Reflect on the different experiences and interpretations.

What can be learned from this is the importance of clarifying any specialized terminology used during talk, as misconceptions can lead to precious time wasted. Using time effectively is a key to success in learning with others.

In informal settings, reflective dialogue with others is characterized by careful listening, active questioning and openness to alternate views and maybe even profound changes to one's beliefs. Mason (2002) argues that to develop professionally you need to increase your sensitivity to noticing what is going on around you and be able to determine possible actions that might result. You may find that terms such as 'mindfulness' 'noticing' and 'active listening' are key features of reflective practice. Consider Sandeep's reflections:

> 66 The best way I see of improving my teaching skills is by continual discussions with my colleagues and talking to experienced practitioners, giving me insight into teaching with the guidance to develop my subject knowledge in a variety of areas, in particular dance, swimming and personalized learning. This has become a strength following discussions with the sports mentor, English as an Additional Language (EAL) support staff, learning support staff, the NQT in PE, my mentor and the professional tutor. The swimming teacher has been particularly helpful, providing great insight into a wide range of pupils, identifying needs and discussing possible solutions.
>
> *(Sandeep, PE PGCE, start of second placement)* 99

Sandeep displays Dewey's 'open-mindedness' and whole-heartedness' (Chapter 1) as she actively seeks support to improve her practice.

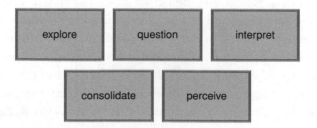

Figure 6.2   Important terms to support reflective talk

Empathy with others

During your training and beyond, staff create time to co-reflect in order to engage in meaningful dialogue with you. They recognize that a beginning teacher with less experience may have a valuable fresh view of the teaching context and practice within it. Many wish to invest time in shaping the identity of new professionals and learn from them. They recognize your views and experiences differ from theirs. These teachers recognize that the development of their empathy with learners is a significant outcome of their own professional learning (Beresford and Devlin 2006). Thus it is important for you to recognize that reflection with others, even more experienced others, is a two-way process from which all parties can benefit. You need to consider not just what you get from, but also what you can give, to the process. Busy professionals, however, need you to take responsibility for your learning by being well prepared for your encounters with them (see Chapter 10).

> Being prepared for reflective encounters with others through initial self-reflection helps you to make the most of support networks.

The role of self-reflection

Before beginning to reflect with others, your self-reflection should lead you to:

- identify and clearly articulate the issue you need help with (see Table 6.1);
- think about the responses you would like in your encounters with others – what should the outcomes be?
- find the 'right person' to help you, seeking advice if necessary;
- accept the constraints of the busy working life of others, and have realistic expectations;
- recognize any weaknesses or personal failings in your professional encounters, for example are you open to constructive criticism, or defensive?
- use previous encounters to build up your preferred 'package' of support (Hawkins and Shohet 2006: 37). What kind of help are you seeking? Early in your training, this may be a prescriptive solution, whereas later you may simply want to bounce your own ideas around with someone else.

Being prepared for reflective encounters with others through initial self-reflection helps you to make the most of support networks. When support roles are undertaken by busy professionals, they can result in reflective discussions becoming a set of 'shoulds and should nots' (Yero 2002). In discussing approaches and possibilities, a 'quick fix' might be to provide you with a list of things to try. This process, however, does not always nurture self-evaluation and thoughtful reflection. It is more likely to occur if you come along with a 'blank sheet' or series of questions that those supporting you need to fill or respond to.

Using 'critical incidents' to stimulate your learning

In the case of Michael below, a specific 'learning moment' provided the impetus for his learning:

> 66 I attended an after school session about 'out of seat learning' and how to improve attainment levels through classroom management. I learned that seating plans can be useful to help lower ability pupils work alongside the more able students. I'd really like to explore this idea further.
> *(Michael, mathematics PGCE secondary, start of second placement)* 99

Michael collected ideas on this theme through informal discussions with colleagues in the department, his pupils, and the teaching assistant (TA). He then had a very clear agenda item for discussion with his mentor. What is significant here is that talking about something that happened to you with others is a really good way of:

- making your learning visible to you and to others;
- identifying what you need to do to build on your learning;
- providing evidence of professional growth and development, for example for assessment against the Q or C standards.

Consider Julie's reflective comments, below, about her experience of planning and organizing a Personal, Social, Health and Economic education (PSHE) day in a secondary school:

> 66 I became involved in planning and delivering a PSHE day with a focus on organizing a drink awareness session for Year 10 students. This was in a workshop format that would be repeated throughout the day, so all the Year 10 students would participate in a range of interactive activities. The team included one experienced school nurse, two trainee school nurses and two trainees. Our combined skills and knowledge soon got the planning buzzing, and not only did I add to my knowledge about the physiological effect of drink but gained insight into the psychological effect on families. This included valuable confidential information from the experienced school nurse about some pupils I found difficult to engage in lessons. The ideas we came up with were great for the day, but resulted in a major breakthrough for some of the students in PE. The knowledge gained from this partnership helped me see beyond the bad behaviour to the 'cause and effect'. More

importantly it supported me to try new approaches and explore different ways of engaging some very challenging pupils. The reflective partnership continued through the rest of the placement, the nurse gaining insight and skills in teaching and delivering information to the pupils from me, while I gained quality ideas on a range of medical conditions such as **ADHD**, **Asperger syndrome** and others specific to pupils I teach. Thank you school nurses.

(Julie, PE secondary PGCE, start of second placement)

Reflective task 6.4   Using critical incidents to develop your learning

1 Use the reflective questions in Table 6.2 to help you explore ways of exploiting your own learning through critical incidents.
2 Add your new ideas to your map sketched earlier.

Table 6.2   Using critical incidents to question and reflect on professional learning

Self-reflection (adapted from Brookfield 1995)	Reflection with others into practice
At what moment (in a critical incident) did I feel most engaged with what was happening? What action did I find most affirming or helpful? Who was involved? Why did this go well or not so well? At what moment (in specified situation or time period) did I feel most distanced from what was happening? Am I listening carefully to the reflection on this issue? Do I need to rethink the way I have interpreted this incident? How did this make me feel about my own practice in relation to the practice of others? What about the critical incident has surprised me most?	How will the process of reflection on this incident influence practice? What do I need to know about the context in which I found myself, and who can tell me? What would others have done in this situation? Am I aligned to the thinking of other colleagues? What aspect of practice may be changed/continued on the basis of this experience? Am I placing enough/too much emphasis on this incident? How can a negative experience have potential for a positive outcome on my practice? What does this incident tell us about my professional learning? What have you learned from this experience and how will it influence future practice? What interventions or support by others I need to address unexpected issues?

Summary

The learning organizations in which you train and work provide rich ground for your professional learning. This chapter has encouraged you to tap that source by helping you to identify the types and purposes of support available to you and to build up a 'map' of your present and future learning needs. Case studies and reflections of beginning teachers illustrate the personal qualities and reflective skills needed to maximize these learning opportunities, and through the reflective tasks you have been encouraged to develop approaches to working with, and learning from, a range of significant professional others.

Conclusion

This chapter has emphasized the importance of incorporating formal, semi-formal and informal opportunities for reflection into your support network and the utilization of these reflections to inform your learning experiences. Personal reflection can be empowering, encouraging ownership of events, outcomes and future actions. Reflective practice with others is a skill that needs practice. It can consist of complex layers and manoeuvres, and needs to be based on trust, confidentiality, agreed boundaries and ground rules. Exchanges on an 'any time, any place, anywhere' basis with others can be helpful, but need reflective 'filtering'. 'Practical wisdom' to make the most of your daily encounters will come through conscious reflection.

Key learning points

In order to maximize your professional learning you need to:

- understand the formal, semi-formal and informal networks of support within and outside the organization in which you are working;
- recognize that the needs of the learners are of paramount importance and all your professional learning is geared to ensuring that you meet the professional standards to the highest level possible. 'Support' is a complex concept that includes consideration for you as a person but is more focused on your development as a competent professional;
- appreciate the value of communication with colleagues and peers, and reflect on the impact of your relationship with them;
- use reflective processes to identify your priorities for learning and to 'sift' the ideas and advice given.

How can you use reflection to develop creativity in your classroom?

Lesley Mycroft and Paul Gurton

> *Prospective teachers who are trained in thinking and teaching creatively and in creative problem-solving will be better prepared to value and nurture the same creative characteristics in their classrooms.*

(Abdallah 1996: 52)

A key issue for any beginning teacher is the ability to think outside the box. In an age where there is a plethora of web-based and paper 'resources' that support teaching at every stage and in every subject, it is sometimes hard for new entrants to the profession to see beyond the subject content and focus on the needs of the learners. Fundamental to good practice are teaching approaches that actively engage learners and support the development of understanding within, across and through a subject area. Honing these skills takes time and experience, but it also requires a flexible and creative approach – a willingness to experiment and take risks, and, importantly, an understanding of one's self as a learner too.

This chapter begins by discussing what 'creativity' might mean for you. It then goes on to provide some definitions of this complex notion. It is structured to help you see how to use reflection to develop creatively, and also how to be creative in your reflections. The following questions will be addressed as the chapter progresses:

- What is meant by 'creativity'?
- What is the relationship between creativity and reflective practice?
- How can creative thinking support the development of **learner-centred** approaches?
- Why is collaboration so important in the creative process?

Defining creativity

Reflective task 7.1   What does creativity mean to you?

Before you read any further pause for a moment and note down what you think creativity means.

Now consider Figure 7.1. How do your definitions (or descriptions) compare to those given? Are they similar to a child's or the experienced teacher's? Or maybe there are some elements in common with the definitions offered by de Bono (1992) or NACCCE(1999).

How you view creativity is likely to determine how you teach, so you need to reflect on your understanding of the term and what it means to you.

Creativity is regarded by governments as a desirable quality that, in individuals and organizations, makes a positive contribution to economic progress (Newton and Newton 2010). As such, it is encouraged around the world (NACCCE 1999 is a good example from Britain). Yet, as can be seen from the definitions in Figure 7.1, it can be interpreted and applied in many different ways. How you view creativity is likely to determine how you teach, so you need to reflect on your understanding of the term and what it means to you. The complexities

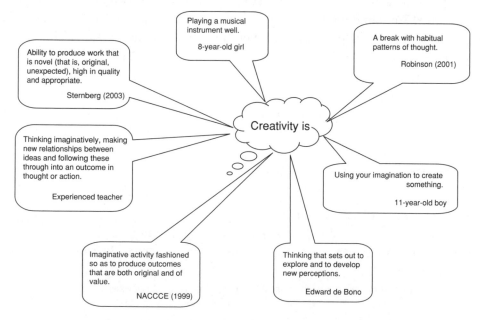

Figure 7.1   Defining creativity

of the notion of creativity are studied by philosophers and psychologists as well as educationists. Research (for example Newton and Newton, 2010) and literature reviews (for example Craft 2003; Bleakley 2004; Grainger et al. 2004) in the field of education have proposed various definitions of creativity. The picture that emerges is what Grainger et al. (2004: 243) have called a 'complex and invigorating cocktail'. From these studies emerge several points relevant to your understanding of creativity as a beginning teacher.

What is creativity?

It is easy to confuse and conflate 'teaching creatively' and 'teaching for creativity' (Grainger et al. 2004: 245). At its simplest level, 'creative teaching' might be viewed as having a fantastic PowerPoint, but if all you do with this is present it to learners, there is no creative process beyond your initial production of the resource. In reality, if you are a creative person, you are likely to teach creatively, and engender creativity in your learners. The following distinctions should help you to shape your understanding of 'creativity':

1 The distinction between ideas that are new in terms of human history (such as the invention of the steam engine) and ideas that are new to our own previous way of thinking (Boden 2001: 95). Not many of the pupils you teach over a lifetime will make important scientific discoveries, but in your lessons they can learn to be creative thinkers by constructing meanings, explanations, hypotheses, arguments and ways of doing things that are new to them (Newton and Newton 2010). Equally, as a beginning teacher, being creative in your classroom implies doing something that you have not tried before, even if it is 'old hat' to more experienced colleagues!

2 The distinction between 'creative' and 'reproductive' activity (Newton and Newton 2010). Tables 7.1a and b give some examples of these. It can be argued that some 'raw material' in the form of knowledge and skills is required before creativity can be triggered, and yet the teacher can be creative in the way that this raw material is presented and processed. You may find it useful to study Table 7.1b and think about the extent to which the described activities have the potential to promote 'productive' or 'creative' thought, and then to reflect on whether your planned tasks are 'reproductive' or 'creative' and whether you have the struck the right balance between the two.

The literature on creativity raises, in various forms, these important questions:

• What do creative teachers do?
• What do creative learners do?

Table 7.1a Reproductive and creative activity

Reproductive activity	Creative activity
Recalling, recycling or gathering information without materially adding to it, for example by talking about, listening to, reading or watching something.	Using existing information in a new context and working out where the gaps are in knowledge and understanding, for example by discussing and comparing information with others. Devising ways of finding things out. Thinking of reasons for and reasons why.
Following instructions, using **algorithms**, applying rules.	Working out rules from a given example; devising strategies for applying them in new contexts.

Source: After Newton and Newton 2010

Writers list variously the features of learning and teaching that are 'creative' (Grainger and Barnes 2006; Bleakley 2004; Cremin 2009). Beghetto's definition (2007), cited in Newton and Newton (2010: 1990) suggests that the general focus of creativity is on 'the ability to offer new perspectives, generate novel and meaningful ideas, raise new questions and come up with solutions to ill-defined problems'. Thus we can see the link between 'creative teaching' and 'teaching for creativity', for if our learners are to acquire the characteristics of creativity defined above, then as teachers we must model and demonstrate them in the classroom. Bleakley (2004) offers an interesting but complex **typology** of creativity. He points out that there is a serendipitous aspect to it (knowing how to exploit

Table 7.1b Stimulating reproductive and creative thought in primary science lessons

A child uses given scientific information to imagine what life is like on Mars.
The child watches a video showing what life on Mars would be like.
Children discuss in groups the question: is there life on Mars? They make use of their existing knowledge about Earth and space.
A child finds out from a book why the image in a mirror is laterally inverted.
The class watch a teacher-led PowerPoint presentation showing why the image in a mirror is laterally inverted.
The child thinks of a reason for the appearance of an image in a mirror, but not in a plastic tea tray.
A child devises a practical experiment to see if roughness causes friction.
A child follows an experiment from a worksheet to see if roughness causes friction.
Children discuss in groups why it is important to know whether roughness causes friction.

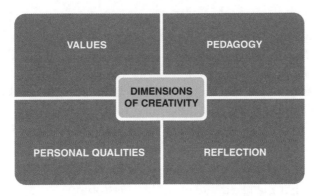

Figure 7.2a Dimensions of creativity informed by Grainger & Barnes (2006)

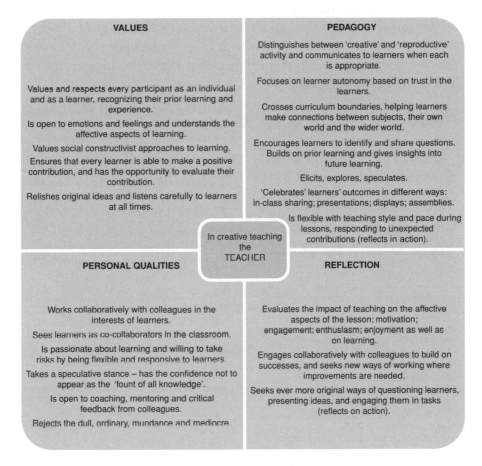

Figure 7.2b Exemplifying dimensions of creative teaching

the unexpected learning opportunity); what he calls 'accidents of discovery' (2009: 472). He also suggests that creative teachers actually take a strong stand against ordinariness, what he refers to as 'the mundane, literal, dull, mediocre, mechanical, trivial, habitual, predictable and routine' (p. 473). Cremin (2009) reports on research undertaken by Grainger and Barnes (2006) on the qualities of creative teachers, in which they identified three dimensions of creativity:

- personal characteristics of the teacher: their values and attitudes and how they perceive their role;
- pedagogy: what the teacher does in the classroom;
- ethos: what the 'creative' classroom looks and feels like.

Within each dimension they described the core characteristics that shape creativity. For the purposes of this chapter, we have adapted Grainger and Barnes' model and included the dimensions of values and reflection (Figure 7.2a), identifying what the teacher brings to each of the dimensions (Figure 7.2b) and what impact this has on the learners (Figure 7.2c).

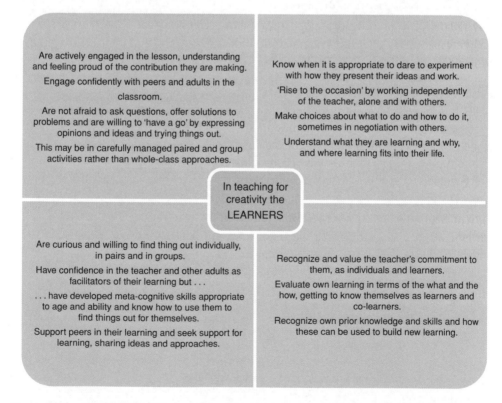

Figure 7.2c Exemplifying dimensions of teaching for creativity through what learners do

Reflective task 7.2   Exemplifying dimensions of creative teaching

1 Consider the following reflections:

66 I'm keen that through my teaching children are encouraged to clarify their thinking, reflect, negotiate, take turns, communicate, listen to others.

(James, BEd primary, second teaching practice)

As a teacher, I should not assume that the pupils are 'blank pages'. They all have previous knowledge and life experiences. This can help them to develop their understanding of new knowledge as well as help others.

(Frank, one-year MFL PGCE trainee, start of final teaching practice)

My Year 8 class is proving quite difficult. I am beginning to think that their teacher last year must have been quite didactic, as whenever I want them to think something through they just say, 'Sir, why don't you just tell us what to put?' I am struggling to get them to think for themselves and work things out.

(Jim, secondary science NQT, three months into new school)

When I first met my BTEC class, I thought 'What can I do with this lot?' There was such a mix of ability and motivation, with some barely interested in the subject. I had expected just to be able to give them the benefit of my knowledge and experience, but that clearly wasn't going to work. The class teacher sent them off to the computers to find things out. This meant that there were no discipline problems as such, but they didn't really learn anything either. I have decided to get them into a routine. We are beginning every lesson with a clear statement of outcomes, then some group work on key concepts relating to the outcomes – what they know, what they need to find out. Then each is assigned something to research, and they have time-limited access to computers, then come back and share the information with the class. My mentor was sceptical, but I think it is starting to work! Today some of the toughest looking lads gave a great little presentation and were really quite proud of themselves! I'd like to think I am helping them to be more confident about their own ability to work independently, share their ideas and ultimately be responsible for their own learning.

(Suki, PGCE, final teaching practice)

2 Think about your own aspirations as a teacher. What do you want for your learners? Using the dimensions of creative teaching in Figure 7.2b, write a short statement to summarize this.

From the above, we can suggest the values that each beginning teacher might be bringing to their classroom, such as valuing social constructivist approaches to learning (James) and recognizing prior learning and experience (Frank). Jim and Suki demonstrate similar values, but in putting them into practice came up against difficulties. For example, they faced the potential conflict between knowledge and creativity (Boden 2001: 95), when the transmission of knowledge is seen as the most efficient way of ensuring that the curriculum is covered. Suki had to work twice as hard because her way of working was different from that of the department, so at first she had little help. As Bleakley (2004: 468) highlights, innovation that is not embraced by the organization can be burdensome on the innovator.

Exemplifying dimensions of teaching for creativity

Reflections such as the above should help you to identify and make concrete your own values and characteristics as a teacher, and the extent to which you are developing 'creativity'. However, what really provides evidence of creativity is the response of learners and evidence of their learning. The following statements are drawn from one visiting tutor's written feedback on different lessons observed in secondary PGCE MFL:

1 Pupils are really enjoying the 'hunt' for the key words. They are sharing ideas both about how to do it and what to make of the vocabulary as they discover it.
2 I am delighted to see you 'taking a risk' by presenting the language first and then getting pupils in groups to work out what it means, rather than spoon feeding it to them. Why do you think some are better able to deal with this than others? I don't think it's always a question of ability. We will talk about this.
3 The 'Bonjour ... au revoir'[1] task is a really creative way of getting them to practise pairs of words with opposite meanings. It's a great differentiation tool too, as more able pupils are really wracking their brains to remember vocab they learned last year, and many are thinking very creatively beyond the 'core' vocab. I love the 'Bonjour petit frère au revoir paix'[2] I've just heard!

Reflective task 7.3   Exemplifying dimensions of teaching
                        for creativity

1 Look at the above examples alongside Figure 7.2c. What aspects of learner behaviour and outcomes suggest creative approaches to learning and teaching?

---

[1] 'Hello-goodbye', such as 'Hello rain, goodbye sun' to practise weather items of vocabulary.
[2] 'Hello little brother, goodbye peace.'

2 Think about a recent lesson that you have taught. What evidence do you have, from learners' responses, work and learning outcomes, of teaching for creativity?

3 In the light of the above, what changes could you make to your lesson to engage learners more creatively?

Suki (see above) persevered because of her own strong values linked to her intuitive sense of how 17-year-olds might work. Her reflection-on-action gave her confidence that her students were learning and responding well to this new way of working:

> 66 I wanted to start with a whole-class discussion about the last lesson, what they learned themselves and then what they could add to their learning from the presentations. I had to do a bit of 'blue sky' thinking to keep them in their seats though. So I thought: 'what if I forget the subject knowledge for now, and focus on their **meta-cognitive skills**?' So I gave them each two post-it notes, and put up two posters at opposite ends of the room. One said '**I NOW FEEL MUCH BETTER ABOUT** . . . .' and the other '**NEXT, I WANT TO LEARN TO** . . .'. They had to discuss in groups first and then write a comment to stick on each poster. I got a mixture of cognitive ('I know more about mental health problems') and meta-cognitive responses ('Not as hard as I thought to explain it to the class') so during feedback I was able to discuss both the knowledge and the skills they needed. The second poster was brilliant! They gave me so many ideas about what they needed to know and how they wanted to work.
>
> *(Suki, PGCE PCE psychology, final teaching practice)* 99

From Suki's reflections, we can deduce that her students were gaining confidence and trust in her, valuing this new approach to learning and sharing their ideas and opinions. They were beginning to see the links between this lesson, prior learning and future needs, and were responding well to Suki's creative approach to their learning. She had been willing, and able, to 'take a risk' even though she had been warned by her mentor that her students 'would only behave' if allowed to 'work' on computers all lesson. In the end, the department recognized the value of these approaches and adopted the model in their scheme of work.

For Marek, the taking of risks did not come quite so naturally. After a successful first placement with a Year 4 class, he was in his final placement, now six weeks into teaching a Year 2 class. Feedback from his mentor and tutor was positive; he planned well, and he 'taught' well too. However, he was not yet taking full account of the learners; his mentor set targets that included:

- make your lessons more interactive;
- be more creative in your approaches, so for the children there is more of a 'wow' factor.

Marek planned and taught a mathematics lesson on measurement where the learning outcome was that the children should begin to make reliable estimates of length. Marek planned for them to estimate and measure in centimetres, using objects in and around the classroom. Many aspects of his lesson were good. However, during feedback with his mentor, he came to understand that some children had not grasped the concept of length, and a few struggled with the notion of 'estimation'. They had left the estimation column blank on their worksheet, filling it in later so that the estimated and the actual were the same. He explored 'next steps' for these children with his mentor, encouraging him to 'take a risk' and be more innovative.

At first, Marek was reluctant to do this; he was being graded 'good' for his lessons, and although a 'very good' would be great, he did not want to slide to 'satisfactory', or worse, by 'losing control'. His mentor reminded him of his very good relationship with the class, urging him to exploit this, and pointing out that she and her colleagues would judge his attempts to be creative very favourably. Thus Marek could see that creative approaches carry a calculated risk, not a disaster warning! Wragg (in Wilson 2005: 188) identified risk in taking a step in an unknown direction:

> "Creativity embodies risk in the sense that if you've done something a hundred times you've got a pretty good idea of how it will go. If you've not done it before, then you don't have any idea of how it will go and it may go badly. . . . The challenge is not so much having an idea because most people can either have an idea of their own or get one from someone else. The challenge is when you're trying out the idea to make it work."

Marek explained to his mentor:

❝ I want children to enjoy what they are doing and for it to have a relevance to their experiences outside of the classroom. ❞

She wanted Marek to address the Q standards at the highest level, particularly with regard to innovation (Q8), and gave a few pointers:

❝ Try and make a link with this and the work that the children have been doing in geography where they have been making their own maps of the school. They could perhaps do some 'big' measuring using metres?
(Marek's mentor, PGCE primary) ❞

In his next lesson Marek did start taking risks. As a result of the discussion with his mentor, but using his own ideas, he devised a series of activities including estimating and measuring the length of throwing bean bags in the school hall, and using a trundle wheel to measure the length and width of the school playground. His focus here was on learner-centred teaching to ensure children were able to develop a concept. Although convinced of the value of the activities to children's learning, Marek confessed to some trepidation:

> 66 I don't know whether it will work. They may just start throwing the bean bags all at once! 99

Reflective task 7.4   Calculating the risk

1 What could have gone wrong with this lesson?
2 How might Marek's plan have mitigated any risks (reflection *before* action)?

However, fears of chaos in the classroom were allayed through a process of thorough planning and effective use of the support of his TA and the obvious enjoyment the children took in the lesson. His lesson evaluation read as follows:

> 66 At last I feel that my aspirations and the practicality of classroom teaching are not running against each other. Today the children were able to learn in a practical context and do something meaningful! All children had a pretty good go at estimating and measuring both throwing a bean bag up the hall and recording their estimates and the real measurement of the perimeter of the infant playground. I feel this is a significant step on from the work yesterday in the classroom. I could also check their understanding by the questions I asked during the activity and the plenary.
> *(Marek, one-year primary PGCE, six weeks into his final placement)* 99

Perhaps a final judgment on the effectiveness of this taught lesson came several days later when one of the boys in the class explained during a 'share and tell' session that he had been using his knowledge gained from this lesson to estimate how far he and his friends could kick a ball on the field outside their houses after school. He even asked to borrow a trundle wheel!

**Reflective task 7.5   Reflecting on how to develop creativity
                        in your classroom**

Depending on your current stage of development, consider how you would respond to the questions in Table 7.2. You will need to refer to Figure 7.2.

Table 7.2   Reflecting on how to develop creativity in your classroom

If you are beginning your teacher training	If you are at least half way through your training	If you are a newly or recently qualified teacher
Your focus at present will be on learning to articulate learning objectives and getting to know your classes. Focus at this stage on Figure 7.2b.	Having gained experience and confidence in earlier placement(s), you now need to establish yourself in a new context. Continue to focus on Figure 7.2b but with an eye on 7.2c.	Once you have established yourself (see columns 1 and 2) your reflections should be on what learners do. Focus on Figure 7.2c.
Values Are you learning the name of everyone in your class? Your aim is to ensure that everyone can make a positive contribution in your lesson. This will take time, but reflecting on this in your early evaluations will help. Do you listen carefully to learners? Sometimes they provide insights that will support your subject and pedagogic knowledge.	**Values** Do your learners have an opportunity to evaluate the contribution they make to your lessons, both formally and informally?	**Values** Are learners actively engaged in the lessons, understanding and feeling proud of the contribution they are making? Are you creating a classroom environment where learners feel confident to 'have a go' and try things out, knowing they have your respect?
Personal qualities Are you flexible and responsive to learners? Can you distinguish between the 'dull, ordinary and mediocre' and the 'creative'? Are you working collaboratively with your mentor and other teachers, TAs and peers?	**Personal qualities** In what ways are you planning for learners to be agents of their own learning? Do you see them as co-collaborators, that is, learning with you and each other, rather than being 'told' facts? What 'risks' are you taking in developing creative approaches and how are you calculating the risk? Are you ready to reject some of the 'dull' in favour of more creative approaches?	**Personal qualities** Are learners catching your enthusiasm? Are they curious and willing to find things out? Do they have confidence in you? Do other adults in the classroom have confidence in your ability to plan their contribution? Are your learners developing meta-cognitive skills appropriate to age and ability? Do they know how to use them to find things out for themselves?

Table 7.2   (*Continued*)

If you are beginning your teacher training	*If you are at least half way through your training*	*If you are a newly or recently qualified teacher*
Can you recognize the impact of creative approaches on learning in lessons you observe?	Can you evaluate the impact of creative approaches on learning for groups and individuals?	Are learners willing and able to share ideas and help each other? Are you confident enough in your subject knowledge to support them individually in doing this? Are you ready to take a persistent stand against the dull and the mediocre?
Pedagogy Can you give an example, from a recent lesson you have observed, of 'creative' and 'modelled' activity? Can you recognize the appropriateness of each in different learning contexts? Are you considering other ways of using questioning than teacher-led approaches? Can you evaluate the affective aspects of your teaching?	**Pedagogy** Are you seeing the links across subject boundaries and highlighting them where appropriate? Are you helping learners see the relevance of their learning? Have you established a clear framework for managing behaviour, so that you are developing trust in your learners? Do you 'celebrate' learners' work to make them aware of what they are learning? Are you exploring different ways of doing this with colleagues? Are you sharing ideas creatively to explore new ways of questioning, presenting ideas and engaging learners? Are all learners motivated to learn and enjoying your lessons? Are you focusing more on the learner and less on you as the teacher?	**Pedagogy** Do learners sometimes experiment with how they present their work? Are they sometimes encouraged to do so? Are they able to work productively in different ways: through talking, listening, working together and working independently? Do they sometimes have a choice in what they do? Are they aware of their developing cognition and meta-cognition?

Creativity and reflective practice

So far in this chapter we have attempted to define 'creativity' both as creative teaching and teaching for creativity, and suggested ways that you can use reflection to develop creative approaches to your teaching and to evaluate the impact of this on the development of your learners as creative individuals.

Elements of the creative process can also be applied to reflective practice. In the final section there are short case studies to illustrate how others have used reflection creatively.

Using self-knowledge through collaborative learning creatively to enhance your teaching

A first step in the process of developing self-efficacy is the understanding of one's self as a learner too. Collaborative working is as important for you as it is for your learners; it helps you to see yourself as others see you, and it allows you to share ideas and give and receive constructive criticism in a non-threatening way.

Case Study 7.1　Jas and Sarah: creativity in collaboration

In her first school experience, Jas undertook a paired placement where she and a fellow trainee worked as partners in the same classroom. Following a period of shared planning, joint teaching, alternately leading the lesson and taking a support role, Jas and her peer partner, Sarah, wrote each other a message outlining strengths. Sarah's message to Jas included:

> 66 Your activity ideas are spot-on for this age group. Children couldn't wait to get started on the DT pizza recipes with the promise of actually making and eating some at the end. But Aman and Jacob really struggled to start writing and we weren't sure how to help them. What can we talk about to make that better? I think it's the same for me . . . .'
> *(Sarah reflecting on Jas's teaching, BEd primary, first teaching practice)* 99

The two trainees talked further about how to adapt their teaching to make it accessible for all children. They developed creative solutions through collaborative thinking.

Reflective task 7.6   Using collaborative reflection creatively to enhance your teaching

---

1 Identify some aspect of your practice that you would like to develop. For example, giving space and freedom to learners to ask as well as answer questions.
2 Sit down with a peer or colleague and a sheet of paper or some Post-it notes, and a pen. Share ideas about what you have done and could do, discussing advantages and pitfalls.

Thinking creatively to develop teaching ideas

Creativity is about having new ideas *and* being willing and confident to try them out. This is not easy for the beginning teacher grappling with subject, curriculum and pedagogic knowledge all at once and for the first time. At some point, however, you will be 'ready' to let your own creative thinking lead you to new ideas to try out. If you are not naturally a creative thinker, or if you are looking for strategies to help your learners become creative thinkers, you may want to consider 'thinking hats'. Edward de Bono (2000), known for his approaches to creative thinking, summarizes how the use of these metaphoric hats can help children (and adults/teachers) think in different ways about their and others' situations and problems.

The hats can be used singly, in pairs, or each one sequentially depending on the time available and the purpose for the thinking. 'Green hat' thinking is particularly focused on innovative and creative idea generation. The intention of the hats is to encourage thinking in different directions for different purposes. The green hat way of working includes considering alternatives and (possible) changes. Really creative thinkers probably put this hat on first! For example, when planning a lesson about advertising slogans, the 'green hat' thinker might come up with a list something like this:

> **❝** We could take them all down to the shopping centre.
> We could get them to interview passers-by about whether they have noticed the slogans and if it has made them buy.
> We could get pupils to design their own slogans as alternatives.
> They could take these out with them and put them up next to the real ones.
> Pupils could evaluate the slogans they see and say which they like best, and why.
> They could translate the slogans into three different languages. **❞**

Table 7.3 De Bono's 'thinking hats'

Thinking hats	Associated reflective questions	Examples of where the questions might be applied
White hat Involving objectivity, without emotion	What are the facts? What do I know about this situation? What (further) information do I need to get?	Examining data on learners, such as reading age, statement of special educational need Collecting evidence in the classroom, for example peer or mentor notes all interactions between teacher and boys/girls to collect objective data on gender bias
Red hat Involving emotions, feelings, hunches, intuition	What do I feel about this right now? How did I feel when …? How would I feel if? How do I think learners felt when …? How would learners feel if …? What if I …?	Evaluating a lesson Reflecting on classroom ethos and its impact on learners Sowing the seeds of a new idea when planning
Black hat Involving caution, truth, judgments, drawbacks	Would this work? Is it safe? What are the disadvantages? Who can help?	Thinking through a new approach or when teaching a new topic Trying out something you have seen pay dividends for another teacher
Yellow hat Involving advantages, benefits, strengths	What are the advantages of doing this? Who would benefit?	Putting theory into practice, for example thinking through an idea about peer assessment, or using a social constructivist approach to teaching
Green hat Involving exploration, ideas, suggestions	What is possible? What are all the different possibilities? How could this be even better?	Putting learners into new learning groups Considering a new text book or learning resource Planning an out-of-school activity
Blue hat Involving thinking about thinking	How did my thinking develop as I applied the different hats in turn? How does my experience now compare with the day I started this placement? And how did I reach this point?	Reflecting on the thought processes you have been through Evaluation of teaching placement and considering overview of progress

Source: After de Bono 2000

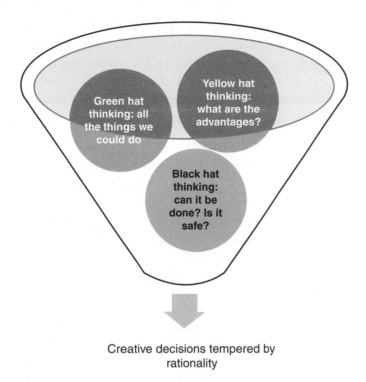

Figure 7.3   Selecting and using thinking hats to funnel creative thinking

Sometimes this kind of creative thinking can be stimulating for others, but it often needs 'funnelling' so that the more outrageous possibilities are tempered by reality. This is where, in turn, the black hat (Is it safe? Can it be done?) and the yellow hat (What are the advantages?) can lead to creative but rational conclusions (see Figure 7.3). In the example above, the head teacher may think with the metaphorical 'white hat' on. (What does the law say about this? How much time have we got? How much will it cost and who will pay?). After the event, the blue hat of post-experience evaluation will be needed by all involved! The red hat, to do with emotion and feelings, could be described as being metaphorically 'stuck' on the head of those who let emotions rule their thinking ('We can't do that, I'm too tired!', 'Let's go for it, it's exciting!'), and forcibly placed on the head of those who never consider the role of feelings in thinking processes ('How will the learners feel about this?').

From the example above, we can see how valuable de Bono's metaphor might be with learners as you try to encourage their creative thinking. From 5-year-olds thinking about what is a healthy breakfast to 18-year-olds exploring the causes of the First World War, the 'thinking hat' metaphor can encourage the development of meta-cognitive skills. In your own work, you may find it helpful to keep de Bono's hats in mind, as the example below illustrates.

'Blue hat' thinking relates to meta-cognition. As it is 'thinking about thinking', this is exactly what the application of reflection involves. Knowing oneself as a learner, then trialling new ideas that emerge for supporting other learners, is a key act of 'blue hat' thinking. Applying yellow, then black and finally blue hat thinking will help you confirm or reject each initiative. The 'bonding medium' in this is personal reflection, as exemplified by Kelly in Case Study 7.2.

Case Study 7.2   Kelly: Thinking creatively to apply theory to practice

Kelly reflected in the middle of her course that learning should be meaningful for children, providing real life experiences so that they can make links. 'I've read about this in Piaget and Montessori', she says. So here is the joining of her ideas as she builds pedagogical and subject knowledge. Kelly took her ideas forward into her school practice. She planned a Year 3 primary science lesson with the learning intention: 'to investigate the properties of materials in relation to magnetism', and devised an activity for one adult-supported group to walk around the school exploring different materials with magnets, having made an initial prediction about what might be magnetic. Her reflection included the following: 'children did well with their predictions as their experience grew'.

At another point in the week, the lesson was classroom based, with children thinking about how the properties of magnetism affect their own lives. Kelly 'accidentally' spilled a box of paper clips on the floor. The children had to think about a quick way of picking them up. In groups, they had to come up with at least one other use for magnets at home or in school, and their ideas were collected on a poster.

> 66 When I spilled the paper clips, someone said, 'get a magnet, Miss!' I was really pleased, even though they all got excited and started shouting out. I then said: 'That has made it so easy! What else could we pick up like that? Would it work for beads, do you think?' From here they went into groups to talk about it, thinking back to what they had discovered in the practical. They came up with some good ideas. While they were working, I thought to myself how great it would be if we could pick up beads with a magnet, and that got me thinking about a task for tomorrow where they can imagine a giant magnet that could pick up anything they wanted it to. Will check with my mentor whether this will 'get in the way' of the science though. They are only just learning about what is magnetic and what is not. Not sure whether this would consolidate or confuse. . . . 99
>
> *(Kelly, BEd primary, second teaching practice)*

Kelly's reflection-in-action was sparking creative ideas, but she needed to check these with her mentor. Thinking in collaboration with others is essential, as creativity in teaching is rarely a solitary process. Bouncing ideas around with others is an invaluable creative tool.

Summary

In this chapter the terminology associated with 'creativity', and the difference between 'teaching creatively' and 'teaching for creativity', have been explored. Case studies of trainee and newly qualified teachers, as they grapple with these concepts and develop their subject and pedagogic skills, illustrate ways of reflecting for creativity and reflecting creatively.

Conclusion: 'Creativity is just good teaching, isn't it?'

Well, yes! Beginning teachers, concerned about 'letting go', are tempted to use **teacher-centred** approaches as the best way of controlling behaviour. Fear of challenge, or lack of security in subject knowledge, are also contributing factors. Experienced teachers may adopt teacher-centred approaches because of a lack of time to prepare creatively, or because they are over-focused on themselves as authority figures. The absence of a constructivist approach, building on prior learning and developmental needs, can hamper the assimilation and accommodation of new concepts. These ideas stem from the seminal work of the Swiss educational theorist Jean Piaget (Atherton 2010).

We cannot claim to be creative teachers until we have put the learner at the centre of everything we do. When we do this, we become better teachers. However experienced a teacher is, every day provides opportunities to evaluate and improve. Within this constant challenge is the promise that learning can remain fresh and alive for you as well as those you teach.

Key learning points

- Teaching creatively and teaching for creativity are separate but related concepts that are often conflated.
- 'Modelled' or reproductive activity has its place alongside 'creative' activity; teachers need to reflect on the appropriateness of each and the inter-relationship between them.
- 'Creativity' is something that is new in the teacher's or the learner's thinking. It is unlikely to be creative in world terms (but you never know!).
- Creativity is not an isolated activity; we are more creative when sharing our ideas and bouncing them around with others.
- Thus learning and reflection can be more productive if conducted collaboratively.

CHAPTER 8

Are you a fatalist or an idealist?

Lesley Cartwright

> *God, grant me the serenity*
> *To accept the things I cannot change;*
> *Courage to change the things I can;*
> *And wisdom to know the difference.*
>
> (Reinhold Niehbur, the Serenity Prayer, c. 1934)

Introduction

This chapter examines the concept of self-efficacy, through which beginning teachers maintain and develop a degree of belief in their own ability to succeed in the classroom. It acknowledges the danger of 'idealized' self-belief. Beginning teachers can sometimes enter the profession with a missionary zeal to 'make a difference' (Chapter 3). They are often baffled as to why others have apparently failed to do this up to now, and set out with great optimism, believing that they will be able to make a positive impact quite quickly. At the other end of the continuum are those with a more fatalist approach. They are somehow drawn into a blame culture; they 'blame' external circumstances for what is not going well, and feel that that they have no power or ability to change anything. Larrivee (2000: 298) calls these 'innocent bystanders', or 'victims' in the classroom, because at best they stand aside from what is going on, feeling themselves powerless to control it, ('the class has a bad reputation with all teachers') and at worst they take what is happening in their classrooms as a personal affront ('this lot have got it in for me'). Reflective practice is the mechanism by which beginning teachers develop optimum self-efficacy by shifting their position along this fatalist–idealist continuum.

In this chapter, you are invited to consider your position along the fatalist–idealist continuum and to apply reflective practice in order to shift along the continuum to a realistic conception by which self-efficacy can be achieved.

How are you travelling?

Picking up the theme that learning to teach is like a 'journey' (Chapter 5), how do you/did you view your own journey? Prospective candidates for training, invited to explore what they think this journey will be like, proffer statements such as 'teaching is hard work' and 'I know this will be a challenging time'. Behind this common rhetoric lie different conceptions of the journey. A few envisage it as a bus ride. They are in no doubt that it will be a long and arduous one, with some very bumpy stretches, but at least they will be safe inside the bus. They travel in the hope and belief that when they reach their final destination and get off the bus, they will be handed QTS. Of course, during the journey, their passive staring out of the window contributes very little to their learning, so although they are going through the motions, collecting a little professional knowledge as it naturally arises along the way, they are not actually developing the skills of a teacher, and can fail to meet the standards.

Most beginning teachers, however, understand that the journey towards QTS is more like a mountain trek in which they have to take an active, participatory part. The destination, in the form of professional standards, is clearly visible on a distant horizon, but the travellers recognize that these standards represent a set of complex practical behaviours and associated theoretical understandings that cannot be acquired passively or overnight. They know that, irrespective of support provided, they have to take each arduous step themselves, and that there are no short cuts. So what is it about those who make this journey successfully? What personal skills and characteristics do they bring with them on the journey, and which ones do they acquire along the way? Most importantly, *how* do they acquire them?

> Beginning teachers approach their new role from a position of tacit knowledge that will depend on the nature of their previous experience.

All those making this journey have access to professional knowledge in various forms, and to classroom experience. However those who make the journey 'on foot' take responsibility for their learning. They make good use of the professional knowledge available to them, processing it in context. They reflect on what and how they are learning, and forge their own pathways that link theory with practice in a way that those who 'stay on the bus' cannot possibly do. They develop a degree of self-belief in their own ability to succeed in the classroom.

Where are you starting from?

All beginning teachers will start out at some point along the idealism-fatalism continuum (see Figure 8.1), moving towards a position where they have a realistic view of what can be achieved in any classroom.

Explaining idealism

Marie, a few weeks into her course and two days into her first school placement noted that:

> 66 Yesterday I met my special needs Y8 class. I can't believe that some of them can't read! They have obviously never been given materials that interest or motivate them. My target will be to ensure that the work I do with them inspires them to try harder. They are lovely – not disruptive at all, so I am sure they could learn given the right environment.
> *(Marie, three-year MFL BEd, 2 days into first placement)* 99

Marie had a very optimistic and uninformed view of what she could achieve, and started her journey from a position of what Furlong and Maynard (1995) have called 'early idealism'. She was applying her experience of being in a girls' selective school to an entirely different context. She had never come across 12-year-olds with poor literacy skills, and was unaware of the possible reasons for this. Marie, in this context, is clearly at the 'idealism' end of the continuum.

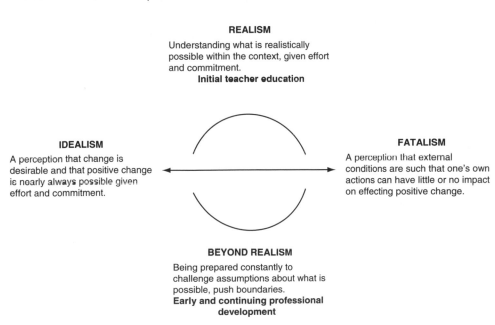

REALISM

Understanding what is realistically possible within the context, given effort and commitment.
Initial teacher education

IDEALISM

A perception that change is desirable and that positive change is nearly always possible given effort and commitment.

FATALISM

A perception that external conditions are such that one's own actions can have little or no impact on effecting positive change.

BEYOND REALISM

Being prepared constantly to challenge assumptions about what is possible, push boundaries.
Early and continuing professional development

Figure 8.1 The idealism-fatalism continuum

Explaining fatalism

John, however, was at the other end:

> 66 I can't see what I'll be able to do with this lot. My mentor told me that even the class teacher has trouble with them a lot of the time, especially when she has them just before lunch. They can't wait for the bell to go so they can get out of the classroom.
>
> *(John, one-year MFL PGCE, one week into first placement)* 99

At a similar stage in his development, he too did not have enough professional knowledge and understanding to see beyond what was immediately obvious to him, but unlike Marie, he felt powerless to change what he perceived to be inevitable. He was starting his journey from a position of fatalism.

Where do these ideas come from? At its simplest level, because we have been to school, and observed teachers doing the job for upwards of 13 years, we have an implicit sense of what teachers do. Eraut (2004: 253) calls this kind of knowledge 'tacit knowledge': 'throughout our lives we make assumptions about people, situations and organizations based on aggregated information whose provenance we cannot easily recall and may not even be able to describe'. Furthermore, Eraut's research suggests that we often use this knowledge uncritically, either because we do not have time, or because we have little inclination, to look for better solutions. It is unsurprising, then, that beginning teachers approach their new role from a position of tacit knowledge that, depending on the nature of their previous experiences, will make them inclined either towards an idealized or a fatalistic view of teaching.

The idealist-fatalist continuum does not represent ideas that are mutually exclusive. Without reflection, an idealistic view of teaching can be turned into a fatalistic one, as the beginning teacher strives to justify why their early optimism about what can be achieved is hitting the rocks when classes do not respond in the way they had expected. Inevitably, beginning teachers' performance in the classroom often falls short of their hopes as they discover that they are a long way from being the teacher who is 'idealized' in the professional standards!

After a teaching experience in which their lesson plan goes awry, pupils fail to respond in the expected way and relationships break down, beginning teachers are often obliged by the requirements of their course to 'reflect' on the lesson either through a written evaluation or discourse with the observer. Frequently this process is charged with emotion as the trainee struggles to come up with what Atkinson (2004) calls 'causal strategies' to explain the 'problem' and defend their position. They 'blame' themselves, the learners, their tutors and even the course itself (Atkinson 2004: 389), and the 'solution' they come up with may not be grounded in established theories about teaching and learning. The following is a good example of this.

Jane, a struggling trainee, was still demonstrating a tendency towards fatalism in the following lesson evaluation:

> 66 The PowerPoint was really good. It took me ages to prepare and it really showed the planetary system well, with clear illustrations and explanations. But after the first 10–15 minutes the pupils became very restless and didn't really want to listen to me. Their concentration levels are far too low for what is supposed to be a top set. I tried asking questions but they just shouted out silly answers. They were so immature.
>
> *(Jane, one-year science PGCE trainee in sixth week of placement)* 99

Her difficulties sprang partly from the fact that she had not yet learned to take responsibility for what was going wrong in her classroom. She was still 'blaming' the pupils for the disruptions that occurred, focusing on the idea that their concentration levels were 'too low'. These 'classroom myths' are what Larrivee (2000: 301) calls 'self-created assumptions'. She reminds us that teachers must 'continually challenge the underlying beliefs that drive their present behaviour' in order to turn their assumptions into realistic solutions to real problems.

Examples of self-created assumptions might be heard in any staff room. Comments such as: 'they are always like this when it's windy' or 'group work never works with this lot' are made by well-intentioned teachers hoping to make disheartened colleagues feel a little better, and what's wrong with that? Well, what is wrong is that such sentiments are often echoed in trainee teachers' early reflections, and this can have a limiting effect on their development. We run the risk of the classroom myth ossifying our practice and of limiting our expectations of what is, ultimately, possible. Larrivee (2000: 301) argues that these limiting expectations 'can set teachers up for disillusionment and a loss of a sense of self-efficacy'. What she means by this is that if we limit our perception of our own effectiveness, we often don't search for and find appropriate solutions to our problems and we lose a belief in ourselves that we can change things for the better.

Towards realism

At the start of their journey, both Marie and John were making assumptions about what was possible without the benefit of professional knowledge, particularly pedagogic knowledge (see Chapter 1). Marie, observing a class where a number of pupils had moderate learning difficulties, had assumed that they had had insufficient exposure to effective teaching. She believed that her desire to teach them well would be sufficient to make a difference. John, on the other hand, observing a lesson where some pupils were disruptive and few were engaged in the lesson, jumped to the conclusion that this class would be unresponsive to anything he tried to do with them. Well into her training, Jane could not see that in presenting a lengthy PowerPoint of the planetary system, which did not take into account prior learning or actively engage her class, she was creating problems that would not have arisen with a more constructivist approach to the lesson. Arriving at a realistic self-belief required Marie and John to develop an understanding of the professional context in which they found themselves. They also needed to apply their developing professional knowledge to reflect on the situation. They needed to seek advice about what questions to ask, and how to interpret the answers, from tutors or mentors. Through reflective conversations, they were able to address the questions in Table 8.1.

As professional knowledge and understanding develops, so professional learning becomes more sophisticated. Table 8.2 illustrates how Marie and John might have responded to these situations at a later stage of their training.

Table 8.1 Fatalist and idealist views in early training

Early teaching experience	*Questions Marie needed to ask* Who is the special needs coordinator (SENCO)? What special needs do pupils in this class have? How many pupils in this class have an individual education plan (IEP)? What do these plans tell me about the strengths of and targets for these pupils? How can my teaching support these targets?	Once Marie knew what questions to ask, and how to respond to the answers, she was on her way to making a difference – but within a more realistic framework. She could begin to learn how to pitch her teaching so that she could challenge pupils appropriately. For example, by understanding the basic principles of formative assessment she could gain a better understanding of how to help her pupils make progress.
	Questions John needed to ask Who else teaches this class? How do they behave in other lessons? What is the behaviour of individuals in other contexts, e.g. around the school, in assembly? What expectations do different teachers have of these pupils and how do the pupils respond?	Once John began to see, from observations of these pupils, that their behaviour was influenced less by external factors such as the weather and more by the expectations that different teachers had of them in varied contexts, he began to take responsibility for their behaviour by applying the basic rules of classroom management he had been learning. He slowly gained control over what happened in his classroom.

Table 8.2 Developing realism later in teaching

Later teaching experience	*Marie* I will need to identify the causes of learning difficulty for my pupils. They could have problems with one of more of the following: • communication and interaction • cognition and learning • behavioural, emotional and social development • sensory and physical development. I need to know what additional and specialist support is in place for my pupils and how I can use this to optimize my planning, teaching and assessment for these pupils.
	John I will need to ensure that my learning objectives for these pupils are realistic, and that they are appropriately differentiated so that all pupils can learn and make progress in my lesson. I need to ensure that I communicate the learning objectives clearly so that pupils know what is expected of them. I need to have clear strategies for monitoring and assessing their progress, so that they can see a purpose in what they are doing. I need to consider a range of teaching and learning strategies that will bring variety and pace to my lessons.

Reflective task 8.1   Towards realism

Refer to McGregor's adaptation of Shulman's model (Figure 1) and the Q standards (Appendix 1).

1. What subject and pedagogic knowledge is Marie using in her reflections? How will this help her to make a more realistic assessment of what her pupils can achieve?
2. What pedagogic knowledge is John using in his reflections? How will this help him to take more responsibility for what happens in his classroom?
3. What would you advise Jane to think about in relation to her teaching in order to have more realistic expectations of her class?

If we limit our perception of our own effectiveness, we often don't search for and find appropriate solutions to our problems, and we lose a belief in ourselves that we can change things for the better.

Starting from very different places, both Marie and John were on a journey towards **realism.** Marie was now able to see that there was a range of cognitive, developmental and emotional factors affecting the academic attainment of her Year 8 class, and that once she had ascertained what these were in relation to each child, she would be able to build her own pedagogic skills, with the support of special needs experts, to personalize their learning. John learned, when he saw the class working well with teachers, that they responded to clear expectations in respect of their behaviour and learning, and that as long as their tasks were focused and related to clear objectives, the enjoyed working in small groups and pairs. For both Marie and John, their initial teacher training programme was equipping them with the tools they would need: theories of teaching and learning that they could apply in the context of their teaching, and the skills of reflective practice (see Figure 8.2). Thus they would be able to:

- use subject and pedagogic knowledge to analyse contexts realistically;
- set realistic targets for themselves and for their pupils;
- apply their developing professional skills to the achievement of these targets;
- reflect on the extent to which targets have been met, and what professional learning has taken place (see Figure 8.2).

In reflecting on the above, both trainees were well on the way to addressing the need for high expectations, but from a position of realism. Beginning teachers

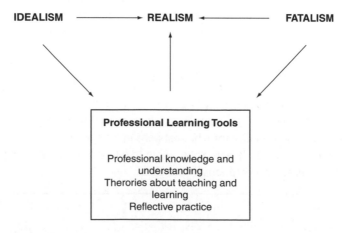

Figure 8.2 Towards realism

often believe that this standard is difficult to evidence (see also Chapter 5). It is certainly true that it cannot be demonstrated with a single task, a typed sheet slipped into your teaching file. Case Study 8.1 illustrates various ways you could evidence the development of your professional attributes.

Case Study 8.1   Alison: high expectations

Alison was in her final few weeks of a Design and Technology PGCE. As part of her final assessment, she was required to plan, teach and evaluate a sequence of lessons that would incorporate all the professional skills standards and demonstrate that she has a creative and constructively critical approach to innovation (Q8). She selected a Year 11 class who had had little exposure to practical work because of the perception that their behaviour was too poor, and planned a practical project (making a candle sconce) with them:

> When I first discussed my ideas for my scheme of work with my mentor he was surprised and pointed out that he thought I was being a little ambitious with these particular students. His view of the group was a negative one that had been built up over the previous months and on seeing him work with the students there seemed to be a lot of antagonism between them. I, on the other hand, had a great deal of enthusiasm and naivety and was ready to take on the world.
>
> *(Alison, one-year D&T PGCE, in the final weeks of her*
> *second placement)*

Despite the language she used in her introduction to this assignment, Alison was not starting from a totally idealistic position. She understood the need for high expectations tempered with a sound knowledge of the class:

> I used a wide range of assessment strategies to establish the students' range of knowledge in this topic. This gave them confidence about what they could already do and helped them understand the planned learning objectives. My next step was to impress upon the students my expectations of them in regards to their behaviour and the quality of work that I was expecting and then I used demonstrations and discussion to show the expected outcomes. The students' reaction to this approach was outstanding, and I was impressed by how they thought out the next steps and applied prior knowledge to the task.

Alison was using her developing understanding of assessment for learning and behaviour management to identify realistic learning objectives for her class. She understood the need to build on prior knowledge and model the outcomes in order to give her pupils confidence. Nevertheless, she was taking a risk; she was banking on a hunch (see 'red hat thinking' in Chapter 7) that behaviour could be improved by giving her pupils a sense of progression and achievement. But it was an informed risk, underpinned by her developing knowledge of D&T pedagogy. Reflecting on an incident where one student became very disruptive when his work went wrong, but responded well to practical help and encouragement, she notes:

> 66 I was in a better position to deal with it, having taking on board the comments made by Barlex (2007). I was confident that to encourage the student to undertake this aspect of the practical work would help towards his emotional development by increasing his confidence and self-esteem. 99

In this reflection-in-action, Alison had applied her developing professional knowledge drawn from theories about D&T pedagogy. Later, reflecting on action, she was able to summarize her professional learning:

> 66 This incident made me very aware that students' behaviour issues can be driven by many different reasons and a lack of confidence or insecurity in their own skills or knowledge can be masked by such behaviour. It can be as important to give students the confidence to fail as it is to give them the confidence to succeed, as there is so much that can be learnt from making mistakes that will inform their problem-solving skills. 99

Reflective task 8.2a Thinking about Alison's situation

1 What professional values does Alison demonstrate in this context?
2 What pedagogic knowledge does she apply?
3 What does she learn as a result of working with this class?
4 How did Alison avoid adopting a fatalist approach to her work with this class?

Reflective task 8.2b   Reflecting on action

Having reflected on the above questions, imagine yourself back in a recent classroom-based situation and reflect on similar questions:

1 What was the context?
2 How did you respond, and what professional values did your response suggest?
3 What professional knowledge did you already have? Were you able to apply it to this situation?
4 Were you aware of any professional knowledge 'gaps' and how you might fill them?

Reflective task 8.3   A fatalist or an idealist?

Read Case Study 8.2. Is the trainee more of an idealist or more of a fatalist?

1 How would you summarize her expectations of her pupils?
2 What professional learning needs to take place in order for this trainee to move along the continuum towards realism?

Case Study 8.2   Fay: attitudes to learners

In evaluating her assessment practice, a secondary English trainee considers how to avoid domination of whole class discussion by certain individuals. She questions the effectiveness of a 'hands-down' approach and the provision of thinking time:

> 66   I have frequently found that with a lower ability year eight class, this time does not make any difference as if the pupils don't know the answer, no amount of time will help them think of it.   99

In the same reflection, she also questions the usefulness of peer- and self-assessment for lower ability pupils arguing that:

> 66   If some pupils are not able to use, for example, complex sentences in their own writing, how are they going to be able to identify them and offer areas for improvement in others?
> *(Fay, one-year English PGCE trainee, after four weeks of teaching practice)*   99

In reflecting upon her practice, the trainee is limited in her exploration of possibilities for developing this practice further with particular groups of pupils because of her view that their progress is fixed and that any development is outside her control. She does not consider that her own actions or attitudes might be limiting the pupils' abilities to engage in the assessment practices in question.

Reflective task 8.4a

What questions would you advise Fay to ask of her mentor or university tutor in order to further her professional learning?

Reflective task 8.4b

Read the following extract from one trainee's self-assessment of her profile at the end of her training year. She begins by describing the strategies she used to ensure that one class developed a deep understanding of the learning objectives for lessons, and how this understanding led to improved engagement and learning.

> 66 During my NQT year I would like to develop this practice and consider how I can use these techniques to engage all pupils. The practice has worked with my Year 7 class and has engaged all of them successfully but I have not been able to develop it so much with my Year 8 group – a far more challenging class with many attention-seeking boys. It is often easy to develop learning strategies with classes with fewer behaviour management issues but I hope to challenge my thinking on this during my first year of teaching. All children deserve the same standard of education and I hope to focus on developing my good practice with more challenging groups; considering how pupils can be engaged and what their needs are.
>
> *(Louise, one-year English PGCE, end of training)* 99

1 Where on the idealism-fatalism continuum would you place Louise?
2 Why?

This NQT is clearly accepting responsibility for her own effectiveness as a teacher and recognizes the need to 'challenge her thinking' in respect of what is possible. She has at her disposal a wealth of professional knowledge gained from theory and practice during her training year. She is demonstrating strong professional values relating to inclusion and high expectations. Fay, on the other hand, has not yet reached this point. She needs to challenge her perception of her learners and believe that she can make small, progressive changes in their learning. For example, she is quite right that 'no amount of time' will help learners answer questions if they do not know the answer. However, she is currently allowing her thinking to stop there, at some point near the fatalist end of the continuum. She needs to ask her mentor (or peers, other colleagues) about other forms of questioning, such as putting learners into pairs and giving 'talk time', or asking differentiated questions, or questions that elicit the answer.

Hannah's approach was from a more idealistic starting point. She had initially pitched her expectations too high, but quickly applied her pedagogic knowledge to change this:

> 66 It was pointed out to me, during the first few weeks of my teaching, that my expectations were too high of some students and that their unwillingness to participate was not because they had bad attitudes, but because they felt out of their depth. Since then, I have made many changes with my approach towards planning tasks and lessons, for example planning more kinaesthetic activities.
>
> *(Hannah, one-year MFL PGCE, four weeks into final placement)* 99

Hannah was supported by teaching colleagues who helped her identify the reasons for some students' uncooperative stance in her classroom. This was helpful in enabling her to find solutions. Hannah was well on the way to believing in herself as an effective teacher.

Towards self-efficacy – which way?

In order for you to make real progress on this journey, you have to get off the bus and decide for yourself which way you need to go. The direction you take will depend on your starting point, how you feel about yourself as a teacher and what assumptions you make about the contexts in which you will be learning to teach. Do you have a rosy view of what you will be able to achieve as a teacher, or are you more inclined to think that the situation you go into could limit what is possible? Are you more of an idealist, or more of a fatalist? Once you understand this about yourself, you will be able to take steps in the direction of *realism*. This should be your goal during your training year. In your induction year and beyond, you should be thinking and acting in terms of *beyond realism*: being prepared to challenge assumptions about what is possible for you and your pupils.

'The wisdom to know the difference': beyond realism

By the end of their training programme, successful teachers will have, to a greater or lesser extent, achieved the Q standards and will have reached a stage of realism, whereby they can apply their professional knowledge and skills and, through the process of reflection, achieve what is realistically possible in any given context. However, it would be complacent in the extreme to assume that this is where the journey ends! Indeed, some beginning teachers who show the potential to be very good or outstanding practitioners have already begun the next phase of the journey before the end of their initial training. They are constantly pushing the boundaries and challenging the assumptions about what is realistically possible. They are moving beyond realism. In other words, these professionals never ask 'are we nearly there?' but are more likely to wonder 'what's that over there?' and go on an exploratory detour. They are likely to engender creativity and test pedagogical ideas. They talk with pupils about why they find learning particular things difficult, or what teaching approaches might encourage them to want to learn more. Such teachers will take their pupils on different learning adventures, perhaps involving risks, but certainly leading to deeper understandings and increased self-esteem for all concerned.

Reflective task 8.5   Are you a fatalist or an idealist?

In this task you will be thinking about where you would place yourself on the idealism-fatalism continuum, and why. First, study the likely characteristics relating to the idealism-fatalism continuum (Figure 8.3), then choose the task more appropriate to your stage of development from Table 8.3.

Fatalist
- Relies on 'tacit' knowledge acquired informally
- Accepts what is observed or what people say at face value
- Has an emotional, often negative, response to situations
- Tends to blame external factors for what is going wrong, such as the ability of the class, the time of day, what happened in the last lesson
- Perceives that some learners are beyond help
- Often feels that advice given by mentors or tutors is 'confusing' or is the wrong advice

Towards realism
- Begins to apply developing professional knowledge to given contexts
- Questions what is observed and said, seeking alternative possibilities to what on the surface may appear obvious
- Begins to take resposibility for what happens in the classroom
- Begins to use information about the context, for example learners' social background or prior attainment, to improve own practice
- Reflects in and on action
- Refuse to give up on learners
- Actively seeks advice and uses it reflectively, selecting what is appropriate in a given context.
- Has belief in own ability to improve practice

Idealist
- Relies on 'tacit' knowledge acquired informally
- Has an emotional, often over-enthusiastic response to situations
- Has a naive and uninformed view of what is achievable
- Tends to be blind to external factors, dismissing them as having little relevance to their own expectations
- Often feels that the advice given by mentors is 'confusing' or is the wrong advice
- Rejects what is seen and what people say in favour of a more optimistic view

Beyond realism
- Applies professional knowledge to gain a deep understanding of given contexts
- Critically examines own classroom practice, believing that improvements can be made
- Has a clear sense of what can be realistically achieved in a given context
- Is persistent, consistent and insistent in expectations of learners' work and behaviour
- Has a strong sense of self-efficacy
- Works hard to develop self-efficacy in learners

Figure 8.3 Characteristics displayed along the fatalist-idealist continuum

Table 8.3 Are you currently an idealist or a fatalist?: Suggestions about what you could do next

Early teaching experience	i.	You are beginning to develop an impression of your school through walking about, a pupil trail, engaging with teachers and other professionals, observing pupils in lessons and about the school, etc. Jot down your thoughts, and in particular how these first impressions make you feel.
	ii.	What do you think are the implications for your own practice? How do you see yourself shaping up as a teacher in this context? Jot down your thoughts.
	iii.	Reflect on the definitions of fatalism and idealism explored in this chapter. Where would you position yourself on the continuum, and why?
	iv.	Given your position on this continuum, what do you need to consider in your early development as a teacher?
Later teaching experience	i.	Using the information you have about this school (Ofsted report, school policy documents, schemes of work, observations, and so on) make notes on how you see your teaching developing during your time here. What will you need to consider in key areas such as behaviour management, pupil attainment, teaching and learning style, special needs?
	ii.	Negotiate with your mentor an opportunity to observe teachers across the school who are known to have high expectations of themselves and their pupils. If possible arrange to co-observe a lesson with your mentor or other class teacher.
	iii.	Following the lesson, and in 'learning conversations' with your co-observer and the teacher, identify the teacher and learner behaviours that are associated with high expectations.
	iv.	Go back to your early notes. To what extent has this experience affected the way you feel about your own practice in this school? Have you shifted your thinking about what you think you can achieve? If so, why, and in what direction?

Summary

In this chapter your attention has been drawn to the need for you as a beginning teacher to develop self-efficacy. That is to say, you need to understand that you can have a positive impact, through your actions as a teacher, on what goes on in your classroom. The road to achieving this is not an easy one; it requires first an ability to know yourself and your personal responses to new classroom situations. Beginning teachers often have, to some degree or another, a tendency towards either idealism or fatalism about what they can achieve as a teacher. Early reflection on your own position on this continuum will give you some insight into how to shape your thinking as a teacher. Later, your developing knowledge and understanding, applied to the specific context in which you are working, will help you to engage in the kind of reflective practice that will give you a belief in yourself as an effective classroom practitioner.

Conclusion

By using reflective practice to assess your position in the fatalist – idealist continuum, you can develop your self-efficacy. You can head beyond realism and be well on the way to building learners' confidence so that your high expectations of them become expectations they have of themselves.

Key learning points

- Self-efficacy comes from a belief that you can make a difference in your classroom.
- This means having realistic expectations of what is achievable.
- In the absence of subject, pedagogic and curriculum knowledge, expectations may be based on either an idealistic or a fatalistic viewpoint.
- Reflection on where on the fatalism–idealism continuum you are starting is an important first step.
- From there, you will be able to make appropriate use of your developing knowledge and understanding to reflect on how to improve your practice and enhance learning.

CHAPTER 9

Frameworks to make small changes with big impact: how can detailed reflection improve your practice?

Lesley Cartwright and Lorraine Thomas

> *Change comes from small initiatives which work.... We cannot wait for great visions from great people, for they are in short supply at the end of history. It is up to us to light our own small fires in the darkness.*
>
> (Charles Handy, in Brighouse and Woods 1999: 109)

Introduction

When you first enter teaching you may feel overwhelmed by the documentation with which you need to be familiar. There is a vast array of statutory and non-statutory guidance relating to what and how you should teach, and how you should monitor the improvement of your learners' attainment and achievements. Linked to this are the frameworks and standards that inform your professional learning and career development. The development of progressive career standards (detailed in Chapter 2) can sometimes give the impression that you are set on a smooth path that is taking you onward and upward. However, occasionally you will feel that your skill as a teacher is a little like the stock market; it can go down as well as up! Changing schools, moving from trainee to NQT, or having to teach a new subject or age group, are all transitions that can leave you feeling less skilled than before, even though plenty of professional learning is still taking place.

This chapter begins with an exemplification of just such a situation. A model of reflection that will help you identify, implement and evaluate small changes is explored, and frameworks to help you develop your practice are provided. These should be particularly useful at transition points in your early career. The focus for reflection is lesson evaluation, or more specifically, key aspects of a lesson where you would like to make a small change. For illustration purposes, three areas that often exercise beginning teachers have been selected: learning objectives, behaviour management and questioning. The conclusion reached is that minor changes can often result in significant improvements in the classroom.

Case Study 9.1a   Transition from training to induction

At the end of her training Jo was selected for observation by an external examiner because of her excellent outcomes. She had very good subject knowledge and was enthusiastic about her subject and teaching.

She planned meticulously, using a range of teaching, learning and assessment strategies that engaged her classes. She modelled tasks well and gave good explanations. She used a range of differentiated questioning techniques that included all learners. She was consistent in her implementation of the school's policy for behaviour management. For example she made clear to pupils when they could work in pairs using 'quiet partner voices' and when they were expected to undertake 'silent individual work'.

In her final teaching practice, Jo was mentored by a very well-established head of department whose positive influence reached deep into every classroom. Fast forward to two terms later, however.

Case Study 9.1b

Jo is half way through her induction year in a new school, and for the most part is teaching alone. She is starting a lesson with Year 8, and is taking the attendance register. She has asked for silence, but doesn't get it; two boys at the front in particular are fooling around. She yells a warning, hands on hips. The two boys burst out laughing, and turn, grinning to share their triumph with the rest of the class. Jo is left feeling helpless in the face of such unseemly behaviour.

Developing 'practical wisdom'

Lunenberg and Korthagen (2009) recount a similar experience. Mary, doing well under the guidance of the class teacher during training, finds behaviour management much more problematic when teaching alone. They go on to document how Mary came to improve her practice over the next few years, developing what they call 'practical wisdom' (p. 226). They define this as 'the sensitivity for and awareness of the essentials of a particular practice situation that shape our perception of this situation' (p. 227). In other words, it comes from the day-to-day application of reflection-in-action during our teaching experiences, which we then process through reflection-on-action. Thus we develop a 'bank' of responses and behaviours, and learn how to adjust them in different contexts. This is what we call 'experience'; practical wisdom, for Lunenberg and Korthagen, is how we use that experience in new contexts. They place 'practical wisdom' in the here and now, relating only to the present context. Jo's 'practical wisdom', like Mary's, becomes more apparent over time (see Case Study 9.1c)

Case Study 9.1c

In her third year of teaching, Jo has just instructed the class to work in silence for three minutes on a written activity. Her active questioning and good modelling have given the class the confidence and capacity to do the work. While she is bending over a desk, checking that the weakest members of the class are able to make a start, she senses something and half turns, noticing that the girls on the back row are passing a magazine under the desk. She straightens, looks directly at them, raises a quizzical eyebrow. The girls return to the task in hand.

During her final teaching practice, curriculum and pedagogic knowledge (see Chapter 1) were uppermost in Jo's mind, and much of her success was due to her ability to evaluate her practice in relation to her 'theoretical' learning. However, in her first year as a teacher, without the support of a mentor, there were moments when Jo lost sight of this relationship and allowed her feelings of frustration to dominate her thinking. Once she pulled back from this, and began once again to reflect on action using pedagogic and curriculum knowledge, she began to develop 'practical wisdom' in the new context. Lunenberg and Korthagen (2009) see the value of practical wisdom in its interaction with theoretical knowledge and practical experience (see Figure 9.1). We can see this interaction underpinning Jo's professional behaviour in her third year of teaching, as shown in Figure 9.2.

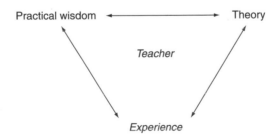

Figure 9.1 The triangular relationship between practical wisdom, theory and experience
Source: Lunenberg and Korthagen 2009: 229

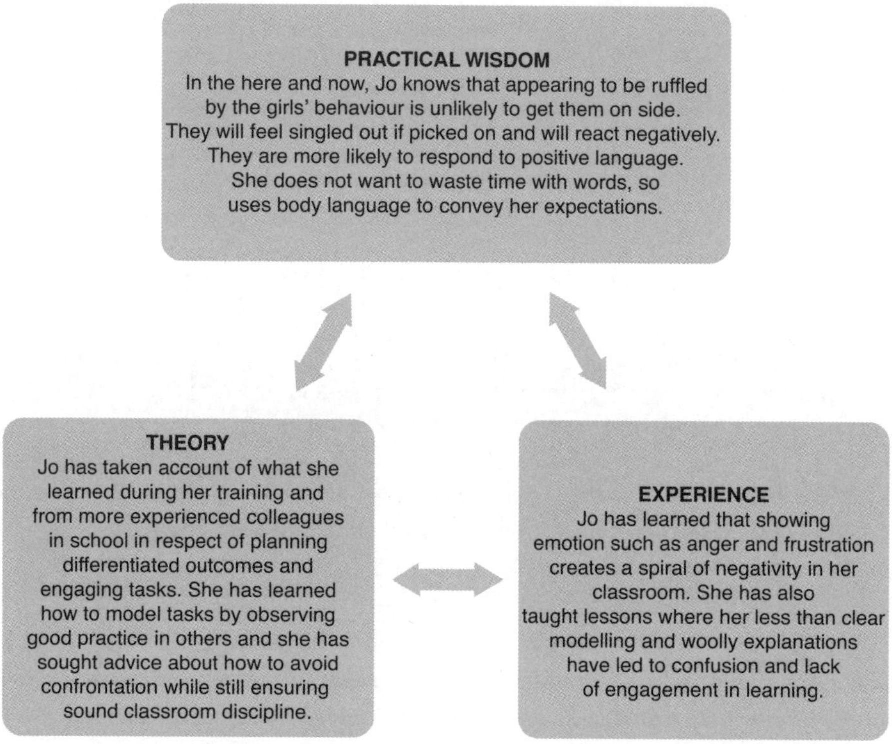

PRACTICAL WISDOM
In the here and now, Jo knows that appearing to be ruffled by the girls' behaviour is unlikely to get them on side. They will feel singled out if picked on and will react negatively. They are more likely to respond to positive language. She does not want to waste time with words, so uses body language to convey her expectations.

THEORY
Jo has taken account of what she learned during her training and from more experienced colleagues in school in respect of planning differentiated outcomes and engaging tasks. She has learned how to model tasks by observing good practice in others and she has sought advice about how to avoid confrontation while still ensuring sound classroom discipline.

EXPERIENCE
Jo has learned that showing emotion such as anger and frustration creates a spiral of negativity in her classroom. She has also taught lessons where her less than clear modelling and woolly explanations have led to confusion and lack of engagement in learning.

Figure 9.2 An example of the triangular relationship between practical wisdom, theory and experience

Lunenberg and Korthagen (2009: 235) affirm that 'Reflection seems the vital instrument for making the connections between experience, theory and practical wisdom.' Quoting from earlier work by Korthagen (2001) they emphasize that 'A teacher's professional learning will be more effective when the learner reflects *in detail* on his or her experiences' (p. 235). We cannot know the detail of Jo's reflections, but she has made considerable progress as a professional since her induction year. If we consider the above model, she may have begun her reflections by thinking about her *experience*: how various situations made her feel; how she thinks they made her pupils feel; what she has discovered will work with any given class and what is unlikely to be effective. Alternatively, she may have begun by seeking answers to questions such as: how do I impose my expectations about behaviour on this class? In this case, her starting point would have been *theory* from a range of sources. Finally, she may have started from the point of *existing practical wisdom.* This will be based largely on her prior experiences and she will need to explore key questions about the extent to which it is valid in the given situation. For example, if her own education was very formal, she may value an authoritarian approach to discipline and will need to deconstruct her ideas in the face of classes who are clearly not responding to this method.

The frameworks used in this chapter are based on the premise, similar to that of Lunenberg and Korthagen (2009), that there is an interrelationship between theory, experience and the development of practical wisdom, and that *detailed reflection* is the key that unlocks this relationship. Detailed reflection can make a very big difference to a small part of the beginning teacher's practice, but there can be a snowball effect in that minor changes can lead to big improvements, in class control or effective learning, for example.

Case Study 9.1d   What Jo did in her induction year

Following the incident when taking the register, Jo felt miserable all day. She recognized that losing her temper had been counter-productive, and that she needed a more focused strategy. 'I've tried doing what you do, and giving them the "stare",' she said to her induction tutor, "but it just doesn't work when I do it!" Jo and her tutor discussed this. Why did it work for the more experienced teacher? Through reflection, Jo came to realize that it was because this teacher had built up a reputation with her pupils. A few terms ago, she would have said to those boys: 'if you continue to talk you will have to sit separately'. Because, when they did talk, she moved one of them to the other end of the classroom, they soon understood that their actions would have consequences, and learned to respond to the 'look' that reminded them of this. Jo was reminded that she needed to clearly communicate expectations of her pupils' behaviour, beginning with silence during the taking of the register. From these small beginnings she was able to 'grow' her reputation for having consistently high expectations of behaviour. From Case Study 9.1c we can also see that Jo was then able to apply effectively the pedagogic skills that had been evident at the end of her training.

Brighouse and Woods (1999: 109) have also noted, in the context of school improvement, that 'tiny differences in input can quickly become overwhelming differences in output'. They call these small interventions 'butterflies' after the work on chaos theory that describes how the 'butterfly effect' can result in significant affects at the later time or place.

Case Study 9.2   Engaging learners in the lesson objectives

Chris was an NQT in secondary PE. He was feeling unhappy that his sixth form BTEC students were not engaging with the learning objectives of the lessons; they were not taking responsibility for their learning and were expecting Chris to do all the work. He writes in his reflective journal:

> " To improve the quality of learning, self- and peer-assessment are important in AfL [assessment for learning] because they allow pupils to involve themselves in their own and others' learning (Black and Wiliam 1998; Casbon and Spackman 2005). The Assessment Reform Group (2002) has noted that learners must have their self-assessment skills developed by the teacher so that they have the capacity to be in control of their learning. When in charge of their learning, pupils must continually engage in self-assessment so that they are responsible for their own achievements and learning (Stiggins 2002). Additionally, independent learners should be able to identify the next steps needed for their learning (QCA 2007). However, pupils must be reminded of their learning goals and only assess their progress according to that criteria (Black et al. 2004). With all this in mind, I made a change to the way I ended my lessons. This involved sitting students in pairs at tables free of resources and asking them to discuss two things they had learnt in the lesson. By planning carefully the questions I asked, I was able to get in-depth answers about the theory learnt, with some remembering how it linked to past learning. I was satisfied with this different type of questioning because it allowed me to check the understanding of students. Past research has also found that a range of questioning techniques consolidates pupils' learning (Capel 2004).
>
> *(Chris, PE NQT)*

Reflective task 9.1

1 What was Chris's 'butterfly'? What small change did he make to his practice?
2 What pleased him about the outcome?
3 What do you think was Chris's starting point in the relationship between theory, practice and practical wisdom?

Chris recognized his responsibility for helping his students become reflective and independent learners, and saw the value of self-and peer assessment in this process. He decided to start with two small changes in his lessons: he would give more thought to how he would question pupils about what they had learned, and he would 'clear the decks' of books and paper so that they were forced to think and talk about the questions he posed. Immediately his students were more engaged in their own learning, and gave him in-depth responses to his questions. However his ideas are clearly underpinned by his knowledge of theory about assessment and about PE pedagogy. His reflections do not really tell us where he started this process: how, as Lunenberg and Korthagen (2009: 232) put it, he has gone 'through the triangle'. Perhaps his starting point was *theory*: the knowledge he had about AfL; or maybe he started from a recognition that he was not making the most of his plenaries (*practical wisdom*). Finally, he may have already discovered, with another class, the benefit of more focused questioning (*experience*).

Lesson evaluation: reflecting in detail

According to Lunenberg and Korthagen, it is the detail of reflection that is most important.

> "The more specific the analysis of a small part of a lesson is, the more a student teacher is supported in developing practical wisdom, as he or she is then supported in developing *sensitivity to the particulars of educational situations.*"
>
> *(Lunenberg and Korthagen 2009: 235)*

They urge student teachers to reflect on the 'thoughts, feelings, needs and actions' that they have about a context, and, equally important, the thoughts, feelings, needs and actions of their learners. (See Chapter 4, Figure 4.1 for a series of reflective questions to help you to concretize these, drawn from Korthagen and Vasalos 2005). Understanding your own feelings and those of your learners will help you to gain the practical wisdom to improve your practice. If you are to reflect in this much detail, then it stands to reason that you cannot do so for every minute of every lesson that you have taught. You will no doubt be expected to complete a lesson evaluation in a standardized format provided by your training provider or school. The sheer number of such forms that you are asked to complete can mean that the action of lesson evaluation is reduced to a set of technical operations. For example:

1 Were the learning objectives appropriate? ☑
2 Were the learning objectives met? ☑
3 Were pupils engaged? ☑

If you felt that that in general the lesson 'went well', you might be tempted to tick all the boxes without further reflection. At best, this can lead to stagnation of practice. At worst, you can be lulling yourself into a false sense of security!

Reflective task 9.2   Reflecting on learning objectives

Refer to Figures 9.1 and 9.2. Starting from any one point on the triangle, use the questions in Table 9.1 to reflect on a lesson that you have taught recently. You must go through all the points on the triangle!

Of course, many trainee teachers plan their learning objectives really well, and have a carefully constructed lesson plan. Yet the lesson goes awry, because of behaviour problems. Amy was in this position:

Case Study 9.3   Dealing with low-level disruption

Amy was half way through her second week of her first teaching practice. Her mentor was happy that her planning was sound, and she knew that she had some good ideas for pupil learning activities. However, she was not yet 'pulling it off' in the classroom. There was quite a bit of low-level disruption and Amy was beginning to think that, as she was working so hard, this must be the pupils' fault – they just would not listen! Amy was not facing up to the responsibility she had for her pupils' behaviour. First, she needed to reflect on the situation. She needed to identify what might be realistic expectations for this class, and she needed to ask herself what she could do to improve the situation. At this point Amy was becoming fatalistic, believing that nothing could be done, and that all her efforts in planning were being wasted. Her mentor suggested that she observe the class with another teacher. From this she was able to see that:

Several pupils in this class were indeed inclined to chatter and disinclined to work, but. . . .

when given plenty of short, manageable tasks with immediate, positive feedback and . . .

with a clear framework of expectations about when they could talk, when they needed to listen and when they had to work in silence . . .

. . . their behaviour was much better.
   Amy reflected:

> 66   As soon as I saw the class with Mr X I realized that they could behave and do their work. I had observed them before I started teaching them but somehow hadn't registered what they were like with other people. It was only when I went back and reflected on the difference in their behaviour with a teacher who had a different approach that I realized I might be able to do something about things after all. This was a key learning moment for me. Now, I understand about the

Table 9.1 A framework for reflection on learning objectives

	If you are part way through your teacher training	If you have almost completed your teacher training	If you are an NQT
1 Starting from **experience**	**Were the learning objectives appropriate?** What happened during the lesson to provide you with evidence of this? What evidence do you have that learning took place? What experiences have you had in previous lessons that might inform this lesson?	**Were the learning objectives appropriate?** What evidence did you look for to ascertain whether the learning objectives were met? What evidence do you have of this?	**Were the learning objectives appropriate?** What evidence do you have that all learners were engaged? Was there a different response from learners of different abilities? Why was this?
2 Staring from **practical wisdom**	**How well did learners engage?** How do you think your learners felt when you presented the learning objectives? How did they react? Did all learners have the same reaction? How has this gone in other lessons, and what have you learned from that?	**How well did learners engage?** How did you feel about the learning objectives? How did the learners feel when you assessed them against the learning objectives? How did they respond?	**How well did learners engage?** How did you feel as you were presenting/demonstrating/questioning the whole class? How do you think the class felt? How did they react? How did you feel when learners were working independently or in pairs? How do you think they felt? How did they react?

Table 9.1 (Continued)

	If you are part way through your teacher training	If you have almost completed your teacher training	If you are an NQT
3 Starting from **theory**	**How realistic were your expectations of pupils of different abilities?** What is the ability range of this class? What are their attainment levels in this subject? What would you expect most learners to be able to learn and do in this lesson? What would more able learners be able to learn and do in addition? What support do less able learners need to meet the core objectives? Do any learners have a specific learning difficulty and special need? Did you address this when planning the outcomes?	**How realistic were your expectations of pupils of different abilities?** How well do you know this class? Do you need to go back to the questions in column 1? What formative and summative assessment strategies did you use to ascertain whether the learning objectives were met? How did you monitor the engagement of learners during tasks?	**How realistic were your expectations of pupils of different abilities?** How well do you know this class? Do you need to go back to the questions in column 1? What formative and summative assessment strategies did you use to ascertain whether the learning objectives were met? How did you monitor the engagement of learners during tasks? What were the learning outcomes for all abilities? What does this mean for your future planning? Were the tasks congruent with the learning objectives?

> value of being strict but fair and respectful. I don't get it right all the time, but this class is much better already and I can see that my planning and preparation are worthwhile because they are enjoying my lessons now.
>
> *(Amy, one-year PGCE MFL, week 2 of first teaching practice)* 99

Reflective task 9.3   Reflecting on behaviour management

Refer to Figures 9.1 and 9.2. Starting from any one point on the triangle, use the questions in Table 9.2 to reflect on a lesson that you have taught recently where behaviour had a negative impact on learning. You must go through all the points on the triangle!

From the framework in Table 9.2 we can see the relationship between behaviour and learning. A key fact of classroom life is this: pupils cannot learn if they are not behaving, but they will not behave if they are not learning. As a beginning teacher you learn how to plan, how to differentiate, how to set up tasks, how to monitor and assess learning and so on. You also learn that rules and routines, **sanctions and rewards**, are necessary for good behaviour management. Through reflection, you can learn how to bring these elements together. Once you can do this, your teaching will be more or less successful, depending on context and the stage of your development. Where it is less successful, you need to be able to deconstruct your lessons in order to identify what you can do to make things better. Often, a slight change will make a big difference; the trick is in recognizing what that small change should be. The Lunenberg and Korthagen triangle (2009) is really useful here. Let us imagine that your well-planned lesson was unsuccessful because learners arrived 'high as kites' from assembly with little inclination to work, and chattered through the lesson, failing to engage with much of what you tried to get them to do. You know what happened in the lesson, and you might have a little moan about it with a colleague at break. You have entered the triangle from experience. You also know how you feel about it. However, if the reflection stops there, you will not really be on the road to solving the problem. By taking the practical wisdom aspect a stage further and asking yourself what effect your words and actions had on the class, you can begin to see the lesson from the learners' perspective. By applying your curriculum and pedagogic knowledge, you can then begin to analyse the relationship between behaviour and learning. From here,

Table 9.2 A framework for reflection on behaviour management

	If you are part way through your teacher training	If you have almost completed your teacher training	If you are an NQT
1 Starting from **experience**	**How did learners behave during this lesson?** What happened when they entered the classroom? How long did it take them to settle? Was the disruption low or high level? Who was disruptive? Were there any 'ringleaders'? What did you do about this? What was the response from the class/individual? What happened during question/answer sessions? Did pupils listen to you and to each other? How much work was accomplished? Were the learning outcomes achieved? Have you taught lessons that have started promptly and smoothly in the past? What contributed to this? What are your personal values about discipline and control? Do they match those of the school?		
2 Starting from **practical wisdom**	**How did you and your learners respond?** How did you feel when your learners arrived in the classroom/as you were starting the lesson? What did you do? How do you think this made your learners feel? How did they respond? How did you react to behaviour problems as they arose during the lesson? How did this make you feel? What effect did this have on the class as a whole and on any individuals? Were there any positive moments where what you said or did resulted in a more settled atmosphere? Overall, did the lesson interest, engage and motivate the class? Were they aware of what learning had taken place? What evidence did they have of this?		

3 Starting from theory

What rules and routines did you have in place to meet, greet and seat the class? What expectations did you have in your head about their behaviour? Did you communicate them to the class? How?

How did you plan the routines for giving out and collecting resources and equipment?

What routines did you have for keeping pupils on task? Were they allowed to talk or not when they were working? Did you convey this expectation to them? How long did you expect learners to take over each task? Did you impose this time limit on them?

How did you monitor their work once they had started a task?

To what extent did you use praise and rewards?

To what extent did you threaten sanctions? Were they realistic? Did you carry out any threatened sanctions?

What routines did you have for dismissing the class?

What expectations did you have of this class in respect of behaviour and learning? Were they realistic? (See column 1.) What understanding did you have of prior learning? Were your learning objectives realistic? Were they appropriately differentiated? Were learners clear about what they were learning and why? Did the tasks and activities relate well to the learning objectives? Did you demonstrate and model the tasks and activities clearly?

Did you provide a variety of learning opportunities, for example collaborative learning, individual work?

Did you use a range of questioning techniques? Did you give pupils thinking time? How well were your questions differentiated? Did you target your questions at individuals?

Was your subject knowledge secure? Did you structure the learning appropriately? What sort of questions did learners ask? Were you confident about answering them?

What proportion of the lesson was teacher led? How appropriate was this?

How well do I know this class? To what extent do you need to consider the questions in columns 1 and 2?

To what extent are your expectations of this class congruent with the whole-school policies on behaviour and learning?

What is the whole school/ department policy on monitoring and assessment? Did you use appropriate assessment for learning strategies during this lesson?

To what extent do you embrace collaborative working practices to ensure a safe and consistent learning environment for all learners?

Did you apply your pedagogic knowledge to this lesson, for example the principles of good practice in teaching this subject, learning styles and strategies, differentiation strategies and supporting special needs?

> Pupils can't learn if they're not behaving . . . but they won't behave if they're not learning!

you can take small steps to achieve big improvements. For example, you may become aware that you are not setting a time limit for tasks, and start to do so. After all, learners will take as long as you give them to get something done, plus a little longer still! Or you may not be making clear when they may work collaboratively ('quiet partner voices') and when they must work independently ('silent individual work'). Or maybe you are expecting them to be silent for far too long, so they are not silent at all! Only through detailed reflection can such things be unearthed, and once they come to the surface you can deal with them. Another example of detailed reflection can be seen in Case Study 9.4.

Case Study 9.4   Avoiding shouting out

When Joseph's university tutor observed a lesson towards the end of his first teaching practice, she noted the following in her written feedback:

> 66 I can sense your frustration as you try to deal with pupils calling out answers to your questions, and you are starting to let this show. 99

In the verbal feedback that followed, the following dialogue took place between Joseph and his tutor:

Joseph Yes, I was feeling frustrated. They are so enthusiastic; they all want to talk at once!

Tutor All? Are you sure all of them were answering?

Joseph Mmmm. Well now you mention it, maybe it is the same kids every time.

Tutor So what were the others doing?

Joseph Listening, I guess. I'm not sure. . .

Tutor Do you think everyone achieved the learning objectives?

Joseph I think so. They could all answer the questions ok.

Tutor But you've just said only some were answering questions.

Joseph Well, the class teacher says some of them are not very confident.

Tutor So what could you do to give them more confidence?

Joseph I need to ask questions they can answer. But the problem is that the others just shout out the answers.

From this circular discussion, the tutor went on to elicit from Joseph how his open, blanket questioning was inviting shouted responses; he was not targeting his questions at individuals. He admitted that once he got a correct answer from somewhere in the room he moved on, allowing himself to believe that the class was now clear about that point. What is more, he could see that because learners got away with shouting out, their general behaviour deteriorated as the lesson progressed. His tutor negotiated a two-pronged strategy to help Joseph. First, he had to establish a classroom rule: no shouting out. This needed to be backed up with clear and consistent routines discussed with his mentor: *listen carefully to the question; think about the answer; put your hand up if you know the answer. I will choose someone to answer. Listen carefully to the answer given.* Second, he needed to think about how to structure and differentiate questioning. This way he could target closed questions to less able or less confident learners and more open questions to more able learners.

This reflection drew on Lunenberg and Korthagen's triangle (2009, see Figure 9.3) in a way that helped Joseph understand his own frustration, have

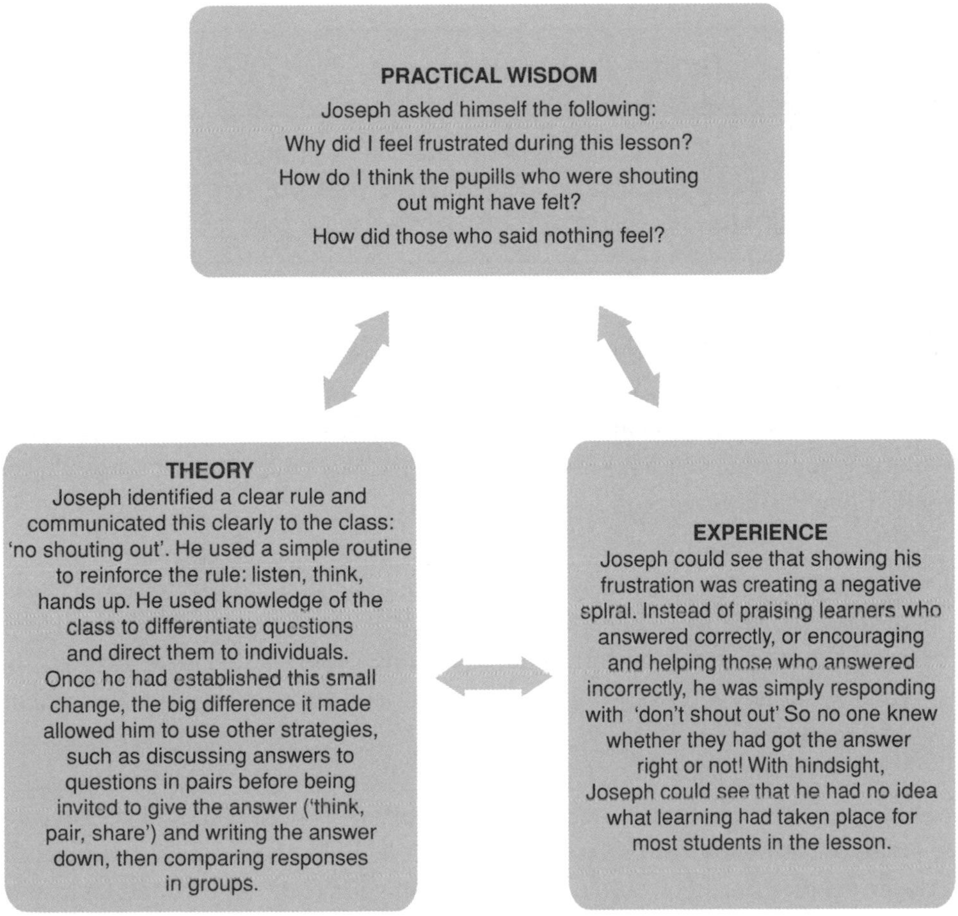

PRACTICAL WISDOM
Joseph asked himself the following:
Why did I feel frustrated during this lesson?
How do I think the pupills who were shouting out might have felt?
How did those who said nothing feel?

THEORY
Joseph identified a clear rule and communicated this clearly to the class: 'no shouting out'. He used a simple routine to reinforce the rule: listen, think, hands up. He used knowledge of the class to differentiate questions and direct them to individuals. Once he had established this small change, the big difference it made allowed him to use other strategies, such as discussing answers to questions in pairs before being invited to give the answer ('think, pair, share') and writing the answer down, then comparing responses in groups.

EXPERIENCE
Joseph could see that showing his frustration was creating a negative spiral. Instead of praising learners who answered correctly, or encouraging and helping those who answered incorrectly, he was simply responding with 'don't shout out' So no one knew whether they had got the answer right or not! With hindsight, Joseph could see that he had no idea what learning had taken place for most students in the lesson.

Figure 9.3 Joseph's reflecting on his questioning techniques

insight into how the class might be feeling, and learn from the experience by applying pedagogic knowledge in the form of theories he was learning in university and conversations with his tutor and mentor.

In his reflective journal at the end of his first teaching practice, Joseph wrote:

> 66 A key learning moment for me was when my tutor pointed out that 'blanket' questions tell you very little about who knows what in your classroom. Once I learned to differentiate the questions I asked and direct them to individual children, I got a much better picture of this. Because I stopped allowing them to shout out behaviour was better and the classroom was much calmer. Also, I could praise the kids who didn't have much confidence and I could challenge the most able with harder questions. 99

Reflective task 9.4   Reflecting on questioning

Refer to Figures 9.1 and 9.2. Starting from any one point on the triangle, use the questions in Table 9.3 to reflect on the quality and impact of your questioning in a lesson you taught recently. You must go through all the points on the triangle!

From the above, you should have a much more detailed picture of how you used questioning in the lesson, how your actions made you feel and the likely effect on the class, based on individual and group reactions. This you can probably do alone (provided you are honest with yourself). However, when it comes to the detail of how to improve, you need to draw on:

- all the resources available to you in school, including the careful observation of more experienced colleagues;
- established curriculum and pedagogic knowledge in the form of learning theory, subject pedagogy, national frameworks for teaching and assessment, and so on.

For this you will need, as Lunenberg and Korthagen point out (2009: 238) the expertise of university- and school-based tutors to help you make the connection between experience, theory and practical wisdom, and to develop your own insight into these connections. If you are lucky enough to be working in what Hodkinson

Table 9.3 A framework for reflection on questioning

	If you are part way through your teacher training	*If you have almost completed your teacher training*	*If you are an NQT*
1 Starting from **experience**	**What happened during question/answer sessions?** How did learners respond? Who was engaged in answering questions? Who remained silent? How much shouting out was there? What did you do about this?	**How well did you differentiate?** Were all pupils appropriately challenged through questioning? How do you know this? What did the answers tell you about what learning had taken place? Have you conducted successful questioning with other classes? What did you learn from this?	**How well did you relate the questions to the lesson objectives?** Were learners aware of why you were questioning them? Were they aware of what the responses told them about their learning?
2 Starting from **practical wisdom**	**What was the learning climate like?** Can you address every learner by name? How did you feel during question/answer sessions? How do you think your learners felt? Do you think everyone felt valued and included during this lesson? Did you praise correct responses? How sensitively did you deal with incorrect responses?		
	Reflecting on action Can you identify one incident during the lesson where you felt particularly confident about your questioning? What contributed to this?	Can you identify one example where you needed to reflect in action, giving a response to an unexpected question or answer? How did you feel about this?	Can you identify one example from the lesson where you may have enhanced the confidence of one of your learners? What contributed to this?

Table 9.3 (Continued)

	If you are part way through your teacher training	If you have almost completed your teacher training	If you are an NQT
3 Starting from theory	**What questions did you ask?** Did you prepare them in advance? What did you want them to tell you about the learning of individual pupils? What did they tell you about the extent to which learners achieved the lesson objectives? **How did you direct your questions?** Did you differentiate your questions? How did you question the most and the least able? How did you use questioning to build learner confidence? How did you feed back to learners, for example praise, encouragement, linking answers to the lesson objectives?	**How did you vary your questioning technique?** Did you encourage written as well as oral answers? Did you encourage learners to discuss their answers in pairs and small groups? Did they have opportunities to present their answers, for example through sticky notes or mini presentations? Did you provide opportunities for learners to rethink their responses to questions, and redraft written work?	**Did you use questioning to explore prior learning?** What do learners already know about this? Did you plan questioning to elicit their prior knowledge, acquired both formally and informally? Were you able to ascertain any misconceptions in order to 'deconstruct' them during your teaching? Did you use multiple questions to elicit and/or establish understanding? Were you aware of the meta-cognitive as well as the cognitive skills they were developing? Did you attempt to make your learners aware of these?

and Hodkinson (2005, in Simkins, 2009) have called an 'expansive learning en-vironment' this will be relatively easy. This is because such schools recognize the value that professional development brings to the organization, and therefore place a high value on individual development. Such schools are likely to have an ethos where issues like those in the case studies above are frequently addressed at formal and informal levels through 'learning conversations', and coaches and mentors are well trained in supporting beginning teachers to address such ques-tions. If you are less fortunate, you may need to turn to other sources for help (see Chapter 5 for more on this). Many training providers 'unpack' the professional standards, providing performance indicators of each one. Ofsted (2009a) has pub-lished descriptors of each grade (outstanding, good, satisfactory and inadequate) as exemplified by trainees in a variety of contexts: their teaching, their teaching files and in their 'explanations', that is, written and verbal communication with tutors and mentors (Appendix 2). In Appendix 3 there is an example of how working with 'progression grids' can lead to reflective conversations about where you are at any point in your development and where you need to go next. By using these and similar frameworks you will be able to take your busy but no less willing mentor with you on a journey of exploration through the reflective triangle.

Summary

This chapter has encouraged you to recognize the value of detailed reflection on small parts of your practice in order to make improvements that will ulti-mately have a major positive impact on how you act as a professional and gain what Lunenberg and Korthagen (2009) have called 'practical wisdom'. Through a number of case studies, the relationship between theory, practice and practical wisdom has been explored, and frameworks for developing detailed reflection on three key aspects of teaching have been provided. In developing frameworks for detailed reflection in other aspects, the reader should engage in an exploration of key questions with university- and school-based experts.

Conclusion

Beginning teachers often slip into a very generalized approach to reflection; they try to examine the whole; whereas the focus often needs to be on the parts that make up the whole. By using the frameworks proposed here to address some of the key aspects of your practice at a micro level, you will be able to develop strategies for reflecting on and improving other areas, thus taking little steps towards a much improved bigger picture.

Key learning points

- Transitions in your professional life, such as changing school or key stage, can lead to what feels like a decline in professional skills.
- Requirements constantly to evaluate your practice can lead to superficial reflection.
- Deep and focused reflection on every aspect of your professional life is not possible. By identifying what is really important at any given point, and reflecting in detail on small aspects of your work, you can ultimately make a significant difference to the bigger picture.
- Using frameworks for reflection can help you to focus on what is important to you in the here and now.
- In this way, you can use your experience to apply 'practical wisdom' in new contexts, so that transitions become easier over time.

How can you make the best use of feedback on your teaching?

Fay Glendenning and Lesley Cartwright

Clearly, students can and do reflect on their own teaching; most students think of nothing else but teaching during their school experience . . . The experienced practitioner can help the student focus on particular dimensions of teaching, 'guiding their seeing', helping them to find a language and encouraging them to discuss and articulate what they know.

(Furlong and Maynard 1995: 185)

Introduction

Whether you are at the start of your training or in your early years as a qualified teacher, you will already be accustomed to the concept of being observed and receiving feedback on your teaching. How you respond to this, and what you learn from it, will have a significant impact on your professional development. This chapter is designed to help you make the most of feedback you receive. In order for you to do this effectively, you need to understand the principles and processes of constructive feedback and appreciate how you tend to respond and what you are inclined to do with the information you receive. You will be guided in understanding how your mentor 'guides your seeing' through the feedback that you receive at different stages of your development. The following questions will be considered during the course of the chapter:

- What can you expect from feedback?
- Why is feedback on your teaching important?
- What types of feedback are there?
- How should you respond to it?

- How can you use reflection to make the most of your professional learning from feedback?
- How can you be more proactive in securing the feedback you need?

Before you read this chapter it would be useful to reflect on the sorts of advice that you may have received in the past and the kind of feedback you would like to receive to support your development.

Reflective task 10.1a   What would you like and/or expect from feedback?

This task would be even more valuable if conducted in pairs or small groups.

1 Jot down your individual thoughts on the following:
   - Why is it important to receive feedback on your teaching?
   - Who could provide feedback on your teaching?
   - What kind of feedback could you receive?
   - Is all feedback equally useful? Why/why not?
   - Can you give an example of feedback that you think has been really useful, and an example of some that has been less useful?
   - Do you think you need different feedback at different stages in your professional learning?
2 If possible, compare your own thoughts with those of peers or colleagues.
3 Reflect on the extent to which there is common ground. It is always useful for you to reflect on the extent to which your ideas are congruent with those of others, and if not, what the reasons for this might be.

Reflective task 10.1b

Read the following quotations from beginning teachers, talking and writing about written and verbal feedback on their teaching. They are all drawn from unpublished research over a number of years.[1] They were collected anonymously, but fictional

---

[1] The authors undertook 'grounded theory' research in order to collect data from trainees and their mentors and NQTs and their induction tutors in 2004–5, 2006–7 and 2007–8. All projects were funded by the TDA Partnership Development Schools Projects and findings disseminated regionally. The outcomes informed the development of initial teacher education and mentor development within the University of Wolverhampton.

names have been added here for ease of reference. Later in the chapter they are quoted anonymously

Lin	I thought that my mentor would comment on how I did during the lesson but I get feedback on how I dress, how I engage with children in the corridor - I never expected that!
Raj	I need to know how I am doing in my teaching. Experienced teachers can make judgments on what I am doing.
Anne	My mentor always writes lots down but has never got time to talk to me after the lesson. Sometimes I need to talk about it to make sense of what he has written.
Amy	My mentor is great and spends time talking things through with me after the lesson but getting something on paper is much harder.
Clare	I thought that we would have lots of time to talk but my mentor is so busy I feel that I'm always pestering her to get some feedback. I really want to talk to someone about how I'm doing and what I need to do next.
Phil	I was really quite pleased with my teaching. Everything had gone very well, and I used the interactive whiteboard all the time, but got no real feedback on this at all. She just kept saying: 'what do you think the children learned at that point?'
Mark	It's hard when you've been observed every week during your final teaching practice, and then hardly anyone seems interested in what you do – you are qualified, so you pretty much have to get on with it.
Ben	Whatever I did just wasn't right. My feedback always started with: 'well, if you'd done it like this it would have been better.'
Jo	It wasn't always good feedback, but it was always constructive. If the lesson wasn't good, it was about me teaching a bad lesson, not about me being a bad person.
Peter	She never had anything good to say about my teaching. It was always 'well, you could have done this, or that.'
Mahmood	It was made clear I had a lot to learn, but I never felt as if I was being judged personally.

1 Can you identify with any of the statements?
2 What themes emerge from these statements? You may wish, in groups, to draw a mind-map to sort features of feedback implied in the above.
3 Compare your identified themes with the analysis below.

Three very general themes emerge from the quotations:

- feelings of general satisfaction;
- feelings of disappointment;
- surprise at the content of feedback.

Raj, Jo and Mahmood are positive about their feedback. Raj communicates appreciation of the input from experienced colleagues; Jo and Mahmood value feedback that examines their teaching but separates their professional self from their personal self. Anne, Amy, Clare and Peter all faced some disappointment; their very busy mentors did not find enough time to give them feedback in the way they would have liked. Lin and Phil are surprised at the content of the feedback; both expected feedback on their teaching, but Lin had not expected her mentor to comment on wider aspects of the professional standards, and Phil felt a little cheated out of positive feedback on how he was doing because of the mentor's insistence on pursuing what his class was learning. As for Mark, as an NQT he missed the regular feedback he had enjoyed as a trainee as his entitlement to support was now much less.

What can you expect from feedback?

This is not an easy question to answer. Bunton et al. (2002: 237) found that beginning teachers in their study had the following expectations of their tutors: 'written comments, suggestions, advice, areas for improvement, praise, encouragement, guidelines and extra points not raised in discussion'. These are very reasonable expectations, and in the pro-formas used to record observations about your teaching there will be guidance setting out your entitlement to feedback based on similar points. While codes of professional conduct may articulate 'good practice' in feeding back to beginning teachers, the fact remains that what constitutes 'good' feedback can be very subjective. Peter above is clearly unhappy with his feedback, but his mentor's approach may have had the good intention of giving him tips to improve his practice. In many of the examples above, a key theme is a mismatch between expectation and reality in receiving feedback. This may well be the case in your reflections in the task above, especially if you have been able to discuss a range of experiences with your peers. Other chapters, especially Chapter 5, have touched on the key aspect of mentor relationships in initial teacher training and professional development. Much recent research in Britain, (Malderez et al. 2007) New Zealand (Ferrier-Kerr 2009), Australia and North America (Mitchell et al. 2007) has focused on the experience of trainee teachers during what is variously called 'teaching practice' or 'practicum', and on the induction of newly qualified or 'novice' teachers. A common theme in this research (for example Hobson et al. 2008: 413) is the significance of the quality of the relationship between the beginning teacher and the mentor. A major part of this relationship is based on feedback on professional learning. Wang et al.'s (2008) review of literature relating to the induction and supervision of new teachers draws on the research of Hall et al. (1995); Luft and Cox (2001) and Williams et al. (2001) to conclude that beginning teachers 'highly regard and expect a formally structured mentoring relationship that focuses on lesson observation and lesson based discussions and that they identify that such activities in their induction affect their teaching practice and learning'.

In a major literature review of mentoring practices across education, medicine and business, Hansford et al. (2004: 10) reported that feedback was found to be beneficial in many studies, but that it needed to be based on 'support, empathy and encouragement' and to be constructive. It is an unfortunate fact of life that this is not always the case. Several studies have explored the variability in quality of mentoring support, for example Cross (1999); Brooks (2000); Maynard (2000); Hobson (2002). A major contributory factor to this variation in quality is lack of time (Hansford et al. 2004) and the tension between one's responsibility as a teacher and as a mentor (Brooks 2000). Anne and Amy in the examples above had mentors who wanted to do their best but were overburdened in their professional role. Hannah is another case in point:

> 66 There were some really good role models in the department. I saw some fantastic teaching, but it was up to me to make sense of it; no one had time to feed back on the lessons I taught, let alone the ones I observed! This is a really good placement if you are able to work and learn independently, but not suitable for someone who needs a lot of hands-on guidance.
> *(Hannah, one-year MFL PGCE at end of first placement)* 99

Hannah gave this feedback in her verbal review of her first attachment. She went on to do well and was awarded 'outstanding' in her final assessment. She had established very strong foundations in what was a challenging, and at times uncomfortable, situation. Her case is a good illustration of the fact that the mentoring relationship is a two-way process requiring positive input from the beginning teacher as well as from the mentor. How you elicit, receive and respond to feedback will have a very significant impact on your professional development.

It is important for you to have realistic expectations of the feedback you will receive and to be proactive in steering and shaping it to meet your needs, even when there are perceived 'gaps' in the reflective conversations you have with experienced teachers. Some strategies for doing this will be explored.

Why is feedback important to you?

Feedback will include any supportive (be it critical or complimentary) comment that an experienced educator makes about your professional conduct and practice. It can be provided by a range of people: a designated mentor or tutor; another experienced teacher; a non-teaching practitioner such as a teaching assistant; a peer, and, increasingly, learners themselves (Fielding and Ruddock 2002). Experienced teachers also value the feedback from parents; although likely to be highly subjective, it can throw light on learners' attitudes. For example, once you learn that 'He loves French. He sings those songs you taught him all night!', you will take quite a different stance on his failure to open his mouth in class.

Feedback provides you with access to the subject and pedagogic knowledge of others. In many cases, this will be linked to experience, particularly of the context in which you are working, thus allowing you insights into others' 'practical wisdom' (Lunenberg and Korthagen 2009; see Chapter 9.) It is feedback that will 'guide your seeing'. As Dymoke and Harrison (2008: 3) explain: 'A mentor helps you to step "outside of the box" . . . and look in at it together.' Your peers, who may have no more 'practical wisdom' than you do, will undoubtedly have their own slant on things, helping you to see your practice differently. Other professionals will have seen your work from a different perspective and can provide excellent feedback at an informal level. Kelly was teaching magnetism to Year 2, and used the insights of the TA to support her lesson evaluation:

> 66 I'm glad I put them in mixed ability groups as the TA told me how much they learned from talking together.
> *(Kelly, BEd primary, second teaching practice)* 99

Another key reason for embracing the concept of feedback is put forward by Hagger et al. (2008: 176). They point out that because beginning teachers are encouraged to adopt learner-centred approaches in the classroom, encouraging independence of thought and responsibility for learning in those they teach, they need to embrace the concept of 'learning to learn' themselves, learning how to process feedback in an appropriate way. This is linked to the notion

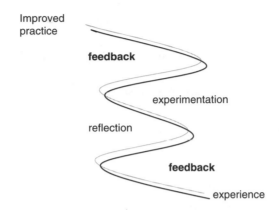

Figure 10.1   Using feedback to enhance experiential learning

that your commitment to becoming a teacher is also a commitment to lifelong professional learning (see Chapter 2). Atkins (1994), cited in Hinett and Weeden (2000: 246), identifies a key characteristic of the lifelong learner as being able to 'reflect on one's own practice and use feedback to assess and manage one's own performance'. Thus feedback is a very important implement in your toolkit for learning to teach. As a beginning teacher you will learn through your reflections on the experiences you have in (and out of) the lessons you teach. These reflections, whether in action, on action or before action in specific teaching contexts, or on your practice more generally, will inform how you plan and what you do in the future. This cyclical action of 'planning, doing and reviewing' or 'experience, reflection, experimentation' (Kolb 1984, see Chapter 13) can sometimes be viewed as a lone process but in reality should not be a solitary activity for the beginning teacher; it is feedback that supports it, ensuring that the 'cycle' is not a two-dimensional wheel that keeps on turning but goes nowhere in particular, but is an upward spiral in which feedback is incorporated to promote improved practice (see Figure 10.1).

Finally, feedback can provide some of the evidence needed to make judgments about your performance as a teacher, and the justification for those judgments, and by the same token it can raise your aspirations:

> 66   I nearly fell through the floor when he said I would definitely get a 'good', and could even get an 'outstanding'. We talked about what I needed to do to demonstrate outstanding features, and I really think I can do it!
> *(Raj, one-year MFL PGCE in the final weeks of her placement)*   99

Thus the value of feedback can be summarized as follows:

- It gives you access to the subject and pedagogic knowledge of others who may be more experienced than you.
- It provides perspectives from other professionals and non-professionals close to your practice.
- It supports your professional development as an independent learner who has to take responsibility for your own learning, just as you ensure that those you teach take responsibility for theirs.
- It provides evidence of your professional learning based on your experience to date, and helps you to seek ways of improving your learning.

What types of feedback can I expect?

Feedback can take many forms: formal or informal, directive or exploratory, context-specific or general (see Figure 10.2).

> How you elicit, receive and respond to feedback will have a very significant impact on your professional development.

It is important to note that the nature of feedback can be any combination of the features shown in Figure 10.2. For example, formal feedback can be exploratory, and informal feedback can be directive.

Earlier chapters, for example Chapter 6, have explored the role of others in providing support and feedback; the remainder of this chapter will focus on written and verbal feedback on your teaching. As a beginning teacher, you should expect to receive feedback on your teaching to help you to reflect on what went well in a lesson *and* what could be improved for the future. It may be surprising for you to find that the feedback can focus on a wider range of professional issues besides planning, delivery and content of the lesson observed. For example, it may refer to more personal aspects such as professional appearance, body language or communication. These expectations lie within the 'professional attributes' cluster of the professional standards for teaching (TDA 2007).

How should you respond to the feedback you receive?

Hagger et al. (2008: 210) acknowledge the range of type and quality of feedback, but emphasize the important role that the beginning teacher plays in the process: 'Notwithstanding this variation, there appear to be different dispositions towards receiving feedback (and critical feedback in particular) and the value that is attributed to it.' Their research identified a continuum in relation to trainee teachers' perception of their professional development not unlike the

Formal	Informal
• designated time and person with planned agenda • linked to formal assessment against professional standards • written feedback is structured, following agreed format • verbal feedback follows structured format with deviations from this agreed as part of the feedback process • includes the negotiation and recording of agreed targets for development • examples: post-lesson discussion of a formal observation; target setting and action-planning meeting	• takes place as the result of collaborative working or as part of support networking • may be provided by colleagues other than teachers, such as TAs or laboratory technicians • may be planned or ad hoc, but is not directly linked to assessment • outcomes are not necessarily recorded but may be written down if both parties agree • can also be an informal moment within a formal observation, such as a verbal comment from the observer to help the lesson along
Specific	**General**
• **context-specific** relates to a given teaching context, for example a single lesson observation, or a series of observations based on a single feature such as starter activities • **subject-specific** addresses aspects of subject knowledge and pedagogy pertinent to the teaching context • **stage-specific** addresses aspects of professional development relating to the current stage of development and immediate future needs • draws on lesson plans, teaching and assessment within the specific context	• relates to specific standards clusters, such as professional values/high expectations across a range of contexts • may focus on overall development rather than one part of it • draws on a range of evidence including teaching, conduct in and around the school, field work, written tasks
Directive	**Exploratory**
• provides written or verbal statements stating what is 'good' and what can be improved • little room for negotiation or comment • can be judgmental in nature, with the provider of the feedback taking a specific stance on how to solve problems • takes little account of the feelings of the recipient • suggestions for improvement are definitive	• facilitates open discussion, exploring different approaches • guides the recipient in drawing conclusions about their practice • elicits ways of doing things, encouraging the recipient to come up with their own solutions • asks open-ended questions and negotiates targets for development • suggestions for improvement are tentative

Figure 10.2   Types of feedback

Deliberative	Reactive
Plans professional learning, accepting responsibility for own development	Reacts to whatever happens rather than planning professional learning
Recognizes the value of looking beyond what happens in the classroom in order to make sense of classroom experience	Relies on experience of classroom teaching to develop learning
Values feedback and makes effective use of it to further learning	Tends to be disabled by critical feedback
Accepts the training context for what it is, capitalizing on what learning opportunities present themselves	Tends to regard the context of the school as limiting learning
Has high expectation of own and their pupils' learning	Is satisfied with current level of achievement

Figure 10.3 A continuum describing disposition to feedback

Source: After Hagger et al. 2008: 167

fatalism-idealism continuum described in Chapter 8. Hagger et al. (2008: 167) refer to a 'deliberative-reactive' continuum, with 'deliberative' trainees aware of and taking responsibility for their own learning needs across a wide range of contexts, and 'reactive' trainees relying on classroom practice alone for their development, with little aspiration to improve from their current level of achievement. Those at the reactive end of the continuum tend to feel 'disabled' by critical feedback, while those at the 'deliberative' end make effective use of feedback to further their learning (see Figure 10.3).

Receiving feedback on observations of your lessons can be a sensitive matter. It is likely that much thought and time will have been devoted to planning the lesson and so receiving feedback that is intensive and critical can be daunting and disappointing. It is important however to get into the mindset of viewing feedback as constructive to your development rather than destructive! Feedback on observations of your lessons assists the process of post-lesson reflection (reflection-on-action) and hence your professional development.

Reflective task 10.2   How do you respond to feedback?

Study Figure 10.3.

1 Think back to some recent feedback that you have received on your teaching, either written, verbal or both. What were the key learning points from this?
2 How did you feel following the feedback session, and why?
3 What 'follow-up' learning did you undertake as a result of the feedback?
4 To what extent is your response 'deliberative' or 'reactive'?
5 If you find yourself towards the reactive end of the continuum, what steps can you take to be more open to feedback?

When your mentors make suggestions for development and offer guidance, as the recipient of feedback you need to be open to listening, accepting, reflecting on, and acting on feedback if progress is to be made. The professional standards for teachers refer directly to the importance of acting upon advice and feedback and being open to coaching and mentoring. Your reflections above should help you to take any steps necessary to make the most of your feedback. You can follow this up by using some of the reflective approaches outlined below.

How can you use reflection to make the most of your professional learning from feedback?

In this section we offer some suggestions, drawing on beginning teachers' reflections, on how to use feedback and advice proactively. We are confining this discussion to feedback on lessons observed, that is, the written feedback and the post-observation discussion. First you need to consider the timing of your feedback. Consider the following:

66 I would like to get the notes straight after the lesson so that I can read the comments and think about what to do about them. If it is too long after, I forget what has happened.
(James, one-year PGCE maths, early in second placement)

I like my feedback straight after the lesson; I need to get it over and done with!
(Clare, GTP maths trainee, first term)

It isn't always possible, but when I can I like to prepare my evaluation of the lesson before I go to the debrief with my mentor. That way I already have a clear idea of what I did well and what I need to improve, so I can be prepared for our meeting.

(Jay, one-year PGCE primary) 99

Reflective task 10.3   Considering the timing of your feedback

1 Which of the above statements is most like your own response to post-lesson feedback?
2 Which is most useful in terms of professional learning?
3 Reflect on whether you prefer to go into your feedback session as soon as possible after the lesson, or whether you prefer time to evaluate before hearing what the observer has to say. Does your preference support your professional learning?

Evaluating your lesson before attending a feedback session can enhance the quality of the discussion as you compare your perception with that of your mentor. However it does require an open-minded approach to be able to deconstruct your own evaluation in cases where it is not congruent with that of the observer!

Next, the location of your verbal feedback meeting can have a positive or negative impact on the value you place on it:

66 I received my feedback in the staffroom, with everyone coming and going. There was another trainee working on a computer only a few feet away. I felt like everyone knew what had happened in my lesson.

(Jane, one-year PGCE maths trainee) 99

Space is nearly always at a premium in schools and colleges, but securing a quiet place for an uninterrupted feedback session not only makes you feel less vulnerable, but conveys the important message that you both take this very seriously. Being assertive about this can pay dividends.

Finally, how do you handle the feedback you receive? Consider Case Studies 10.1 and 10.2:

Case Study 10.1   Building on the positives

Joanne is a PGCE MFL trainee in her first school attachment. Her school is very challenging, with languages not valued by many learners. Joanne has just taught her Year

8 class for the second time. She had several activities planned that she was unable to use because the pupils were unsettled. She is close to tears when the feedback begins.

Mentor	Well Joanne, that was only your second lesson but already you are starting to get them on side. What did you do today that established a routine that you introduced on Tuesday?
Joanne	Well, I got them all to hang their coats up, get their books out and put their bags under the desk.
Mentor	Yes you did! How long do you think that took?
Joanne	Not long, much less time than on Tuesday.
Mentor	What else is a step forward from Tuesday's lesson?
Joanne	I know most of their names now. It helps a lot
Mentor	Yes it does, except that it can encourage us to nag the most disruptive pupils!
Joanne	How could I avoid doing that?
Mentor	Well, using more body language than spoken language will be possible in a few weeks, but first we need to talk about how you can exploit your firm expectations of their arrival into clear expectations of their work . . . . I think it would be useful to begin with ways of presenting new language to them that will engage their interest and enhance their learning . . .

In this short extract, we can see the skilful way in which the mentor, aware that Joanne was upset, began by eliciting from her what she had done well and establishing how she was already imposing her presence on this class, before going on to advise her about pedagogic matters.

Later in your training and during your induction, the 'positives' may be taken for granted as expectations about your performance are raised. This is something you need to be prepared for if you are to have high expectations of yourself!

Case Study 10.2   Reflecting beyond the positive

Jon was an NQT in a primary school. His induction tutor had just conducted a formal observation of his teaching English in Year 5. Jon had a very good rapport with the class, but his rather relaxed approach had been of concern to his mentor on the previous observation; she was not convinced that the children were being sufficiently challenged. Jon's target had been to discuss with the Key Stage 2 coordinator what expectations he should have of the individuals in this class and to use the scheme of work as a starting point for developing differentiated learning objectives that reflected high expectations of children's work. The lesson went well; all learners were engaged and enthusiastic and Jon began the session feeling very pleased with himself.

Mentor	Well Jon, they enjoyed that lesson, didn't they?
Jon	Yes I think they did. They liked the first group activity.
Mentor	What do you think they learned during that activity?
Jon	Well, that different texts are used for different purposes.
Mentor	Can you give me an example of that?
Jon	Well, they were looking at the difference between argument and comment in a text.
Mentor	Who do you think understood the difference?
Jon	They all did really. All the groups sorted the cards into the right pile.
Mentor	Does that mean everyone knew the difference? If you had asked Kieran, would he have been able to tell you what the features of 'argument' and 'comment' are?
Jon	Mmm. Good question . . . .

During the rest of the session, the discussion that Jon had hoped for about his excellent resources and his humorous, relaxed approach with his class never happened. Instead, the focus was on ways in which he could assess children's learning at a deep and meaningful level, challenging them to think and take responsibility for their learning, without losing his excellent rapport with them.

Reflective task 10.4   Responding to feedback

1 How would you feel if you were Joanne or Jon?
2 What is your reaction to the feedback they received?

You may be thinking that Joanne's tutor was more 'lenient' than Jon's. He was pleased that Joanne had used clear routines to get her class settled, whereas Jon's mentor was unimpressed by his excellent rapport with the class and wanted to move him on to a deeper understanding of formative assessment and its contribution to learning. However, consider the stage of development of each of the above teachers; Joanne is at the very start of her training, Jon is in the first term of his NQT year. In our experience, the most useful feedback is stage specific, that is, linked to realistic expectations of what could and should be achieved at the current stage of development. Although Joanne's mentor is keen to help her establish good behaviour management, he realizes that this comes partially through teaching that leads to tangible learning, and is keen to move Joanne on to think about this. As well as being stage specific in his feedback, he is, like Jon's mentor, being subject specific.

Reflective task 10.5   Stage-specific and subject-specific feedback

1 Are you conscious of what feedback you need at the current stage of your professional development?
2 How would you distinguish between general feedback and subject-specific feedback?

In Chapter 1 you were introduced to the types of professional knowledge on which you need to reflect. As well as the general 'pedagogic' knowledge (your beliefs about teaching, your knowledge of your learners and your practical knowledge) you also need to reflect on the 'how' and the 'what' of teaching your subject, your knowledge of curriculum and your knowledge of the key skills associated with the subject. In order to build up these knowledge bases in a systematic way, you need to:

- pay close attention to course content, training sessions and the role of assessment in your work;
- maintain an open dialogue with your tutors and mentors at all stages of your development so that you are aware of your progress and what you need to do next;
- focus less on what you *should* have done in your teaching, and more on what you *could* do in the future, so that you are constantly identifying your learning needs (Hagger et al. 2008).

Some training providers have identified stages of progression towards the standards for trainees to reflect upon and discuss in feedback sessions. It is also important that your feedback is subject specific; it needs to reflect your developing pedagogic and subject knowledge and indicate ways in which you can improve, for example, subject-specific explanations and demonstrations Of course, in an ideal world, your mentor would guide you effortlessly through the processes identified above. However, as we have seen in Chapter 5, few placements are without their problems; schools and colleges are busy places and the dual role of teacher and teacher trainer is rarely adequately resourced. So how can you help yourself through the process of ensuring that your feedback is stage specific, subject specific and meets your needs?

How can you be more proactive in securing the feedback you need?

Are you 'learning to teach, or learning to manage mentors'? Fortunately much has changed since Maynard (2000) used this title for her research into primary trainees' experiences of being mentored in school. In a large-scale, in-depth survey of teacher education in England, Hobson et al. (2009b: 332) reported that 90 per cent of trainees who successfully completed their course rated the feedback on their teaching as good (47 per cent) or very good (43 per cent). Of those who were unsuccessful or withdrew, this level of satisfaction drops to 63 per cent, although the causal relationship is a complex one. How we view the quality of the feedback we receive is to some extent dependent on three factors:

- Our expectation of what school-based training will be like. If our vision is of a kindly mentor who will be always on hand to advise and provide a shoulder to cry on, we are likely to be disappointed! If we add to the mix someone who will always give us positive feedback because she knows how hard we are trying, then we will face double disappointment.
- How well we understand ourselves, and our learning needs, at given points in our development. Linked to this is our capacity for self-efficacy, explored elsewhere in this book.
- How well-equipped we are to steer our feedback, ensuring that if we find ourselves facing problems in a mentoring context we will, like Hannah above, be able to continue to learn.

In the final section of this chapter, we offer some strategies for making the most of your feedback, particularly when you need to take some of the responsibility for making things happen.

Planning a lesson observation schedule

66   My mentor is really busy . . . lesson observations just don't happen.   99

A useful way forward here is to negotiate a lesson observation schedule with your mentor. You can enlist the support of a university tutor or a professional tutor in school if you need to. Arranging for several teachers in addition to your mentor to observe you across a range of subjects or classes will provide broad-spectrum feedback on your work. Such an observation schedule can be very simple (see Table 10.1).

Table 10.1 Lesson observation schedule

Lesson observation schedule		
Date & Time	*Class*	*Observer*
17 November 1.30–2.30	7E2	Mrs Jones

By planning a draft lesson observation schedule in advance of the observation period, you can ensure that the schedule includes a range of classes to be observed and that the observations are undertaken by a range of appropriate observers. Although the nature of school or college life will mean that occasionally lesson observations may not go ahead as planned, the schedule should help to keep everyone on track to ensure that an alternative observation is arranged and that regular feedback is received. As with all aspects of school life; flexibility is the key!

Identifying the focus of the lesson observation

66 I need to know if the alternative ways I have planned of presenting new language to learners is enhancing learning and motivation. 99

As a teacher, you would not plan a lesson without considering the learning outcomes for your class. Equally, you should always consider the focus for your own professional development for each lesson that is being observed, in order that you and your observer can make a point of building this into your feedback. A statement like the one above, shared with your observer before the lesson, will help in ensuring that the observation and feedback match your needs. Of course, you will need to accept that your mentor may also have an agenda, and will be steering your learning in ways that should complement your own perception of your needs. If this is not the case, you need to reflect on and discuss why this is.

Scheduling regular review meetings

We have explored the feedback that may be received following a lesson (reflection-on-action) and the strategies that you might use to get the most from your feedback. As well as receiving feedback on individual lesson observations, it is important also to consider your progress over a period of time. This can be achieved through professional discussions with your mentor, but may be more difficult to pin down than post-lesson feedback.

One way to ensure a focused professional discussion on your progress is to schedule regular review meetings. The frequency of these will depend on your stage of development and course requirements. Often there is a weekly review meeting for a trainee teacher undertaking a school placement and a termly or half-termly review meeting for a beginning teacher in the early years of their teaching career.

The review meeting allows a set time for the beginning teacher and the mentor to meet to discuss reflection-on-practice. This will focus on overall progress and development rather than one particular lesson observation. Planning these in advance increases the chances that they will take place on a regular basis. Many schools now 'ring fence' mentor meetings, protecting the time slot within the school day.

Being focused and prepared for meetings

Both you and your mentor are very busy; neither of you can afford to waste time. Being clear about what you want to gain from any feedback session, and at the same time remaining open minded to what your mentor has to say, will help oil the wheels of the process and ensure that the meeting runs smoothly and efficiently. Many chapters in this book provide you with reflective questions to mull over; use the index to identify an area of particular concern and draw reflective questions from this that will maximize the time available with your mentor.

Dealing with feedback that you perceive to be negative

Most so-called 'negative' feedback is constructive; it is designed to help you to improve your practice. Most beginning teachers are able to accept it in this spirit, and use it to develop their teaching:

> 66 It was pointed out to me by my mentor that I need to start thinking about the lesson from the learner's perspective and not from my own teaching perspective. This has really struck a chord with me. I believe that this has certainly been the case that I have only been concerned with my own performance and coming over as though I know the material inside out.
> *(Joseph, one-year PGCE MFL, four weeks into second placement)* 99

However, no one likes to be criticized. On very rare occasions, a hard-pressed or untrained mentor may feed back in a less than sensitive way, but such moments of weakness are usually overcome and forgiven. Persistent negative feedback is soul destroying, and if you are unlucky enough to be at the receiving end of this you should seek help as soon as possible from a more senior member of staff or university tutor. However, you do need to bear in mind that there is a difference between criticism of teaching and personal criticism, and not everyone is able to distinguish the two (Hagger et al. 2008: 171.) Where there is criticism of the teaching, perhaps it is justified. If you are concerned about being 'picked on', you can introduce some objectivity into your feedback by suggesting the collection of data. This could be undertaken by a peer or other colleague. For example, if your mentor suggests that your classroom language is negative, you can ask someone to keep a tally of negative and positive talk during the course of a lesson. The data collected by such methods are factual and as such can be depersonalized. The information can give you insight into how you are doing. You can ask for your teaching to be co-observed so that you have a second opinion, and you can also record your teaching in order to take the long view of it.

Using recordings to support feedback

66 My mentor tells me that my body language during the lesson is all wrong ... I have tried to put this right but am told it is still wrong. I don't know what to change! 99

To assist in post-lesson discussions, you may wish to take recordings of your lessons to support your own initial reflections and to support professional dialogue with your mentors[2]. Three types of recording will be explored: video recordings; interactive whiteboard recordings; and audio recordings.

'Even short video extracts of lessons can provoke rich and lengthy discussions' (Goulding 2004: 128). A video recording of a lesson, or part of a lesson, allows you to view the lesson again and to see it through the eyes of the observer. This can be a useful strategy for identifying mannerisms and body language that you may wish to change. These are most often things that we are not aware that we do!

Although having a permanent recording of the lesson allows reflection-on-action to take place, the process is enhanced if you evaluate the lesson *before* viewing it, then re-evaluate it in the light of what you see. It can be very enlightening to see how a viewing of yourself can change your perception.

66 My mentor kept saying that I was overusing 'ok?' but I just thought 'yeah yeah' and didn't really take what she said on board. I couldn't believe how annoying I found myself to be, saying 'ok?' in every sentence, when I saw the video! 99

The use of interactive whiteboards provides an interesting way of viewing back the lesson as part of the reflective process. The SMARTboard allows the activity

---

[2]Please note that you will need permission to photograph or record children or young adults. Always discuss your plans with a senior member of staff.

and voice at the board to be recorded and played back. During post-observation discussions, the activity at the board can be played back so that annotations on slides and the associated teacher talk can be viewed again. The viewing together of how you explained a point or modeled a task encourages quality reflective discussions between the mentor and the beginning teacher.

> 66 Hearing myself explain the method, and seeing how I had modelled it on the board, gave me the opportunity to engage with my mentor in a really good discussion about different ways this can be done. It was really interesting! It wasn't just about what I did, and why it only partially worked, but about the pros and cons of other methods. 99

It may assist in the reflective process to audio record formal verbal feedback. This allows for the feedback to be revisited for reflection by the beginning teacher, as is the case with written feedback.

> 66 The mentor feedback that I receive is useful but there is so much to take in. It is good to be able to rewind and listen to it again – to remember everything. 99

Summary

In this chapter we have acknowledged that feedback, in its various forms, can engender a range of emotions that can inhibit professional growth. We recommend developing reflective practice as a way of distancing yourself from the emotional aspects of feedback so that you are more able to use it to positive effect.

Conclusion

Whether you record your feedback sessions or not, there will always be a lot to take in. A recurrent theme of this book is that reflective practice is a powerful tool in building your self-efficacy and establishing yourself as a professional learner. This is needed nowhere more than when accessing and processing feedback on your teaching and your overall progress. The last word here goes to two trainee teachers cited in Hagger et al.'s research (2008):

> 66 I also feel that my learning is directed by me at this stage. I am the person saying 'I'd like to teach more chemistry' or 'I'd like to teach lower ability groups'. I'm asking for more challenges. . . . I'm hoping

that I'll be able to work with the other [student teachers] and we can observe each other.

(science student teacher, p. 168)

" [A]t the moment, because I'm training, I can take a lot of time over working out what I want to be like and what I want to do and try new things and make mistakes ... I've just this time, and I'm learning, and that's the whole point, the whole reason for me being there isn't it?

(English student teacher, p. 169)

Each of the above is demonstrating very high levels of self-efficacy and proactivity, being at what Hagger et al. term the 'deliberative' end of the learning continuum.

Key learning points

- Where feedback is powerful, its power may be negative as well as positive.
- It is important to be able to accept constructive criticism and use it to reflect on what you need to do in the future to improve your practice.
- If we, as teachers, give feedback to learners and expect them to reflect on how to improve their work, we must be open minded and proactive enough to do the same in our own learning.
- The day-to-day demands of teaching often mean that mentors do not have the time to devote to teacher training that beginning teachers hope for. You can mitigate these difficulties by being proactive in using a range of strategies to support the feedback process.

CHAPTER

11

How can you overcome constraints to enhance reflective practice?

Mahmoud Emira and Julie Wilde

Make use of time, let not advantage slip.

William Shakespeare

This chapter is about how as a beginning teacher you can overcome some common barriers to enhance your professional practice. Many obstacles to reflection can be addressed by documenting your views, feelings and thoughts about past experiences and future directions for development. Writing about your deliberations, hopes and desires, however, can be time consuming and many trainees highlight this as a concern. Bolton (2010), Otienoh (2009), Moon (2006) and Jasper (2003) all acknowledge the challenge of time to think, reflect and articulate the processes that inform the development of reflective practice. Craft and Paige-Smith (2008) also suggest that a lack of time may impede the process of reflection and stall the development of practice. It is however, somewhat naïve to suggest that reflective practice will routinely emerge with the provision of more time. In addition to having enough time, beginning teachers need to recognize the worth of written reflections as a useful tool to augment pedagogic development, be motivated to engage in it and have confidence in their ability to reflect. This chapter explores ways in which you can recognize and respond to the factors that constrain your ability to reflect.

Reflective task 11.1   Identifying your personal barriers to reflection

1 What do you perceive to be the major constraints and barriers to documenting your reflections?
2 Can you categorize these as practical, emotional or academic?

Common barriers to reflection may include practical barriers (not enough time, too many other commitments); emotional barriers (it is hard to face up to what is not going well, even harder to sift out what is going well from a perceived 'bad' lesson) and academic (fears that your writing or ideas are not really good enough, or that you do not know enough). Your identified barriers may be broadly similar to this.

'Writing has never been my strong point': academic concerns about reflection

An essential characteristic of self-reflection is 'documenting' your practice (Craft and Paige-Smith, 2008) which can be done in various formal or informal ways, for example: keeping a journal; annotating a diary; scribbling on your lesson plans; rigorously evaluating lessons and sequences of lessons; or collecting and collating varied artefacts of evidence of your progress towards professional standards as you build up a portfolio. Some of this will be paper based but it is increasingly likely to be electronic, as outlined in Chapter 12.

> Capturing professional practice in the form of a journal can support understanding thought patterns (cognitive processes) and thus aid the process of problem solving.

How can you be persuaded of the value of writing a reflective log? First, you should not feel too constrained in terms of how you record your reflections; you can be quite creative with your preferred style of journaling, from hand-written jottings to e-portfolios and everything in between. Second, you need to be assured of the value of this activity. Capturing professional practice in the form of a journal can support understanding thought patterns (cognitive processes) and thus aid the process of problem solving. Beginning teachers can re-visit their journal entries in order to prompt reflective practice by considering what they would do differently in the future. Moon suggests that in its simplest form journalling provides 'interesting data about how we see the world' (Moon 2006: 156). Documenting reflective evidence enables teachers to have ownership of their professional development and as Otienoh (2009) points out, journal writing actively engages teachers in the reflective process. By being able to draw out 'action points' or questions which can be shared with a mentor or significant other, you will be creating time for a much richer and deeper reflective dialogue during meetings (see Chapter 10). Finally, you need to develop your own strategies in order to address concerns about your writing ability and/or the quality of your knowledge base. Journal writing gives you the opportunity to cogitate over theory and how you might apply it in practice (See Case Study 11.1.)

Case Study 11.1   Amy: linking reading, writing and classroom practice

Amy was constrained by her fears about writing. As a graduate mathematician, she had done very little writing since the age of 16. As a PGCE maths secondary trainee in her first term of training, she was faced with the double anxiety of how she could express herself well in her reflective journal and successfully complete written assignments, as well as plan, teach and evaluate! She made an appointment with her university tutor, who showed her how she could use her reading to enhance both her writing and her professional practice by:

- reading a little on each topic but reading it deeply for understanding;
- using what she read as a model for her own writing, for example observing use of references and links between theory and practice;
- seeing how the reading and academic writing are there to enhance practice, not get in the way of it!

66 I had to read a short extract from Hargreaves (2005) about conceptions of learning. I then had to find a piece of writing about maths teaching, and then observe a lesson and comment on the three together. Now I see what 'synthesis' means! Finally I had to say how this reflection would enhance my own practice. From my reading I found out that teachers can either see learning as the achievement of objectives or as the construction of knowledge. When I observed a lesson where the teacher presented different polygons to the children, which they had to copy in their books, I could see that her intention was that they achieved the learning objective of 'know what a polygon is'. I then read Forrester and Searle (2003) who talk about 'folding back' to earlier learning as a basis for new learning. This led me to reflect: how about giving the children triangles, circles and polygons and asking them to pick out the polygons? (They already know what triangles and circles are.) This helps them work out a definition of polygon for themselves. This is what I think Hargreaves means by 'learning as the construction of knowledge'. I will try more hands-on activities in my lessons. 99

Later, in her evaluation of the module, Amy wrote:

 Reading short extracts and using the ideas made me think about my practice more and gave me confidence to write about it as well. 99

Amy gained confidence in her own writing in two ways:

- She changed the way she read by reading less but in greater depth, thinking carefully about the meaning and structure of the content.
- She changed the way she perceived the different elements of her course, recognizing how reading and reflective writing had the power to enhance her practice.

Many trainees, especially graduates of non language-based degrees such as mathematics, science and technology, have concerns about their basic writing skills. Peer support can be invaluable here. Bold and Hutton (2007) found that students who engage in group activities are more likely to have their reflection abilities developed than their classmates who do not take part. Another way of fostering the process of reflection in peer support groups is the brain development (Strong-Wilson 2006) which fosters personal reflection (Bold and Hutton 2007). However, support does not always have to come from groups; it can be sought from individuals. Some people may find it less threatening and even more convenient to comment on each other's work and discuss with more confidence any issue with a peer than in a whole group (Bolton 2005).

Reflective task 11.2

1 What, if any, are your 'academic' concerns about reflective writing? Make a list of up to three.
2 Alongside this, jot down a broad action plan. This might include discussing your ideas with someone, or reading something, or rethinking how you approach your reflection at the moment.

From the above case study we can see the value of building a subject and pedagogic knowledge base upon which to build reflection. Kirby (Case Study 11.2) found that knowledge of organizations is useful in understanding barriers to reflection. He became frustrated with some of the practices in his school.

Case Study 11.2   Kirby: knowing and doing together

> There have been times when I have felt powerless. I think I have some good ideas and can sometimes see where improvement can be made. However I feel held back by 'rules and policies' – I value the profession and the learning experience of my pupils. Sometimes I wonder if I will ever be allowed to think for myself. I had fantastic feedback during my initial teacher training programme on my creative ideas, enthusiasm etc. However when I arrived at the school I soon learned that 'we don't do it like that'. I felt so frustrated.
>
> I spoke to a friend who I met during my training and she explained the 'circles of influence' (Covey 1992). Doing what I can, and accepting what I can not change. I concentrate my energies within the circle of influence and on things I can be proactive about such as MY teaching, MY classroom, MY planned learning activities. Change can be slow but focusing on where I can make a difference, for example making sure MY pupils have a positive and rewarding learning experience, prevents me from feeling negative and ineffective – there will always be things I cannot change and there are plenty of things I can change.
>
> *(Kirby, primary NQT)*

Kirby learned to understand his 'sphere of influence' (Figure 11.1). Your own sphere of influence will be slightly different depending on your stage of development.

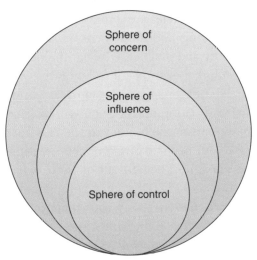

Figure 11.1 Circles of influence
Source: Covey 1992

> **Reflective task 11.3**   Understanding your 'sphere of influence'
>
> Think about an aspect of your professional life that frustrates or troubles you. Using Figure 11.1, locate this problem in one of the 'spheres of influence'. Does this help you to respond more objectively to the problem?

'I really don't have time for all this': good reasons to make time to reflect – and how to find the time

Solving one problem, of course, can lead to another; knowing how to do something still requires you to find the time to do it! The value of collaborative work has been emphasized throughout this book. Not only is it an enriching activity, but it can be a time-saver too. An example of this is to create with your fellow trainees or colleagues a reading group through which reading will be delegated to and shared by group members. This has the potential to decrease the time you and your peers spend on reading and will become a vehicle for the development of reflection in the group (Eckel et al. 1999). Picture for example, in Amy's case above, a 'triangular' reading and discussion group in which one member read the generic Hargreaves article (2005) and each of the other two read a pertinent aspect of teaching and learning mathematics. Individually they would be practising skills of reading and summarizing, and collectively developing skills of synthesizing theory and practice, while at the same time sharing ideas to enhance their practice. Another example of collaborative work that may facilitate reflection on practice is engagement in systematic observations and debates (McCollum 2002). During teaching practice you will have some 'spare' time that can usefully be spent supporting each other in the classroom rather than in the staffroom. You may ask your peers to observe your practice and feedback to you afterwards. To get the maximum benefit out of these activities we suggest that you observe their practice too. The key point here, whether you systematically observe or engage in a discussion about your/their practice, is that reflection should be critical but constructive at the same time. Collaborative work including peer support is not advocated for its own sake; it may become insignificant if it lacks a critical reflection on practice (Campbell and Sykes 2007). Task 11.4 may help you to develop the required level of rigour and criticality when working collaboratively:

Reflective task 11.4　Three-way collaboration

1 Work in groups of three. One person is a 'storyteller', one a 'detective' and one an 'umpire'.
2 Enter into a role play where the storyteller relates a critical incident. This may be about something that went particularly well or particularly badly in a recent lesson you taught. The detective asks questions about the incident. The umpire's role is to see fair play by ensuring that the discussion is open and non-judgmental.
3 After the role play, discuss the extent to which a shared discussion is effective and what limits its effectiveness (such as being over-judgmental).

(after Brookfield 1995)

When time is at a premium, it is helpful to be clear about roles, and about what behaviours have a positive as opposed to a negative impact. Developing mutual respect and empathy saves time in the long run; a lot of time can be spent on dealing with negative emotion.

Case Study 11.3 demonstrates how Eddie realizes the need to make time for reflective practice. He is motivated because he sees the value of reflection in terms of improving his practice for career progression. He moves from documenting evaluations of his teaching practice to asking more reflective questions, and recognizes the need for action as a result of what he learns.

Case study 11.3　Eddie: finding more time to reflect

66 Recently, I have decided that I would like to move forward in my career .... Perhaps head of department or head of house. I know that I will have to show that I am capable of the role so I have had to make time to reflect on what makes me a good teacher and what I can do to become better still. I have learned that I have to make time for reflection. It's Ok to jot ideas down ... but that's not really reflection – true reflection is analyzing the notes; it's the why ...? how ...? what next?. and then thinking and acting upon those thoughts. I make time at the end of some of my lessons to ask pupils to complete evaluations ... what went well etc ... I now use them to reflect upon – a shared activity. The important thing is how the information helps me reflect and develop my professional practice – I really want to make a difference.

(Eddie, in second year as a qualified secondary teacher) 99

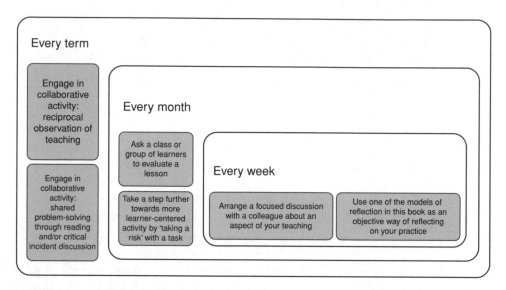

Figure 11.2   Time-saving action plan

Time is a constraint for reflecting and yet reflective practice is a vital part of developing professional practice. Eddie creates time in some of his lessons by asking pupils to complete evaluations. His reflective practice strategy is developed by documenting the evaluations to guide his reflections and he is aiming at using the process to enhance his teaching career.

Reflective task 11.5   Make time to . . .

1 Design a post-lesson evaluation sheet for your learners to complete.
2 Read and make notes on the evaluations through different lenses: a) the learner perspective; b) a teaching quality perspective.
3 Identify an action point which will develop your professional practice, acknowledging why you have decided on the specific action.
4 Share this process in a critical dialogue with a peer, colleague or mentor, or through and online forum.
5 Keep a diary of what you have to do (assessed tasks, meetings and so on), leaving spaces for what you would like to do, then . . .
6 Develop an action plan to use termly, monthly and weekly so that your short-term and longer-term schedules are efficient. See Figure 11.2 as an example.

Table 11.1   Table for reflective questioning

Descriptive level of reflection	*Theory and knowledge building level of reflection*	*Action-orientated level of reflection*
What ... ... have I been trying to achieve? ... has been the response of my learners? ... was good or bad about the experience?	**So what** ... ... does this tell me about myself and my way of working? ... other knowledge am I now able to bring to my role? ... is my new understanding of the role?	**Now what** ... ... do I need to do in order to further improve? ... broader issues do I need to consider if this action is to be successful? ... might be the consequences of this further action?

Source: Rolfe et al. 2001

'It's bad enough at the time, without reliving it again through reflection!': overcoming emotional aspects to reflect more deeply and broadly

Using journalling, action planning and/or your learners' responses in lesson evaluations can all help in developing reflective practice. Applying models to analyse reflective writing is another strategy that can support professional and personal development. For example, building in how you feel can be useful; Reed and Canning (2010: 2) suggest that reflection needs to be an emotional response, complementing the knowledge and understanding we already have about a subject or situation.

Case Study 11.4 demonstrates how Bali has used a variety of strategies to develop her reflective practice skills. Bali was constrained in her reflections by her own negative thoughts. However, she employed a diary (Moon 2004) in the form of lesson evaluations and used a reflective questioning model (see Table 11.1). Bali is a trainee teacher who always reflected on the negatives of her teaching experience. She had started to lose some confidence in her judgements but then learned how to combine writing lesson evaluations with a model (Rolfe et al. 2001) to guide her reflective practice.

Case Study 11.4   Bali: overcoming negative emotions

❝ Previously my reflections were about what went wrong! I used to spend too much time thinking and not enough time doing. All of my energy was taken up by 're-living' the negative parts of my lessons. I went around in circles . . . Making the same mistakes.

My mentor suggested that I keep a diary made up of lesson evaluations from my Year 8 class. He also suggested that I should use a reflective questioning model. By combining my diary of lesson eval-uations and reflective questioning I could identify both the strengths and weaknesses of the lesson. I can balance the negatives with the strengths – I can see how and why they are strengths and what I can do to develop my practice – models help to focus possible targets – so now I do not think about a 'bad' lesson – I use a model and I think what have I learned and what can I do to prevent it from happening again. I decided 'small steps' to change teaching practice and now I can identify them for myself without beating myself up and losing confidence . . . I do not mind being observed by anyone – I know what a good lesson is and I know what to do when I do not achieve what I set out to do. Lesson evaluations and reflective practice models have enabled me to analyse the situation professionally rather than thinking that I am personally ineffective – much healthier for me.

(Bali, secondary science PGCE, second teaching practice) 〞

Bali's reflections had been constrained by 'automatic negative thoughts' (ANTS). However, Bali had a colleague who explained that negative thinking is often due to a 'fear' about the future. She was encouraged to reflect in a way that enabled her to explore her negative thoughts but plan for a 'happy' ending. She used a model provided by Rolfe et al. (2001) to balance negative thoughts with positive outcomes.

Reflective task 11.6   Reflecting objectively

1 Reflect on a recent teaching experience that did not go as well as you would have liked using the questions in Table 11.1.
2 Try to balance negative thoughts with positive outcomes.

Many models for reflection are presented throughout this book, and are useful in that they 'channel' any negative thinking away, leading you to take a more objective view of your practice. If feeling negative is a particular problem for you, see in particular Chapter 4. Kay (Case Study 11.5) found ways of being reflective more objectively.

> ### Case Study 11.5   Kay: standing on the outside looking in
>
> 66 I was finding it difficult to engage in reflective practice without becoming 'judgmental' . . . I began comparing myself to others and was very critical – teachers can get it wrong (or is that being too judgmental again?) The reason I use a model is because I like that my feelings matter as much as my thoughts and practice. Teaching is an emotional profession and having a model to guide me helped to focus why I felt certain ways and why I did certain things – I learned 'triggers' and then I became aware of certain feelings/thoughts so I learned to adjust my practice to ease my feelings and thinking . . . . I have also learned to be more objective, stand outside the situation and look in.
>
> *(Kay, second year of teaching in a primary school)* 99

Kay worked with a model that ensured she was less likely to become too judgmental of herself and of others. A danger facing teachers who move into critically reflective mode is that of being labelled as trouble makers (Brookfield 1995: 228). Kay used an adaptation of Gibbs's (1988) model (see Figure 11.3 and Chapter 13) to explore details of her teaching and learning situation. The reflective questioning helped her to enhance her teaching.

The ability to identify and assess one's strengths and weaknesses (Osterman and Kottkamp 2004) and personal expectations has shown its effectiveness in facilitating the process of reflection (Morss and Donaghy 2000). In their study, Morss and Donaghy found their students were much more able to structure and guide their thinking by evaluating their own strengths and weaknesses. One way of doing this is to assess how your lesson went after an observation by using a model to prompt a critical conversation or by designing activities for pupils to evaluate a learning experience. There are many ways to engage learners in the evaluation process such as:

- asking learners to write one positive and one negative statement about learning on a sticky note which can be placed on a wall;
- asking learners to put comments in either a 'basket' (valuable learning) or a 'recycle bin' (learning which needs to be developed);

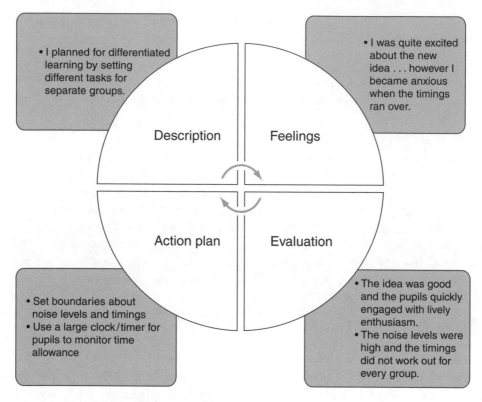

• I planned for differentiated learning by setting different tasks for separate groups.

• I was quite excited about the new idea . . . however I became anxious when the timings ran over.

Description

Feelings

Action plan

Evaluation

• Set boundaries about noise levels and timings
• Use a large clock/timer for pupils to monitor time allowance

• The idea was good and the pupils quickly engaged with lively enthusiasm.
• The noise levels were high and the timings did not work out for every group.

Figure 11.3   Kay's adaptation of Gibbs 1988

- using a 'traffic light' system at points within a lesson indicating red for 'stop I'm not sure', orange for 'let's spend a little more time on this' and green for 'let's get on to the next thing'.

Responses from the learners, 'harvested' during lessons, provide time-saving evidence to be used in reflection and future planning. Not only does this facilitate your reflection but it also bridges the gap between theory and practice (McCollum 2002).

Summary

This chapter has used literature, teacher accounts and activities to help beginning teachers take ownership of their reflective practice, despite the constraints. Ways of overcoming barriers such as lack of time, confidence and motivation have been addressed. The importance of developing your subject and pedagogic knowledge base to build your confidence has been acknowledged, as has the value of using models of reflection to enable you to take a more positive stance. Above all, the value of formal and informal collaborative learning as a means of saving time and developing high quality reflective practices has been emphasized.

Conclusion

Dom provides an apt conclusion to the ideas expressed in this chapter:

66 Developing deep and meaningful reflection is challenging – sharing your ideas and thoughts with others can confirm or challenge your perceptions, values and attitudes – however I think that my commitment to learning through reflection has increased my confidence, improved my teaching practice and I am more relaxed (in a good way!)

(Dom, in second year of teaching) 99

Finally, Marsha provides an optimistic note on which to end this chapter by concluding that all the commitment and effort are worthwhile:

66 For me reflective practice has been time consuming but rewarding none the less. There were times when I questioned my involvement, there have been times when relationships seemed stretched – however the personal and professional development far outweighed the difficulties. Sometimes it is only when you look back and see the distance travelled you realize how much you have achieved.

(Marsha PCE NQT) 99

Key learning points

- The most common barriers to engaging in reflective practice are: lack of time; inexperience or lack of confidence in writing skills; feeling overwhelmed by the knowledge and skills that need to be acquired as a teacher; feelings of isolation; organizational constraints.
- Overcoming these problems takes time, and requires good time management, an open mind and an ability to be constructively self-critical.
- The use of models for reflection can help in making the best use of your time and developing reflective skills.
- Collaborative working, both formal and informal, provides an excellent vehicle for developing reflective practices, and as well as making the process more enriching, can save time.

- It takes time to become a reflective learner (McClure 2002), but the time spent engaging in reflective practice is not wasted. The outcomes of becoming a reflective practitioner may emerge slowly, and should not be rushed.
- The consistent and persistent use of planned reflective strategies will pay valuable dividends in time as your personal and professional growth is enriched.

CHAPTER

12

How can e-reflection help develop your practice?

Sarah Powell

> *Online education may facilitate collaboration and stimulate discussion between people, cultures, institutions, and subject areas. It is like a melting pot for educators. Young professionals who now enter the field of online education should use these opportunities to learn from, and build on, all the experience and controversies that come from this melting pot.*
>
> Morten Flate Paulsen, Professor of Online Education,
> Pennsylvania State University

Other chapters in this book explore and exemplify a range of reflective tools to enhance your professional learning. The assumption, traditionally, has been that such reflective practice is conducted either in a face-to-face meeting with a peer, colleague or mentor, or is a very private affair between you and a sheet of paper. This chapter highlights how technology could support your professional learning and the development of your reflective practice. The intention is to engage you in some thoughts about how you might benefit from the digital age in which you are living, not just at a personal level (which doubtless you already do) but also at a professional level. The chapter draws on the commentary of beginning teachers' experiences of using technology to enhance their professional learning, to consider the following questions:

- Why use e-learning tools?
- What e-learning tools are available? A brief description of a number of tools is given, with commentary from beginning teachers who have used them.
- How can e-learning support reflective practice?

Why use e-learning tools?

'Anyone who can access the Internet can be part of the knowledge-access, knowledge-building, information-exchanging culture, regardless of location' (Loving et al. 2007). The 'e' of 'electronic' is applied more and more to our everyday lives: e-mail, e-billing, e-banking and e-shopping have become everyday activities. The power of technology as an education and communication tool is therefore self-evident. Governments around the world are pledging support for e-learning in schools, colleges and universities and in civic communities. In Britain, for example, there has been a promise of 'integrated online personal support for learners' (DfES 2003: 43) with a target that every learner will have access to a personalized online learning space. E-learning and e-delivery have the potential to offer differentiated and personalized support for learners (Beetham 2005: 7).

> The traditional teacher-to-student transmission model of learning is slowly moving to one that embraces the potential of the information revolution to provide exciting, flexible learning tailored not only to individual learning needs but also allowing 'anytime, anywhere' access to learning.

The traditional teacher-to-student transmission model of learning is slowly moving to one that embraces the potential of the information revolution to provide exciting, flexible learning tailored not only to individual learning needs but also allowing 'anytime, anywhere' access to learning. Beginning teachers are very much part of this revolution. First-hand experience of e-learning during training has been shown to facilitate teachers' openness to new ideas as well as to enhance their reflective and academic skills, to provide a 'synergy between knowing and doing, pedagogy and technology' (Hughes and Purnell 2008).

What e-learning tools are available?

Most schools, colleges and universities subscribe to a 'virtual learning environment' (VLE), of which some are commercially available (for example Moodle) and some are exclusive to the organization such as WOLF (Wolverhampton Online Learning Framework). Many teacher training institutions now make use of VLEs, providing structures through which trainee teachers can communicate with each other and with tutors. Thus 'communities of practice' described by Wenger (1998) can take on a whole new dimension once they are no longer confined to physical spaces and set times, but become 'asynchronous' learning environments. These virtual communities complement rather than replace face-to-face contact with tutors, mentors and peers. They may be organized formally through VLEs or develop organically through social networking sites and informal blogging. The advantages and disadvantages of both formal and informal e-communities of practice are explored in this chapter, and suggestions for your own use of them are made.

Webfolios

The webfolio, or e-portfolio, is variously defined in the literature as both a process and a product. Consider your teaching file; it is a collection of everything related to your professional development: lesson plans and evaluations, written observations, informal notes made during feedback sessions, a variety of school-based tasks and activities, maybe 'field notes' and reflections relating to practice, and so on. Imagine this as wholly or partly electronically based, building up as a collection of evidence of your meeting professional standards. Add to this some of the conversations you have with peers, colleagues and mentors and imagine that, instead of being conducted in snatched moments in the school day, they are formally structured but flexibly accessed (early in the morning, after the children have gone to bed, while waiting for your lift home). These electronic exchanges can contribute to your e-portfolio, building up as you develop your professional expertise. Sutherland (2005) sees the e-portfolio as a personal space for learning, providing opportunities to tell our own stories about learning. Lorenzo and Ittleson (2005) expand on this, describing the e-portfolio as:

> "[A] digitized collection of artefacts, including demonstrations, resources, and accomplishments that represent an individual, group, community, organization, or institution. This collection can be comprised of text-based, graphic, or multimedia elements archived on a Website or on other electronic media such as CD-Rom or DVD."
>
> (Young and Lipczynszki 2007: 6).

Webfolios work on the same principle as the 'wikis', such as Wikipedia; that is they are websites that allow for the easy creation and editing of any number of interlinked web pages. They work a bit like a spider's web. Each item can be linked to others by hyperlinks from one page to another. Documents and suggested websites are linked to each other and organized in a way unique to you, enabling you to engage quickly and easily with material to support your professional learning. A page can be arranged to provide easy access to documentation, websites, subject knowledge, images, clipart, music clips and photographs. The example in Figure 12.1 is one created by a trainee to develop their subject knowledge in the area of 'Linguistic diversity and language development'.

There are clear advantages to being able to access all your documents in one place, as anyone who has lugged half a dozen files around school and college will

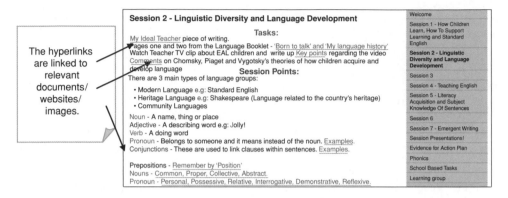

The hyperlinks are linked to relevant documents/ websites/ images.

Session 2 - Linguistic Diversity and Language Development

Tasks:

My Ideal Teacher piece of writing.
Pages one and two from the Language Booklet - 'Born to talk' and 'My language history'
Watch Teacher TV clip about EAL children and write up Key points regarding the video
Comments on Chomsky, Piaget and Vygotsky's theories of how children acquire and develop language

Session Points:

There are 3 main types of language groups:

• Modern Language e.g: Standard English
• Heritage Language e.g: Shakespeare (Language related to the country's heritage)
• Community Languages

Noun - A name, thing or place
Adjective - A describing word e.g: Jolly!
Verb - A doing word
Pronoun - Belongs to someone and it means instead of the noun. Examples.
Conjunctions - These are used to link clauses within sentences. Examples.

Prepositions - Remember by 'Position'
Nouns - Common, Proper, Collective, Abstract.
Pronoun - Personal, Possessive, Relative, Interrogative, Demonstrative, Reflexive.

Welcome
Session 1 - How Children Learn, How To Support Learning and Standard English
Session 2 - Linguistic Diversity and Language Development
Session 3
Session 4 - Teaching English
Session 5 - Literacy Acquisition and Subject Knowledge Of Sentences
Session 6
Session 7 - Emergent Writing
Session Presentations!
Evidence for Action Plan
Phonics
School Based Tasks
Learning group

Figure 12.1 An illustration of the ways that web links can be developed to support learning about language

know! Feedback from trainees suggests that once they have mastered the (simple) technology, the fact that they can access material quickly and easily contributes to their ability to be organized, as Lauren testifies:

> 66 Having immediate access to the materials was useful especially when I was in school and needed help with prepositions. When it came to revise for the exam I trawled through the pages and used the links I had already set up. It did help rather than having all my paperwork in different folders. I am definitely going to add to it for next year.
>
> *(Lauren, Early Years BEd trainee, first year)* 99

Reflective e-learning through this kind of multimedia resource can be stimulating, motivating and at first glance very informative. However there are disadvantages too; the plethora of information on wikis can contain ill-informed and biased materials as well as valid and reliable resources. Suppose Lauren's information about prepositions had been gleaned from a peer's ideas about what they are, and this peer had got it wrong?

Reflective task 12.1

1 What do you need to bear in mind when using information online information such as websites and wikis?
2 How will you use your developing academic skills to verify the information you find online? How will you ensure that any information *you* post is valid and reliable?

Webfolios present the practitioner with the capacity to act quickly on their reflections by offering the flexibility to adapt and restructure their e-portfolio through the use of a range of technical presentation tools. The developing practitioner is therefore provided with the opportunity for 'constant' reflection rather than the 'periodic' reflection offered by more traditional paper-based portfolios. This approach offers a readily available framework that can support convenient continual improvement (Fletcher et al. 2007). This may of course be seen as a disadvantage as well as an advantage; once armed with 'anytime, anywhere' technology, when do you switch it off, so that you can switch off too?

ePersonal development planning (ePDP)

Structured personal development plans (PDPs) have a place in professional learning through the negotiation and setting of targets for development based on current performance and future professional need. Technology enables this to be conducted flexibly, and within a learning community that can include peers and colleagues as well as tutors and mentors. Participants engage in critical reflection on their professional development and share their reflective thoughts through asynchronous online discussions with their tutor and/or with peers. Unlike many web blogs, the *e*PDP within organizational VLEs (such as PebblePAD at the University of Wolverhampton) is a closed environment. Contributions are by invitation only from the PDP owner. This allows work to be shared within a trusted learning community that can be as small as two or as large as desired; as with all social networking programs there are different levels of access to ensure this privacy. This non-public forum allows confidences to be shared and a sense of trust to be developed. There is very positive research evidence, for example from the University of Wolverhampton, that such engagement enhances beginning teacher experience, as stated by Emma:

> 66 The ongoing dialogue with my peers and tutor was fundamental in my development as a reflective writer and new teacher. It was a creative collaborative learning space, a lifeline on what could sometimes be a bumpy road.
>
> *(Emma, PCE PGCE trainee, cited in Hughes and Purnell, 2008: 151)* 99

As well as having the capability of asynchronous access, online exchanges within and between trusted groups have other obvious advantages. Loving et al. (2007), reporting on an evaluation of an online learning community for trainee teachers in the US, found that 'most participants (community college faculty members, mentor, and intern teachers) recognized the value of blogging as a platform for sharing resources and ideas and reflecting on personal experiences'. They acknowledge two aspects of the professional blog: the **conceptual,** where participants deepen and enrich their professional learning through their shared information and reflections, and the **affective**, where they support each other's emotional ups and downs during the training process. Laura explains how her online exchanges, reading about how others reflect, helped her to reflect more deeply using Gibbs's cycle of reflection (1998, see Chapter 13, p. 230):

> 66 In the past I tended to reflect upon incidents by jumping straight in and thinking what I could have and should have done when things have gone wrong, completely missing out the beginning three stages of the cycle: feelings, evaluation and analysis.
>
> *(Laura, PGCE PCE trainee, cited in Hughes 2010: 205)* 99

Tom greatly valued the opportunity to commit his feelings to the blog:

> 66 The PGCE has brought out the following feelings and experiences. I have been stretched mentally. I have also experienced anxiety, disappointment and frustration and at times I have felt blind. The e-portfolio has been a sort of picture frame where I can look and retain my thoughts electronically.
>
> *(Tom, PGCE PCE trainee, cited in Hughes 2010: 206)* 99

Jen also supported the value of having a Webfolio to support her reflective thinking.

> 66 I have been able to create a journal called 'My Journey' to help me reflect on everything that I did at the beginning of the course to now. I am able to write at any time of the day of how I am feeling happy or sad. I do feel happier when I have reflected on what I have learnt and decided on the next steps to take. 99
>
> *(Jen, third year Primary BEd trainee)*

Reflective task 12.2

1 To what extent do you value the opportunity to share conceptual ideas with your peers, such as how to apply Gibbs's model of reflection? Would this be easier for you to do online or face-to-face?

2 To what extent do you want to commit your personal feelings to written form, as a blog? With whom would you be willing to share these, and what do you perceive to be the advantages?

Collaborative webfolios and collaborative e-reflections

Online collaboration has been going on since email first hit our computer screens; trainee teachers have sent out many a late-night plea along the lines of 'has anyone got any ideas about how I can explain right-angles to my class tomorrow?' Increasingly, schools, colleges and universities are harnessing this potential by making online collaboration a compulsory, and often assessed, part of the course. Working collaboratively, supported by an electronic network, learners have opportunities to collectively apply skills or knowledge to a task. This can contribute to each developing deeper appreciations and understandings through learning together. There is the added benefit of extending the time available for interactive learning outside of the classroom. It allows for the re-processing of information given through reading, or reviews of activities developed out of the school experience in a taught session. 'Creating a shared understanding is simply a different task than sharing information. It's the difference between being deeply involved in a conversation and lecturing to a group' (Schrage 1995: 5, cited in Evans and Nation 2000). The 'blog' is part of the bigger picture. It can be conducted as part of a formal exchange of ideas. For example, reflective journals written by trainee teachers at the University of Wolverhampton are semi-structured, with stage-specific prompts given to support thinking at and about key points in their professional development. The responses are read online by a tutor and an e-learning dialogue ensues. On a wider level, special-interest groups can conduct blogging activities through a VLE; for example, anyone teaching learners with special needs might share ideas and exchange experiences, or primary trainees teaching maths for the first time may value subject knowledge advice from their specialist peers.

One such learning community was developed by an Early Years group on the penultimate placement of their course. It uses social constructivist ideas by exploiting dialogic exchange between participants. Not only do members exchange ideas to consolidate understanding of given knowledge, but they generate new 'adaptive' knowledge (Kilpatrick et al. 2003). As Roberts (1998: 45) explains: 'The social constructivist perspective recognizes dialogue, talk, to be central to teacher learning'. Below, some trainees comment on the value of collaborative e-learning for them:

> 66 I have found that my understanding of subject material has improved quite a lot through blogging and through the use of Webfolio. . . I've been able take the lecture material and collate it with other resources and ideas tied in with collaborative work, and kind of mould it into . . . what's actually useful for me personally.
>
> *(Jane, Primary BEd, year 2)* 99

66 It has helped me to clarify things and go back to take stock of what I've learnt in the day and also it's enabled me to guide other people within my learning group and that's helped my own understanding a lot as well.

(Peter, Primary BEd, year 2) **99**

66 I find that blogging makes collaborative learning much easier. Last year on placement we were working individually, miles away from our colleagues and we were brought together through a blog so we could share our experiences, the hard bits, the celebrations and the issues that we were facing we could share.

(Julie, Primary BEd, year 3) **99**

Reflective task 12.3

1 What advantages do you see in being part of a formal or semi-formal blog?
2 If you are in training, what opportunities for professional learning does blogging present?
3 If you are an NQT can you see an advantage to setting up a blog, perhaps with colleagues in other schools, or former trainee peers?

There are clearly advantages of sharing the positive aspects of experience in the form of ideas, resources and knowledge, and the negative aspects through the unburdening of feelings after a lesson that did not go well. However blogging, even in a controlled environment, has its disadvantages. It can 'liberate' the individual to learn asynchronously. However, not everyone feels comfortable in committing their feelings, thoughts and ideas to the ether. Professional learning communities therefore require a sensitive and respectful stance between participants. This is not always easy, especially when we want to challenge another's ideas. In face-to-face discussions, we have the opportunity to 'read' others' body language and respond accordingly, or we can 'change tack' in our argument to explore less controversial avenues. However, research to date tends to allay these concerns; when writing becomes a social practice rather than an individual activity, more care is taken in the style and content. Wheeler and Wheeler (2009) have found that bloggers present what Goffman (1959) defined as the 'front stage' version of themselves, with one of their trainees commenting: 'if anything it probably makes me write better. On the wiki you know that everyone can read your work so you make yourself as intelligent as possible'. Yang (2009) found that students using blogs paid much more attention to spelling and grammar because they knew their work was being scrutinized by others. It is always wise to re-read the content of your blogs, emails and so forth before pressing the 'send' button!

Reflective task 12.4

1 Reflect on how you tend to address and respond to other people in face-to-face working groups. Are you measured and thoughtful, or do you tend to speak first and think afterwards? How do these attributes transfer to online communications? What do you need to consider when using collaborative e-learning tools?
2 How confident do you feel about your writing? How could blogging and other forms of e-learning enhance your confidence?

Social networking

As trainees of the twenty-first century you are familiar with applications such as MSN Chat; Blackberry Messenger; Facebook; Skype; Bebo; Yahoo and Twitter. Facebook alone has brought us a different 'digital space' and 'Facebooking' is now a recognized term. Beginning teachers can perceive reflective practice as a solitary activity, especially once they begin a teaching practice or become an NQT. Social networking can allay some of these feelings of isolation. There are confidentiality and professional issues surrounding the use of social networking sites like Facebook. In some schools, head teachers forbid their staff to have Facebook accounts. As with all e-learning tools there are advantages and disadvantages for all such sites. You need to use your professional judgement. As a beginning trainee, Facebook (or similar) can assist you as a reflective practitioner as it can facilitate online support from friends and colleagues.

> 66 I have used Facebook to create threads of discussion with friends to help with assignments. We have also used it to discuss our placement and share ideas. We agree never to mention schools or names of teachers or children. I use to it receive advice as well as giving help to my friends.
> *(Patricia, Early Years BEd trainee, final year)* 99

E-support for collaborative lesson planning

Lesson planning is a key aspect of teaching, and a daunting and time-consuming task for the beginning teacher. A semi-formal system of online peer evaluation of lesson plans can be useful because it draws knowledge and understanding and blends it with the creative thinking of a group of people, thus 'pooling' teaching ideas and their underpinning theories.

Trainees who have used peer e-feedback tell us that it has increased their awareness of different teaching strategies and supported the development of related subject knowledge. When lesson plans have been peer-reviewed, trainees feel more confident about their teaching, and anecdotally suggest that their lessons are more successful.

> 66 Once we completed our plans, we sent them to each other via email, which enabled us to give constructive criticism and make amendments. The outcome was a lesson plan that I can now use and just adapt it to suit my children's learning needs.
>
> *(Karen, Primary BEd, year 3)* 99

The process of peer-review was appreciated by Stephen as he valued the input given.

> 66 I can use other trainees' advice, ideas and resources within my lessons and improve the delivery of the lesson. It deepens your reflections on practice when you consider someone else's viewpoints.
>
> *(Stephen, Primary BEd, year 3)* 99

Reflective task 12.5   Feedback on lesson planning

1 Send your lesson plan to a friend/several friends on your course. Use the suggested guidelines to provide constructive and purposeful feedback.

   See Figure 12.2 for guidelines to support the process of peer-reviewing your friend's lesson plan.

2 Select two or three questions to put to your peers, such as: 'are the learning objectives clear enough?'; 'How do you recommend I assess this group?'

3 Invite your friend to do the same. Study their plan carefully in the light of their questions. What subject, curriculum and pedagogic knowledge are you utilizing in order to respond?

Guidance for peer-review
Use the prompts below to review your peer's planning

---

1 In the planning is the **structure** clear? Can the reviewer clearly identify the different components of the lesson (teacher input/main activity/plenary)?

2 Are the **learning objectives** specific to the year group? Are they a learning objective or an objective explaining the task? Are they child friendly using 'I can' statements?

3 Does the planning include specific opportunities for **assessment for learning** to be completed by the teacher? Are the success criteria clearly defined? Are pupils also given opportunities to reflect on their learning – peer/self assessment?

4 In the main part of the lesson (independent activity/teacher–led group) are the activities motivating and engaging? Does the planning take into consideration the different learning styles? are the children working in their books? On sheets? Creating posters? or is it a speaking and listening activity? What happens when a child finishes their work? Is there an extension activity?

5 Thinking of **differentiation**, are all groups' needs catered for? Will the resources for each group provide the appropriate support? Are the key questions suitable for this lesson?

6 Look at the **resources**, would you add any to enhance the lesson further? Teaching assistants and other adults are a valuable resource, how are they being utilized?

If you were to teach this lesson, what would you add? What other activities could you suggest? Could you deliver the lesson based on these plans? By providing constructive criticism you are enhancing your peer's planning. Try three stars and one wish (three strengths for each area and one suggestion for improvement).

Figure 12.2   Guidelines for peer-review of lesson plans

By engaging in reciprocal peer evaluation, you should both be able to benefit from a deeper review than seems possible as you stare at your own lesson plan!

Podcasts

Podcasts are repositories of audio and video materials. These can be downloaded to portable media players that can be taken anywhere, providing the potential for 'anyhour and anyplace' learning. Podcasts can be a vehicle in which trainees can 'read', 'review' or 'reflect upon' material outside the traditional learning environment. They can be a significant aid for auditory learners. To augment their reflective learning, some trainees have listened to tutor presentations and lectures as well as producing their own podcasts to capture their thoughts, after discussion sessions, school-based training, teaching experiences and even at the end of the academic year. The choice of format used to capture these thoughts synchronized with their preferred learning 'style' whether it is visual or auditory. You may wish to consider whether the use of podcasting or audio recordings has the potential to enhance your own learning.

> 66 I have used audio recordings when speaking with my Attachment tutor when receiving feedback after a lesson. The mp3 files gave me the 'time' to play back and reflect on strengths and my areas for development. I think it benefits the aural learner.
>
> *(Julie, Primary BEd, year 3)* 99

Electronic record of professional development

Increasingly, as illustrated above, beginning teachers are collecting and storing electronically a range of evidence of their progress towards the professional standards. Now add to this the collection of lesson observations in electronic format and the myriad ways in which classroom outcomes can be recorded (for example, digital photographs of classroom displays and students' work; audio feedback from mentors; video clips of key aspects of teaching). What you have is a flexible and useful mechanism for monitoring your experience, an evidence base for logging your developing knowledge understanding and skills, as well as a possible 'vehicle for reflection' (Moon 2006). As a beginning teacher, this system would support your professional development in an ever-changing technological educational climate.

How can e- learning support reflective practice?

So far in this chapter there have been suggestions that the application of e-learning tools sits well with social constructivist theories of learning, and has the potential to extend reflective learning and enhance the professional development of beginning teachers, provided that they reflect on the possible pitfalls. The chapter is concluded by illustrating the benefits of e-collaboration as a means of promoting critical and creative reflection (Ghaye and Ghaye 1998) on the stages of teacher development (Furlong and Maynard 1995). See Case Study 12.1.

Case Study 12.1 Primary trainees reflect on the 'novice to qualified teacher' continuum

1 Primary trainee teachers were introduced to the concept of 'stages of development' on the journey to QTS. This included an adaptation of the Furlong and Maynard (1995) staged model and that of Fuller and Brown (1975). This included (1) early idealism; (2) personal survival; (2a) survival concerns; (3) dealing with difficulties; (3a) teaching situation concerns; (3b) pupils concerns; (4) hitting the plateau; and (5) moving on. The studies indicate that some beginning teachers only become concerned about their pupils' learning at a relatively late stage in their own professional learning. Initially they are more concerned with their own successful performance. On analysis of Furlong and Maynard's model (1995) there would appear to be a considerable gap in expected student attainment between what they believe trainees should be achieving or feeling between stages two and three and three and four. These stages are not defined stages in the stages of student development (Furlong and Maynard, 1995: 76–89) but are in-between stages appropriately labelled Stage 2a 'assembling the pieces' ('What pieces are missing from the QTS jigsaw puzzle?') and Stage 3a 'fitting the jigsaw pieces' ('If I try this orientation will I succeed?')

2 Primary BEd trainees were asked to respond to a post in a blog inviting them to reflect on their own stage of development, and to identify and describe any 'in-between' stages that they felt applied to them. The outcomes were illuminating; not only did trainees share their ideas, but they felt reassured that their own feelings were similar to those of others. Articulating their own stage of development engaged them in high quality, deep reflection.

> 66 As it has been a year since I was last in a school, and my next placement is a further two months away, I would like to call this point of my degree 'Plodding along' as I feel like I am just waiting until I go on my next placement. I have learnt a lot from lectures but looking back over my experience I feel that I learn best kinaesthetically, so I am itching to get back in there and put my learning into practice. 99
>
> *(Lisa, Primary BEd, year 2)*

> 66 The reason I have called it 'The calm before the storm' is because there are many concepts and stages to learn, it is like braving a storm until the storm calms and the concepts are understood. The subheadings that I have included within this stage are: 'seeing the concept' and 'grasping the concept'. ... being introduced to the concept and grasping what is expected of me. 99
>
> *(Mark, Primary BEd Primary, year 2)*

Reflective task 12.6   Reflecting on your stage of development

1 Consider the following, depending on your stage of development:
  a If you are at the start of your training, consider whether you are at the stage of 'early idealism' (aspiring to be outstanding) and to what extent you have progressed to recognizing the problems you face and are dealing with 'personal survival' (recognizing teaching is not as easy as first supposed and requires essential strategies to survive).
  b What 'sub-stages' might there be as you learn to deal with the problems you face in school, in order to do more than merely 'survive'? How would you describe these stages?
  c Once you can deal with most difficulties or immediate challenges, how do you become more than a 'good enough' teacher? How do you set yourself challenges to 'move on' from the 'plateau'?
2 Reflect on how this shared activity has encouraged informed reflection through the synthesis of theory and practice.
3 What other aspects of your professional learning could you develop in this way?

Emerging from the framework of stages of student development and the trainees' e-reflections is an e-supported framework for beginning teachers adapted from Furlong and Maynard's work in 1995. It shares thoughts from trainees' personal Webfolios and suggests e-activities for the beginning teacher (see Figure 12.3).

The timescale of these stages is not definitive and the stage you are at will depend on the experience you bring to the course, your ability to reflect effectively and how you act upon advice given to you. You may also revisit different stages as you continue to develop along the continuum from a beginning teacher to a qualified teacher.

Reflective task 12.7   Using e-tools to support you as reflective practitioners as you reflect on your stage of development

1 Create a blog to share your ideas with friends and ask for their contribution.
2 Send a lesson plan and use the guidelines to provide constructive criticism
3 After a lesson, create a podcast providing feedback on a lesson; highlighting three key areas of success and three areas for development.
4 Video part of your lesson to play back and reflect on. What else can you see happening?

Stages of e-reflection	**Stage 1: Vision** **Stage 2: Survival** *Additional Stage 2a ~ 'assembling the pieces'* *'What pieces are missing from the QTS jigsaw puzzle?'* **Stage 3: dealing with the jigsaw pieces'** ***Additional Stage 3a ~*** ***'fitting the jigsaw pieces'*** *'If I try this orientation will I succeed?'* **Stage 4: emerging teacher** **Stage 5: moving on**
Trainees' responses to model	*Stage 2a* *'I thought it was excellent to put the theory I had been taught into practice but also some of the theory that I didn't fully understand at the start of the year actually made sense within the school settings.'* *Stage 3* *'I feel more confident to make the "natural connection" between the theory learnt in lectures and read in books to my own school based practice'.* *Stage 3a* *'I found it very rewarding when the children understood something which I had taught them, and yes although it may sound corny you can almost see the cogs ticking round and then suddenly a light bulb turns on and their faces say "I get it!"'(BEd, Year 2)*
Suggested e-supported activities	Share your successes/limitations and thoughts or future action. Write an entry sharing your successes, hyperlink these thoughts to your favourite track, music or artwork. How could you use podcasts with the children? Diary extract . . . to add to at several stages throughout the course. Reflective entries with 3 key learning points and 2 aspects identified for further action. Ask your mentor/tutor to provide you with feedback (mp3 file) so you can reflect on the lesson. Webfolio for subject knowledge. Collaborative Blog to support peers, share resources, give moral support. Video clip of yourself teaching. Each time your review the clip . . . 1) look at your use of subject knowledge; 2) use of your voice and body language; 3) current behaviour and classroom management. Review lesson planning. Share feedback and if a peer is teaching the same year group. Plan together. At interview share how e-learning and e-activities have supported you as a beginning teacher

Figure 12.3 A progressive e-supported framework for the beginning teacher

Source: Adapted from Furlong and Maynard (1995)

Summary

In this chapter we have illustrated ways in which the new digital age can provide different media and platforms to support your reflective learning. Technology now allows us to communicate, in real time and asynchronously, with others at a distance, so that we can build personal learning communities and participate in formal ones. Technology also allows beginning teachers to build portfolio evidence of their developing knowledge and skills, mapping their progress for themselves and their assessors.

Conclusion

Throughout this book you have been able to access practical ideas to help you to think about and improve your understanding of teaching and its practice through reflection. If the university, college or school where you are training or working is already involving you in formal and semi-formal e-learning activity, this chapter will have provided a rationale for this and some encouragement to participate with enthusiasm. If it does not, perhaps you have been inspired to set up your own, informal social learning networks.

'Reflection, reflection, reflection, I'm thinking all the time, why do I need a theory or model of reflection?'

Vanessa Dye

Our ideas are only intellectual instruments which we use to break into phenomena; we must change them when they have served their purpose, as we change a blunt lancet that we have used long enough.

Claude Bernard

Introduction

By now you may be feeling overwhelmed by the many models of reflection presented to you. What approaches should you be taking, when and why? The purpose of this chapter is to:

- help you to see that reflection is a stylized form of thinking that will help you to develop new skills, knowledge and sources of information from your experience(s);
- guide you in recognizing which tools of reflection are appropriate to your needs at any given time.

This chapter will prompt you to look more deeply into reflective practice, considering how your own ways of thinking can lead to obstacles, as well as openings to new learning. Models and tools to help sharpen your professional practice are illustrated with examples from trainee teachers' reflections.

The chapter title paraphrases a conversation between a trainee and his assessor. The trainee poses the question: 'so how is "reflection" different from the thinking I do anyway?' (Ottensen 2007). This is a good question. As sentient beings we are thinking all the

> Reflection is more than thinking: it requires action on that thinking as part of a cycle of improvement.

time, after all. However, as Jarvis (2006) reminds us, not all thinking is reflective. Reflection is not simply educational jargon for thinking. As you read about and consider the ideas and activities suggested in this chapter, you will begin to identify and engage with a number of different methods that scaffold varied perspectives of reflection. These are organized into the themes outlined in Table 13.1.

Table 13.1   Perspectives of reflection

Themes	Foci
1 Extending early notions of reflection	a Reflection and theory-practice links b Using basic models of/for reflection c Writing a learning autobiography d Journal writing
2 Deepening reflection through critical incident analysis	Looking at significant events that have made you 'stop and think'
3 Using a staged reflective model	Using Gibbs's reflective cycle

Theme 1: extending early notions of reflection

a Reflection and theory-practice links

Perhaps the most useful explanation of *reflection* is the mirror image. When we look in a mirror, we may be prompted to take some action to improve what we see, especially first thing in the morning! Just as we recognize the need to comb our hair, or shave, or whatever is needed to improve the image we see, so reflective thinking should inform the development of action. It moves us on to thinking about the image we hope to see, and how we should act to change the current situation. As indicated in previous chapters and cited by Kuit and Reay (2001), there are many approaches to help beginning teachers become reflective. Early reflective activities may focus on personal accounts; many of these are used throughout this book. These help you to know yourself, and frame your development, as a new professional. It is also worth noting that your reflecting abilities and experiences are unique to you. Just as you will differentiate in your teaching, so you will note how the way you reflect differs from that of your peers and mentors. This is as it should be. Different learning and cognitive styles (Coffield et al. 2004), mean that we all experience learning differently. In this way reflection has great plurality of meanings (Ghaye et al. 2000), and what suits one person may not be as useful to another. Larrivee (2000: 296) captures an important maxim when she states, 'The process of becoming a reflective practitioner cannot be prescribed.' This does not mean that prescribed reflective activities are not valuable. Indeed, as a beginning teacher you are likely to be directed and guided in your first approaches to reflection and the reflective process. It does mean that you need not feel anxious if a particular tool for reflection does not work for you. There is likely to be another reflective approach that will.

Johns (2000: 107) says: 'when I commenced reflection, I did not draw on any reflective practice theory to guide my practice because such theories that did exist made no practical sense because they were grounded in an obscure language'. Like Johns, we have seen beginning teachers grapple with the body of theoretical knowledge concerning reflection. It is unsurprising, therefore, that some see attempts to define the word reflection as rather pointless, or think they know what reflection is: 'Reflecting, reflecting, reflecting. I think all the time, don't I? I mean, it's not like I don't think. What is it with this reflection thing that makes it so important?' (Ottensen 2007: 32). Yet defining 'reflection' is more problematic than Ottensen's student suggests. You need to consider the direction of your reflection and how you wish to develop. Perhaps you want to extend your teaching repertoire, or build a better relationship with your class. It may also be that your definition and use of reflection will change over time and in differing situations. It is sometimes easy to fall into the trap of using terms in a rather blasé way; thinking about your teaching (in an unfocused way) after the event can be defined rather loosely as reflection. There is so much to reflect upon related to preparation, enactment, follow-up, assessment and even longer term monitoring. All this needs concrete and tangible ways of reflecting that extend and deepen your understanding of the teacher you want to be.

But beware: from the start of your teacher education programme you will become inculcated into a constant climate of reflection and reflective practice, and it is easy to be sucked into it 'being the thing to do' (Bolton 2005: 1). The pervasive use of the reflective practice model can also give rise to a potentially flawed **truism** that everyone can reflect, can't they? The manner in which reflection is woven into the teacher education curriculum can lead to the simplistic assumption that reflection is easy. As a beginning teacher, knowing that reflection is not necessarily an easy process or activity may be a relief; particularly if you struggle to unpack ideas into reflective journals, or try desperately to act on feedback that your reflective writing is too descriptive.

As a beginning teacher you will also be wrestling with both educational theory and teaching practice and trying to make sense of the relationships and what they mean to you. Educational theory and teaching practice are not always comfortable bedfellows, although the seminal work of Lewin (1951: 169) suggests otherwise: 'there is nothing so practical as a good theory'. However, Day et al. (2006) remind us that there is a great deal of scepticism about the value of theory for practitioners, and that sometimes practitioners view 'theory' as unhelpful, unreal and irrelevant. This is because it needs to be situated and applied in a context. For example, you may read about some potentially useful tactics to manage a boisterous group but until you experience such a situation you will not be able to test out the ideas. For a reflection to have a coherent framework, it must connect personal experience with teaching ideas and educational theory.

Reflective task 13.1   Building 'theory' into your reflections

Theory informs us that 'positive reinforcement' (praising) of students helps learning to occur (Petty 2009).

1 Select a lesson you are going to teach where an individual or a group of learners has low self-esteem, does not engage with learning, and so on. Think about how to praise learners: 'good', 'well done', 'what an improvement' and so on, for their contributions and efforts.
2 During the lesson, reflect in action about the impact this is having, and how it is changing their behaviour.
3 After the lesson, reflect on action about the impact on individuals, groups and the whole class.
4 Now consider if using so called 'positive reinforcement' is a valuable theoretical tactic to use in practice.

This is how you will start to build up your armoury of tactics of what works for you, and see how the theory links to your practice. It is not really important whether you start with a theory or work from your own intuition about teaching. As you learn more about educational theories you will begin to see that many of your intuitions about what works for you may be grounded in a theory, or developed through tacit knowledge. Reliance solely on either gut feelings or reading about educational theory to guide classroom practice and teaching identity is likely to provide you with only some of the necessary tools to function as an effective teacher. Both theoretical and practical bases are needed to establish greater deep understanding of the teacher role. As a reflective practitioner you will develop your own theories and models of teaching as you encounter new experiences and act on similar experiences (Whitehead 2007). Dewey (1933: 78) cited in Chitpin (2006) argued that: 'We do not learn from experience. We learn from reflecting on experience.'

Working through the commentaries and activities presented in this chapter should help you to:

- see how learning, reflection and experience fit together;
- find a balance of theory and practice;
- understand what types of reflection work for you.

Reflective task 13.2   Creating a simple model of reflection

1 Write the following three words on three separate pieces of paper:

   | EXPERIENCE | | REFLECTION | | LEARNING |

2 Think about a recent learning experience (in any context) and scribe it as a piece of autobiographical text. It may begin with 'What I hoped to achieve was . . . ', 'I learned how to . . . ' or 'I learned that . . . '

3 Draw a diagram of how you learned this, using the three words above. You may need to move the words around, and you can add words, ideas or arrows to denote how they are linked.

   Well done! You have devised your own model for reflection! Perhaps yours looked like a bit like the model in Figure 13.1.

4 Look at the example in Figure 13.1. Can you see what is *description* and what is *analysis?*

Ultimately, *describing* your leggy sweet peas is of little value, but *analyzing* why they might be leggy (they have long roots and need to be planted more deeply) engenders learning.

---

b Using basic models of/for reflection

In activity 13.2, you started to think about some of the key concepts involved in reflection: experience, reflection and learning. It will not surprise you that these words appear in some of the formal theoretical models you are likely to read about, such as Boud et al. (1985). For example, in Figure 13.2 you can start the cycle at any point. Let us suppose that you want to reflect on how you presented the learning objectives at the start of a lesson. Maybe you displayed them on a poster, or read them out. Maybe you referred back to them at key points in the lesson, linked your **plenary** to them. This was your 'experience'. While teaching, and after the lesson, you will have thought about how this aspect of your lesson worked. Perhaps the

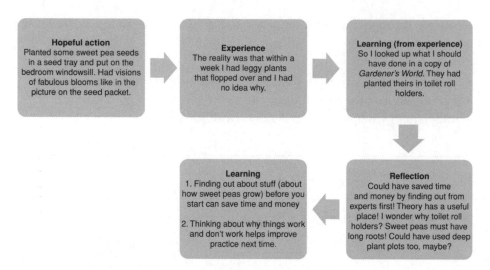

Figure 13.1 A simple model of reflection: growing sweet peas

display helped focus you and the learners, informing them about the intent of the lesson. Conversely, you may have found that your outcomes did not work well because they were poorly worded or set too high or too low, so did not help to steer the session (your 'reflection'). As a result of your reflection you may have gained better awareness of the value, use and explanation of learning outcomes as part of the teaching event, either reinforcing your practice or identifying ways of improving it ('learning').

In your reading you are likely to encounter Kolb's (1984) experiential learning model (Figure 13.3; Kolb and Fry 1984) which uses more elaborate language, but you will see that the models have many similarities. For example, '*concrete experience*' can be considered as synonymous with 'experience' in Boud's model in that it relates to something tangible in your teaching that has prompted you to reflect. However, the phrase 'abstract conceptualization' provides another layer

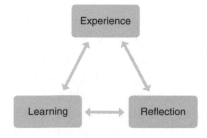

Figure 13.2 A model for reflection

Source: After Boud et al. 1985

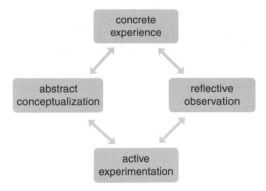

Figure 13.3 Kolb's experiential learning model

Source: Kolb 1984

of reflection. It means that when you reflect and observe things, you will also think more broadly about what is happening and try to build new learning onto pre-existing knowledge. You may then use your existing frameworks and ideas to make sense of the situation. For instance, in reflective task 13.2 you were asked to relate three words about reflection and make sense of them for yourself. This involved a process of 'conceptualization': taking personal meaning from the words and their relationship with each other.

The phrase 'active experimentation' denotes the actions that follow. In other words, as a result of your new experience what can you now do that you could not do before? Reflection moves beyond thinking about something because it involves acting on what has been learned. The model goes on to further concrete experience when you try out something you have learned in an ongoing cycle.

c Writing a learning autobiography

An early activity in many teacher training programmes involves writing a 'learning autobiography', focusing on the 'self' as a learner, and where your ideas about teaching come from (see Chapters 3 and 5). If you have not already does this, you may find it a useful starting point to note your ideas about teaching and where they have come from. Looking back on these notes later, as you gain experience, will provide a basis for *critical* reflection, as you will be able to analyse where the changes in your understanding lie. In the example below, Paul analyses the gap between his early expectations and the reality of his current situation:

> ❝ **Placement**
> My college placement has been a real eye-opener into the world of teaching.
> In my learning autobiography, I thought that I would be teaching highly

motivated individuals in further education, but I have found that some students lack interest in the subject. I was also surprised about the need for 'crowd control' with some groups. This will not just be about teaching my subject, but about inspiring, cajoling and motivating a wide range of different young people.

University sessions

The lectures at the university model good teaching, and provide knowledge and experience that support my teaching development. I have also found it interesting to look beyond my subject to issues about curriculum and learning: the scope is much wider than I realized.

(Paul, one-year PGCE PCE) 99

Through these reflections, Paul is able to link his initial expectations and his early experiences on teaching practice and in university training sessions to develop his professional learning.

So, what is the value in writing a reflective journal for you?

Through revisiting your own learning journey you will think about yourself as a learner, exploring the high and low points. This self-analysis usually engages both cognitive and emotional elements, examining both positive and negative learning experiences to help you understand why you gravitate toward certain ways of doing things and avoid others (see Chapter 5). Jarvis (2006) reminds us that the emotional, or affective, part of reflection is an important part of the event. As discussed in earlier chapters, it is useful to signal that reflection can sometimes be an uncomfortable or painful process, particularly if you consider the experience you are reflecting on to have been a negative one. However, being truly self-aware invariably involves understanding how you feel as well as how you think. Writing things down can help you to embrace the emotional dimension of reflection.

An additional value of written reflection is that it can be revisited at any point and added to, or reflected on further, for different perspectives and comparisons, as skills and knowledge are developed. Learning autobiographies, or reflective journals, often contain defining points that shape us as people. These insightful personal events may also help you to see the value of critical incident analysis as another useful reflection tool.

d Journal writing

Various chapters, but particularly Chapters 11 & 12, have included discussions about writing journals or diaries. This section reviews some points about keeping a reflective journal. Beginning teachers tend to have these initial questions about their reflective writing:

- Why keep a journal anyway?
- What kinds of things should go into a journal entry?
- Who is likely to read it, and why?

Why keep a journal anyway?

In short, keeping a journal helps to review experiences in a more formal way than just thinking about something. Writing about an experience may prompt you to think more carefully, as explaining it and committing it to paper for someone else to understand means you have to revisit key events and think more deeply about them, and the part you and others played in them. I have encouraged my own trainees to use what I have called the SOS model which reminds you to think about 'self', 'others' and 'situation', since these three factors tend to be present, interrelated and important in most experiences:

'Self' refers to you as a teacher: your style of teaching, and the **pedagogical strategies** you tend to use.

'Others' relates to everyone else involved in the situation that you are reflecting about: individual learners and the groups; teaching support; and the presence or absence of observers.

'Situation' identifies the context in which you are working, such as environment, facilities, timing and resources.

Note that while the following extracts contain reflection and discussion about these key elements they do not necessarily use SOS as subheadings to frame journal entries, although you could consider these as an idea for organizing some of your journal entries.

Jenny, who is teaching art in her placement, begins to see the value of reflection:

> 66 An artist's reflection is usually done internally about ideas for work, and often these can be quite personal, so to start sharing my 'reflections' was a strange concept. But doing so gave me the opportunity to 'think out loud'.
> *(Jenny, one-year PGCE PCE, Art, part way through her first teaching practice)* 99

Later she says:

> 66 It was not until I had realized the purpose of the reflection that it began to come more easily, although at times I struggled with what to write, as the process of reflection was exhausting. But writing my thoughts down

enabled me to revisit things. Looking back over what I had written, I could
see exactly what changes I needed to make to improve my practice.

What kinds of things should go into a journal entry?

Sometimes you will be guided by your course tutors to reflect on learning at
key stages of your development, for example planning, behaviour management,
differentiation. You will also be encouraged to write about **critical incidents** (see
Theme 2 below). If you are given a blank canvas, however, it can be difficult to
decide what to write about. This is because it is not always possible or desirable to
separate your personal self from your professional self, and there may be personal
matters which impact on your professional identity as a teacher, and vice versa, as
examined in Chapters 3 and 5. When reflecting you may have a tendency to focus
on the negative experiences that have occurred. Outlined below (Figure 13.4) are
a few ideas to help you to try to focus on the positives as well. See also Chapter 4
on positive experience reflection.

Who will read it, and why?

The short answer to this question is that your reflections will be read by a tutor
whose interest in them is based on concern for your development. You need to
have trust in the person reading your work, and feel able to write openly. This

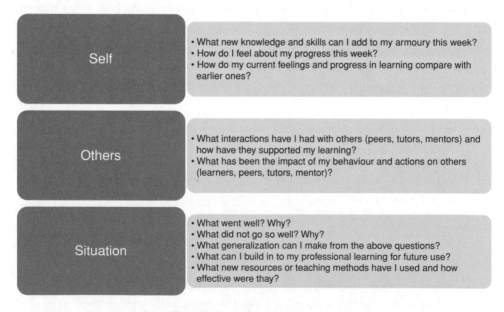

Figure 13.4 Questions for reflective journal writing

is echoed by Bolton (2005: 12) when she says that you should be able to 'do the writing free from the police officer of your mind'. On the other hand, you need to be aware of the need for professional language: 'My mentor thinks he's Machiavelli' is no way to start your reflections! As you write, have a respected professional colleague in mind: someone with whom you feel able to share your vulnerabilities. Thus you might say 'I was upset by the feedback I received, and need to find a way of having more say . . .'. Your diary entries should be written for someone who can give you constructive and developmental support in building your skills, such as how to deal with negative feedback. Even when this is the case, not everyone finds the experience easy:

> 66 Reflective practice seems to perpetuate the current policy climate in education, which is dominated by systems of surveillance.
>
> Through the process I have opened up my professional and to some extent personal identity to the scrutiny of not only peers but also tutors. In my experience this reduces the liberating element of reflection and replaces it with performance anxiety.
>
> *(Sandra, one-year PGCE PCE, towards the end of her training)* 99

The following extract is a brief entry from a trainee's reflection about being observed by both a peer and a tutor in one week.

> 66 Monday I had my peer observation with Emma, which went well. It was a bit strange, mainly because this was a 'developing of ideas' session, which involved some questions and answers, with not much teacher input. Nonetheless it went well, because it drew ideas directly from the students and helped to personalize their learning. The second observation was a bit scary as I knew it was an important observation that would be graded. But I had planned well and made some examples of using wood in art for the students to see, and everything went to plan, particularly my timing of demonstrations and time for students to work on their own. This was really satisfying. It shows that being prepared is a very important aspect of teaching.
>
> *(Janet, one-year PGCE PCE Art, towards the end of first teaching placement)* 99

There is evidence in the above entry of some reference to pedagogic knowledge, for example 'showing examples' to students. The writer is also clear about the importance of good planning. However, the entry does not tell us about the indicators of what 'went well'. Nor does it tell us how useful the examples were, nor does it say anything about the why the session was 'really satisfying'. Deeper reflection would pick up these important points.

Theme 2: deepening reflection through critical incident analysis

At all points in your teaching career, it is highly likely that you will be faced with a situation that you have never encountered, never expected, or are not sure how to react to. Gelter (2003) says the often spontaneous reflection comes about as a result of something which has gone wrong, or when we fear failure. Equally, a classroom event can produce a 'light bulb moment' when we suddenly understand something clearly. This is what a critical incident is. It is something *significant*, which made you stop and think. Tripp (1993) has developed deeper insights into the unpacking of critical incidents, embedding them within the ideological positions emerging through the reflective process, examining particular ways of operating within particular contexts.

Looking at significant events that have made you 'stop and think'

Below is a brief journal entry which uses two ideas, 'self' and 'others' from the SOS model (Figure 13.4), to shape it. Kulvinder writes about the difficulties of trying to follow the college rule about no hats in class.

> 66 **It's only a hat!**
> The college policy states that the students cannot wear hats in class. I understand why, but I'm trying to create an environment where students can be comfortable, and I don't mind. However, students have signed a charter to state they will abide by rules and this is one of them.
>
> My critical incident unfolded when a student refused to take his cap off because another student, who was wearing a net and had injured her head, would not take that off.
>
> SELF AND OTHERS
> I tried to reason and explain to him the college policy and the fact that the other student was not wearing a hat, but he got very aggressive towards the other student and point blank refused. I myself got very angry, but tried to hide it, as other members of the group joined in. I quickly attempted to defuse the situation by asking him either to leave or accept my decision. I also stated if he disagreed with the policy he could book an appointment with the advisory principal.

Looking back I did beat myself up about this incident, thinking I should not have let it escalate. Should I have given in and let him wear the hat as it did not bother me, or was I right to enforce college policy? It's difficult because if I lapse in one area students could think 'right then let me try . . .'

What do you think?

(Kulvinder, PGCE PCE, subject stage of course)

The Internet now allows for much 'any time, any place' collaborative reflection (see Chapter 12). This journal entry was shared in a collaborative blog with peers. Here are a few of their comments:

> I think what you did was fine. You have to stick to the protocols of the college; otherwise the students will just do what they want . . . . .
>
> I would have let him wear it and just got on with the lesson and talked to my college mentor afterwards . . .
>
> Obviously students should be allowed to wear hats on religious grounds, but beyond that surely it is courteous to others to aid total communication, i.e. clearing visual and auditory fields?
>
> If someone wears a hat to keep their head warm, there is no need for it in the classroom as it is warmer. If the hat is a fashion statement then no.
>
> I believe it's around aesthetics and image rather than anything else. It stems from the hoody and the baseball cap brigade and I believe the policy is stereotyping certain students. If you treat students like children they will behave that way. I like to run my classroom like a running business and explain to students that they would not be able to wear them in most organizations.
>
> I believe in freedom of expression, but as a professional I must abide by college policy and be consistent in my enforcement.

Reflective task 13.3   'It's only a hat!' What would you do?

---

1 What would you do in Kulvinder's place?
2 Do you agree with Kulvinder's point that if you do not uphold the procedures and policies then this leaves you open to further challenges in the classroom?
3 If the policy does not impact on the classroom learning should it be enforced?
4 Do you see any value in sharing reflections in the way illustrated above? What types of events would you like to share? What would you prefer to keep more private?

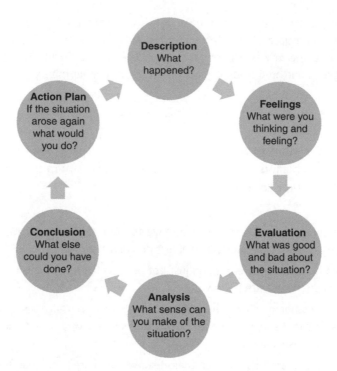

Figure 13.5 Gibbs's reflective cycle

Theme 3: using a staged reflective model

Johns (2000 and 2002) provides the reader with opposing views of the use of reflective models. Reflective models provide cues for enabling the deconstruction of experiences (Johns 2002). On the other hand, he suggests that 'new "reflective practitioners" struggle to fit experience into models (of reflection) that are clearly unhelpful' (2000: 107). See what you think after using a model to reflect.

There are a number of models around. Some of these dwell on the key points of reflection and action (Petty 2009). Whereas others provide useful subheadings to unpack the reflective process (Arygris 1982; Gibbs 1998, in Jasper 2003) still others focus on the use of metaphors to explore experiences (Alsup 2006). It is worth trying different models to see which suits your style of writing and thinking. It may also become apparent as you develop and progress through your course of study and teaching career, that a different model will add some new perspective to your thinking and approaches.

Using Gibbs's reflective cycle

Fiona used Gibbs's model (Figure 13.5), to analyse her experience with the issue of lateness when working with a group she had just started to teach:

66 Step 1 – Description

My concern was the lateness of half the students in the class. In this particular group there were a few students late last week, but in this session six of them were late. One student actually arrived 50 minutes after the start of the session! I can deal with one or two students being late, (as circumstances do arise), but I feel that the lateness in this particular session greatly affected the learning of the group.

Step 2 – Feelings

I felt really disappointed that a number of students arrived late. There was a lot of information in this session; they missed a great deal. I felt that the high number of students being late was related to the fact that I am a student teacher. They obviously believed that I would accept the lateness. I adopted this viewpoint when non-late members of the class commented that the students are not late for their other class, as they have the head of department. Obviously they feel that he will not accept this behaviour. I was also very concerned about the amount of potential learning they would miss.

Step 3 – Evaluation

Although this was a difficult situation for me I think it was good to have the experience, because it made me think of some strategies if this happens again. I also developed a sense of what was acceptable and what wasn't in terms of punctuality. I have decided that lateness is unacceptable. First, it is disruptive, as the lesson has to be momentarily halted for each late arrival, and the students disturb other class members when finding a seat. Secondly, I believe that being late is going to have a detrimental effect on the students' academic achievement. A further meaning I added to this incident was that it indicated a lack of respect for me as a teacher, my lesson, or for their peers.

Step 4 – Analysis

I wrongly made the assumption that the students in the group would have the same attitudes and ideas about lateness as I do: that it is disruptive and detrimental to achievement. However, on reflection it is evident that they do not feel this way. This is clear from the fact that one student found it acceptable to turn up 50 minutes late! The students' perspective and my perspective on time keeping are very different.

Step 5 – Conclusion

The conclusions that I made following this incident were that I may have been partly responsible for this incident, as I had given them the impression that I would accept this behaviour, because I did not pick them up for lateness at the previous session. However, I also think this is a college wide problem as I have had similar experiences with other groups and I have spoken to my mentor about lateness and what can be done to prevent it. I have also concluded that I should not make assumptions about how the students view things as they are typically going to think like students, whereas I am going to see things from a 'teacher' perspective. They will think it's ok to be late whereas I do not find it acceptable.

Step 6 – Action

After this incident I decided to take action during and at the end of that particular session. I spoke individually to the students concerned when they decided to show up for the session and let them know that I did not find it acceptable. I also decided it was necessary to let the whole of the group know what my stance on lateness was to make it clear that I would not be accepting it in future sessions. I made the decision to pass the names of the individuals concerned onto the head of department, and I told the students that from next week anyone who is late will not be allowed in and will be marked absent. This may mean I end up with a very small group but it's a risk I am willing to take to make these students realize just how seriously I take this. On reflection this was the best way to have dealt with the situation as it indicates to the students that they cannot take advantage of me just because I am a student teacher.

(Fiona, PGCE PCE, second teaching placement) 🙶

Here are some comments from a blog shared with peers:

🙶 This is a really important issue, and I have also had some problems with late students. I agree with you, that some students try to take advantage of our student teacher role. Did you check the college policy on lateness too? My college has a rule that no student can attend the lesson if they are more than 10 minutes late. I admire the stance you took in your actions, there's nothing worse than 'punctual' students being disrupted. Echoing your concerns with the head of department was also important.

Wow! I know exactly what you mean and how you feel; I think that as we are trying to give a professional impression we may seem like the 'bad guys'. It is really tough trying to get the right level of respect and approachability as a student teacher.

I totally agree that teacher taught time is very precious and that being late shows disrespect not just for you but for peers as well. It is sad that you needed to spell this out, but it was a good move to make your expectations clear.

This was a good reflection and you managed to handle the situation very well. I urge you to maintain the grip on lateness to the lesson because it is very disruptive. Setting ground rules with your learners is the most important way to tackle this problem.

Also try to give your learners some incentives that will motivate and encourage them to want to attend your lessons early. You can do simple things like give them stars and display them on the notice board. I have learnt this from my mentor and it really works because at the end of a certain period students get a prize for a good record of attending the lesson in time. **99**

Here is an extract from the tutor's comment:

66 High quality learning and teaching also provide incentives. If the perception is that nothing much happens in the first 10 minutes or so of the lesson, there will be no rush through your door! On the other hand, if you have really engaging starter activities that hook your students into the lesson, they will want to be there from the start! **99**

Reflective task 13.4   Using Gibbs' model

1 Can you distinguish between description and analysis in Fiona's reflections?
2 How does the feedback she receives support her emotionally, intellectually and practically? What is the relative value of the peer and tutor comments?
3 Follow the stages/steps of the model for your next critical incident journal entry.
4 What is the value of such a structured approach?
5 Does the structure help you, or does it affect and distort your reflection?

Summary

This chapter has attempted to explore some of the reflective approaches and models available to the student teacher. Reflection is more than loose thinking about your teaching. Thinking is a vital starting point, but becomes reflection only when it leads to an understanding of what actions are needed to change a situation. Through reflection, we heighten our perceptions of our personal and professional self by exposing our values and assumptions, and we develop a greater awareness of situations and the part we play in them, leading us to devise different ways of acting in similar or changing situations.

The chapter has also highlighted the need for teachers to challenge routinized practices, including reflection itself. The message in the title reminds us of two key points. First, you may have puzzled over the difference between thinking and reflection. Secondly, it raises awareness about the reflective practice model as having a high profile within teacher education programmes. This in itself may have caused you to pause for thought about the apparent significance of reflection and reflective practice. Or you may be conscious of your own *tacit* acceptance of it as a dominant part of your professional development. You may wish to ponder on your acceptance, or not, of given models, and you should certainly pause to consider what the benefits are of reflection to yourself, to others, and to the situations in which you operate as a professional.

Conclusion

Reflection is about raising consciousness of you as a beginning teacher and exposing you to other ways of thinking and being. At the heart of any of the 'beginnings' is the need to make critical thinking and reflection an inherent part of your development. It should engage you in a variety of different reflective tactics and enable you to see phenomena and situations as more complex, dynamic and interconnected, opening up several potential approaches for each situation you encounter. Reflecting on small learning moments in your practice will enable you to gain an insight into the bigger picture of this thing called teaching! This is when reflection overlaps with critical thinking (Mezirow 1998; McGuinness 2005; McGregor 2007). Critical analysis and reflection are about questioning the apparent 'rightness' of phenomena, such as education policy, curriculum content or teaching style. This will help you to analyse the pedagogical choices you make. Testing what is sometimes taken for granted will help to prepare you to challenge situations intelligently and analytically. As a bonus, you will be well equipped to think and write at Masters level, as the teaching profession will demand of you in the future.

Key learning points

- Reflection does not automatically support your development in practice or under- standing as a teacher.
- Reflection is more than thinking: it requires action on that thinking as part of a cycle of improvement.
- Different approaches to reflection suit different individuals and/or are needed in different situations. One size does not fit all!
- Opting out of reflection is unlikely to enhance professional development, so recog- nizing its value as a learning process is key.
- Why we do what we do must be constantly challenged through reflection.

CHAPTER 14

Taking the longer term view: how can reflective practice sustain continuing professional development?

Debra McGregor and Lesley Cartwright

> *Knowledge is always gained through action and for action. From this starting point, to question the validity of social knowledge is to question, not how to develop a reflective science about action, but how to develop genuinely well-informed action – how to conduct an action science.*
>
> Bill Torbert

As you have discovered in earlier chapters in this book, reflection to enhance your pedagogic development can be used to describe a range of activities, from individual contemplation to vigorous critical dialogue between several people (Webster-Wright 2009). Throughout the book there has been a focus not only on *how* to reflect but also on what to reflect *about*. Some reflective practice, especially early in your training, or at a point where you change schools and feel that you have to 'relearn' some of the basics, seeks to provide a rapid solution to an immediate problem, such as: 'how do I get them to pay attention?' or 'when I explained it, they didn't seem to get it'. In the long run, however, your reflections need to lead to changes that can transform your practice rather than tweak it. Other chapters have discussed this issue of 'quick fix' versus longer-term solution (see especially Chapter 9). This chapter describes and illustrates approaches you could use to ensure that reflective practice becomes part of the fabric of your professional life. As some of us know only too well, the 'crash' diet can provide a short-term solution to get us back into that outfit for a few weeks, but it is not the answer if we want to be permanently slim and fit. For that, we need to take the longer term view. We know what we need to do, it is just a question of sustaining our efforts to do it! Once we have achieved our ideal weight, maintaining it is not nearly so hard, but does require constant commitment, vigilance and creative ways of balancing the different aspects of our lives. So it is with reflective practice.

Over time your teaching, at one level, gets easier. For example, when planning to teach something for the tenth time, you already have many different ways of explaining and demonstrating up your sleeve; you have a much better concept of learners' misconceptions, a good idea of the questions they will ask and where they will come unstuck. Yet without further reflection you could become complacent. Once the concerns that everyone has at first are by and large resolved, you can ask more far-reaching questions, such as: 'how can I differentiate so that the most able are really challenged?' This chapter considers how you could maintain the 'habit' of reflective practice without allowing it to become routine or mundane, so that your practice does not become a stunted version of what it could be, but blossoms and flourishes, growing from the strong roots laid down in your early reflections. Two approaches to taking the long view are explored:

- developing reflexivity
- using action research

While these two approaches can achieve the same outcome, the ways that you might apply them are quite different.

Developing reflexivity through deepening levels of reflection

Table 14.1 suggests how deepening levels of reflective thinking can move you on in your thinking about critical incidents. If something happens to make you pause and think back to your practice, steps 1 and 2 are routine responses: this is what

Table 14.1 Deepening thinking to develop reflexivity

Level	Reflective level
1st	Being able to identify and describe a critical incident or happening. The *what* of a situation.
2nd	Being able to explain *why* you did it the way that you did or *why* the critical happening arose.
3rd	Being able to recognize there were *different ways* to act in the critical happening or incident.
4th	Being able to devise a way of *finding out* whether one approach was better than another leading up to that kind of critical incident.
5th	Comparing evidence to decide *which approach* worked best, to avoid such an incident arising again, and *why*.

happened, and I think this is *why* it happened. Step 3 requires recognition that alternative responses might be possible: 'what would happen if . . . ?' Stopping at this point would leave us with hypothetical answers only. Step 4 requires us to be creative, to explore other approaches to the problem *and* try them out. Step 5 demands *evaluation* of our new strategies. Thus steps 4 and 5 are taking us into the realms of researching the effects of our (changed or changing) practice; we are asking ourselves questions such as 'what will happen if I try this?' and providing answers through implementing and evaluating our ideas.

These levels of reflection are adapted from Goodman (1984); Stenhouse (1981) and Whitehead (1993) and are linked to notions of **reflexivity.** This can be a confusing term, as the distinction between re-flection, critical reflection and reflexivity is not always clear in literature that sometimes seems to use them interchangeably. Here, we see reflexivity as a particu-larly 'conscious' form of reflection-informed action. As Moore (2004: 148) puts it: '[it is] not just the ability to reflect about what has happened and what one has done, but the ability *to reflect on the way in which one has reflected'*. In other words, reflexive learners are able to understand themselves: the values and beliefs that underpin their actions, and why they think in the way that they do. To become more knowingly reflexive in your practice requires deepening thought to explore the 'whats'?, 'whys', 'what ifs' and 'could haves' of critical incidents, with the added dimension of a critical lens on yourself and how you think, feel and respond in the situation. Earlier chapters in this book have encouraged you to do this, so reflexivity is well within your grasp!

> Reflexive learners are able to understand themselves: the values and beliefs that underpin their actions, and why they think in the way that they do.

Reflexivity can emerge from deepening levels of reflection or a more cyclical approach to reviewing and refining your practice. Reflexivity is about acting on reflections, rather than just proposing what you could have done or might do next. Reflective activity informing actions that are actually taken (Jasper 2003: 100) is a form of reflexivity. It is this kind of reflection informing knowledgeable action that is referred to in this chapter. Consider the developing MFL teacher in Case Study 14.1. How is she becoming more reflexive?

Case Study 14.1   Adèle: improving listening skills in MFL

Adèle was very concerned about her students' ability to work independently. She thought that if she could improve their listening skills they would be better equipped for more autonomous learning. She tried a teaching approach that involved exploring their views about learning a foreign language. She realized through encouraging free responses to her questions that previously her class had learning tasks imposed upon them and that the enjoyment that could be gained from talking and listening activities was never explored. She found that the students were much more interested when what they talked about (and listened to) were purposeful (for example, extracts from the latest movies or popular television where the language is simple, story line appealing and relevant to the students' lives) they were more motivated and keen to be involved. Developing listening skills can be successful if the 'ingredients' of contextualization provide a recipe for motivation' (Alison and Halliwell 2002: 17).

Adèle prepared for the students to watch 20 minutes of 'Les Choristes' because she thought the gist of the storyline could easily be grasped (a challenging boys' boarding school where the head tries a variety of approaches, including developing a choir to improve their achievements). The students would be discussing the same movie and would not be asked to do the activity 'cold'.

Even after all his preparation there were still some students who did not participate fully in the lesson, without the English subtitles accompanying the film, their frustrations in not understanding all that was said became apparent.

Adèle realized this and in a subsequent lesson, before viewing the next part of the movie, she gave the students a pre-listening task. This task meant they had to talk in pairs in 'quiet partner voices' to review what they had seen and to suggest what would happen next. During this time the music from the film played in the background. Then the class collectively shared their views of the film so far. The class responded and engaged much better in this lesson. Adèle presented the outcomes of this approach to her teaching to the other (more experienced) teachers in the MFL department. In reflective discussions it appeared that although the teachers recognized the need for 'pre-listening tasks' they rarely practised them and when they did they stuck to National Curriculum content.

Adèle's reflections at the end of her teaching practice included:

> It has not been easy for me, having been educated in the French system that is very teacher-led, to develop more student-centred approaches to my work. My instinct was to stand there and tell them stuff, and I expected them to do what I said. It was a shock when they didn't! At first I did it because my tutor suggested that getting them more actively engaged would help with the behaviour problems I was having, but now I see that it is not just about behaviour. It is about their enjoyment, being involved in what they do. It has really made me change the way I think about what teaching is. It has given the department food for thought too, which has made me feel very proud!
>
> *(Adèle, PGCE MFL student, final weeks of teaching practice)*

Here, Adèle is thinking not just about her teaching, but about her ideas and beliefs about teaching. She has analyzed why she started out with such a teacher-centred approach, despite her training to the contrary, and why she had to change. She is demonstrating *reflexive* capabilities.

Reflexive activity is based upon reflections on and in action that weave together theory and practice. Rolfe et al. (2001) suggest how this might arise by proposing how reflection that relates to theory can inform subsequent actions (Figure 14.1).

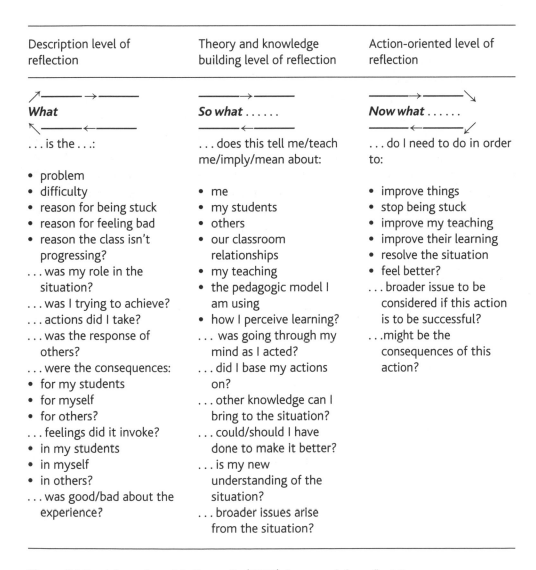

Description level of reflection	Theory and knowledge building level of reflection	Action-oriented level of reflection
What	*So what . . . . . .*	*Now what . . . . . .*
. . . is the . . .:	. . . does this tell me/teach me/imply/mean about:	. . . do I need to do in order to:
• problem • difficulty • reason for being stuck • reason for feeling bad • reason the class isn't progressing? . . . was my role in the situation? . . . was I trying to achieve? . . . actions did I take? . . . was the response of others? . . . were the consequences: • for my students • for myself • for others? . . . feelings did it invoke? • in my students • in myself • in others? . . . was good/bad about the experience?	• me • my students • others • our classroom relationships • my teaching • the pedagogic model I am using • how I perceive learning? . . . was going through my mind as I acted? . . . did I base my actions on? . . . other knowledge can I bring to the situation? . . . could/should I have done to make it better? . . . is my new understanding of the situation? . . . broader issues arise from the situation?	• improve things • stop being stuck • improve my teaching • improve their learning • resolve the situation • feel better? . . . broader issue to be considered if this action is to be successful? . . . might be the consequences of this action?

Figure 14.1 Adaptation of Rolfe et al's (2001) framework for reflexivity

Developing reflexivity through extending reflection

As your experience grows, you are able to use both foresight (unless I do something quickly the consequences could be dreadful) and hindsight (last time I was in this situation it helped to . . .) to deal with problems that arise in the classroom.

Bourdieu and Wacquant (1992), Lawson (1985) and Steier (1991) have derived the meaning of reflexivity from its Latin definition, 'to turn back on oneself'. Thus to be reflexive means to think about our own concepts and values and what they bring to any situation. Like Adèle, we use hindsight from our own experience to reconstruct learning experiences for our learners. Part of the process of becoming reflexive is to recognize how *what* you are *doing* influences your students' learning. In other words you are becoming more self-aware (Yaffe 2010). Being reflexive requires that we apply a social and intellectual consciousness to situations. Adèle had a reason for her approach to teaching linked to her personal biography (see Chapter 3) but developed a conscious understanding of the different social context in which she was working. Reflexivity, then, is about the development and application of self-awareness in order to extend and further our understanding of situations (Matthews and Jessel 1998). Reflexivity can lead to experimentation, as the natural progression from understanding the current situation is to project into the realms of *what if*? If teachers reflect on new approaches in particular ways, and try them out, they can become *action researchers*.

Developing action research strategies

When teachers undertake **action research**, they:

- systematically examine an aspect of their teaching;
- collect information and evidence about the situation;
- evaluate and analyse this information in order to develop and deepen their understanding of that situation;
- use this new knowledge to improve their practice.

Such activity is evidence based and cyclical. Teachers engaging in action research seek to review an aspect of their practice in a focused and systematic way. This practitioner strategy is very useful for teachers studying for a Masters degree, as it deepens their pedagogic understanding and improves their practice while developing their academic skills. McNiff and Whitehead (2005: 1) describe action research as 'a common-sense approach to personal and professional development that enables practitioners everywhere to investigate and evaluate their work, and to create their own theories of practice'. This kind of focused and regular review of an aspect of your professional work can scaffold an ongoing process of plan-do-review that enables you to continue to develop long after your initial teacher education course is completed. As a beginning teacher who is developing this way of thinking and doing, you are smoothing the path to M level accreditation, so that the prospect of completing your Masters degree becomes much less daunting!

As action research often involves a teacher reviewing personal performance to improve their own practice, it is also known as **practitioner research**. Kemmis and Wilkinson clearly link reflection as an integral component of action research when they describes how it is:

> "*a form of self-reflective enquiry undertaken by participants in social (in-cluding educational) situations in order to improve the rationality and justice of a) their own social of educational practices, b) their understand-ing of these practices and c) the situations in which these practices are carried out.*"
>
> *(Kemmis and Wilkinson 1988: 42)*

Increasingly, teacher education courses encourage trainees to engage in action research (but it may not be labelled as such) to assess their capabilities as reflective practitioners while developing their pedagogic skill. Such 'academic' exercises need not be feared. Throughout this book you have been encouraged to appreciate the positive links between 'theory' and 'practice' and you have read many case studies where beginning teachers have demonstrated reflection on the application of well-established pedagogic principles and ideas to their practice. What happens in action research is that this process is formalized, so that it can be written up with some authority in one of several forms:

- an internal report, for example for the 'special needs' action group, or the subject department;
- as part of the organization's self-review process;
- an external report, for example as part of a nationally funded project to investigate practice in key areas of national concern;
- as an academic assignment for accreditation.

Steps in developing action research

The starting point for action research is the identification of a problem you wish to solve. This will give you a broad question, such as: 'How can I make my explanations clearer?' or 'How can I be more creative in my teaching?' These are big questions, and you cannot eat the elephant whole! As suggested in Chapter 9, small changes can have a big impact. In action research, you are likely to take one class, and one aspect of teaching that class, over a time-limited period, trying something out, and evaluating it with a view to further development. In other words, you are taking a deep look at the present, with an eye on the future.

Developing research questions

The next stage is to identify the 'questions within the question'. This means thinking through what you need to find out in order to answer the 'big' question. For the beginner, this is not always an easy process and tutors can help. Figure 14.2 illustrates how some trainees have done this. Note that some questions require some theoretical research, for example, 'what is there in the literature about the use of Socratic circles to support speaking and listening skills?' Some require data drawn from practical sources, for example 'might some of the students with difficulties in sport have dyspraxia?' 'What does my teaching feel like to my learners?' Others are answered through reflection on the implementation of key ideas, for example 'How effective are tasks that relate forces to everyday life in developing understanding?' Not all questions can be identified at the outset of the research. For example the sociology student, on observing how other teachers engage learners in independent research, discovered that one teacher used short independent sessions interspersed with regular, formative feedback, leading to this trainee's final question. Reflection about which approach worked best could be developed into research questions.

Reflective task 14.1   Reviewing your current practice

1 What aspects of your teaching concern you currently?
2 Can you identify the 'big question' and then further research questions?
3 Study the suggested framework in Figure 14.2. How could you develop a strategy for action research to develop your practice to address this issue?

In contrast to other research which attempts to generate new knowledge, action or practitioner research develops unique personalized evidence about aspects of your practice. That is to say, you cannot make claims that because something works for you, it could work anywhere; it is not what we call 'generalizable'. It is a form of evaluative self-reflection on practice (McNiff with Whitehead 2002: 15).

What are your key professional concerns to address (relating to developing your practice)?

Which aspect of your teaching do you wish to focus your action research on?

What are your specific action research questions?

What methods will you use?

What is the context of your study?	Who are the participants in your project?

What data/evidence/observations will be collected? Why?	How will the data/evidence/observations be collected? When? Frequency?

How will you analyse the data/evidence/observations?

What are your anticipated outcomes of your action research? (How do you think you might change your practice?)

Figure 14.2   A planning framework to help develop your action research project

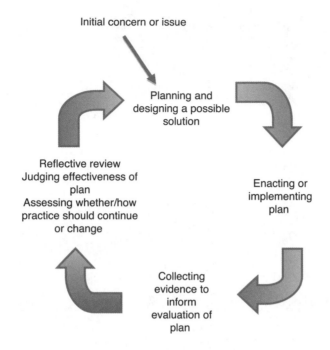

Figure 14.3 Systematic reflective review adapted from the Action Research cycle
Source: McNiff with Whitehead 2002: 41

As indicated earlier, action research is usually cyclical, beginning with a problem or dilemma, from which a plan to solve the problem or develop practice is developed. The action research or self-reflection cycle including the key steps (seen in Figure 14.3) can provide a scaffold for you to sustain the continual improvement of your practice. This cyclical approach of planning, action, monitoring and reflection can sometimes become a little blurred and the teacher-researcher may find action and reflection becoming synonymous. Some areas of action research can also have a longer timescale, with small, incremental change steps being taken, perhaps termly, or each year with new classes, and regularly reviewed before you finally develop an approach or strategy that you are happy with (see Figure 14.4). For example, you may wish to develop your practice by using more differentiation strategies with your class. Over the space of a term, or even a year, you will introduce, one at a time, new ways of doing this. You will evaluate and reflect on each strategy used, using evidence of learners' responses, learning outcomes, the reflections of colleagues, and so on, before introducing the next refined idea. By the end of the academic year, having taken small progressive steps during the year, you will be able to use your enhanced professional development to implement improved differentiation strategies in the future.

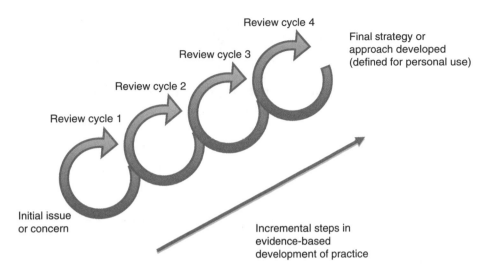

Review cycle 4

Review cycle 3

Final strategy or
approach developed
(defined for personal use)

Review cycle 2

Review cycle 1

Initial issue
or concern

Incremental steps in
evidence-based
development of practice

Figure 14.4 Potential sequence of action research cycles

Source: Adapted from McNiff with Whitehead 2002

Consider the following description of Julie's research to develop her teaching:

66 In preparation to teach about states of matter (solids, liquids and gases) I read about children's ideas in science. Although I anticipated students would have trouble with some concepts in science, I did not realize that it wasn't unusual for learners to think that particles are embedded within materials (rather than the particles being the substance of the material itself), that particles are usually 'round' in shape, that air flows between particles and substances warmed up . . . expanded! Armed with this information before I taught the topic I decided I would use creative writing, concept cartoons (Keogh and Naylor 2008) and questioning to find out exactly what my ten year olds thought about substances before I had them do anything. I wanted to be able to challenge and correct any misunderstandings that this class had.

The lessons I taught involved some interactive practical activities that I designed specifically to address their rather varied views of particles. At the end of the teaching I experimented with different ways of assessing their learning. I interviewed a small group, had them create posters to summarize what they knew about particles, as well as have the whole class sit a test to find out what they had learned.

The most effective method of assessing what they had learned was through interviewing. The most useful way of finding out how their understanding developed was to have them share (and me note on a large poster) any ideas about a topic before teaching them, however, this will not be the best method for all classes all the time.

(Julie, one-year PGCE science, second teaching experience) 〝〝

Action research takes reflection much deeper than just describing what might be happening in a situation, recognizing why it is or is not working and then trying to remedy it. It is an **iterative** process at a much more analytical level in an attempt to effect positive change in a situation. It will involve alternating phases of action and **critical reflection** and, in the later cycles, continuously refining methods, data and interpretation in the light of the understanding developed in the earlier cycles.

Reflective task 14.2   Comparing two different research approaches

1 Consider the following two examples of AR projects in PE, the first applied by Lydia, the second by Christian.
2 Can you identify the steps in the action research process?
3 Are the trainees critical and self-reflective in the same ways?
4 Would it have been helpful if either of them had been more critical earlier on in their research?

Lydia's reflections

〝〝 I was concerned about 14- and 15-year-old girls opting out of physical education, so I decided to develop an approach that helped them improve their participation and performance in badminton. I assessed a range of their skills, useful for badminton, before I taught them their six week programme of lessons. The skills I measured through practical tests included throwing, catching, zigzag running, balancing and jumping. My enthusiasm for my subject was illustrated in the way I prepared, planned and organized the lessons. I began with skill development exercises using fun task cards that I designed and created. These cards really helped the girls work independently in groups or pairs and clearly understand:

- what equipment was needed
- what to do (with diagrams and text)
- how to extend (differentiate) the activities (to develop advanced skills)

Each skill had to be practised for a minute and then the number of times the skill was completed in one minute counted and noted (on a score sheet).

I found that if I did the circuit of practical skill activities with the girls they became more participative, trying to beat my scores. I also found that when they transitioned to conditioned badminton games (although interestingly they didn't recognize it) they were generally more competitive (as confirmed by my mentor). I re-tested the girls at the end of the six weeks and found that most had improved their performance on the practical tests (as judged by the individual scores for each compared at the beginning of the badminton lessons).

(Lydia, one-year PGCE PE trainee, final weeks of teaching practice) 99

Christian's reflections

66 I noticed that the athletic performance of my 10-year-olds, in cricket and tennis, was not very high (ranging from NC level four to five). I thought that if I worked on their thinking about their skills and fitness to help them understand the fundamentals of movement and have them self and peer assess their progress (through applications of AfI) they would then be able to make successful transitions from one sport to another. I developed a questionnaire to find out what they thought they needed to be good at to be successful in sport. I also devised a range of tests to measure their abilities in balance, coordination and agility before and after I taught them about cricket and tennis. I also created a simple AfL chart that they could use to judge their fitness.

Critical reflection of the findings from my project indicated that to try and have the students focus on both fitness (stamina, strength, speed, skill, suppleness) and skills (balance, coordination, agility) did not work. I was trying to assess two quite different aspects of physical education. What I realized was effective, was not what I set out to do. After I had finished teaching the tennis and cricket lessons I realized it saved time and was better for many students to teach them the skills discretely while playing a mini-match (rather than always drilling the skills before a game). Not always telling them how to do things and practising it many, many times meant they were sometimes very creative in the way they moved. I sensed that as Pickup et al. (2007: 11) affirm, a teacher-led approach may hinder their long term interest in sports.

Reflecting on my study, I would say that I needed to consider many other factors like the expertise of the students, the culture of the school, what the students had learned with other staff before me, before deciding the best way to help learners in skill transition or transference from one sport to another.

(Christian, PGCE PE trainee, final weeks of teaching practice) 99

These examples illustrate that action research is not something that you 'bolt on' to other forms of reflection, but is a more specific, more systematic version of it, based on the application of experience and knowledge in a cycle of ongoing reflective activity.

Becoming more specifically critical in the focus for your AR

As you become more experienced, so the research on different aspects of your teaching provides you with your own personalized form of professional development. Consider Della's reflections in Case Study 14.2 about how she sets about improving her questioning skills. How far does she apply an AR approach?

Case Study 14.2   Della: improving questioning techniques

As a Primary BEd mathematics student in her final month of teaching practice, Della was concerned with using her questioning techniques more effectively to support AfL. She had noted that Ofsted (2008: 13) described good practice as 'teachers listened to pupils carefully and observed their work throughout the lesson. They aimed to identify any potential misconceptions or barriers to understanding key concepts and responded accordingly.'

She had also read that 'you will need to listen, observe and question in ways which will enable you to give appropriate feedback or further instruction' (Briggs and Ellis 2007: 66).

She reflectively reviewed the kinds of questions she was asking her students and realized most were closed questions requiring only a one word reply or a yes/no response. In attempting to redevelop her questioning technique she began writing scripts for herself so that her wording of questions was much more open, for example, 'Can you explain how you answered this question?' She found that the students were initially resistant to that style of questioning. Over time, however, they seemed to grow in confidence and offer more explanations. Reflecting again on her development of questioning, she realized that she was often choosing the same students to respond, usually the ones she thought would give the correct explanations. As Lawson (2008: 150) says 'the drawback is that it is easy to rely on a few students to supply all the answers and the rest of the class get used to opting out'. Further cogitation led her to begin directing her questions to those who were less likely to volunteer and then to use a random name generator to choose respondents. Her tutor recognized her increasingly effective use of questions, but suggested she often intervened too early or too frequently and that less able students needed longer to answer. She returned to the literature to search for ways she could assess students' understanding using different types of questioning. Coffey (2007: 196) suggests 'alternative questioning strategies'. These included reframing questions by providing an answer for pupils and challenging them to think of an appropriate question for that answer. Black et al. (2003) recommend that questions that make the students think and which motivate them to want to discuss ideas and questions that require students to predict or consider alternatives are better than those leading to a set answer. These suggestions informed her development of teaching and led her to reflexively refine her questioning techniques.

Reflective task 14.3 Della's reflexive development of her questioning techniques for AfL purposes

1 Can you identify what reflective questions Della was probably asking herself?
2 Consider the adapted Rolfe framework (Figure 14.1) and 'Deepening thinking to develop reflexivity' (Table 14.1). How closely do Della's actions correspond with these two scaffolds?
3 If you were concerned about your questioning skills, how could you develop an action research approach (see Figures 14.1 and 14.2) to improve them?

Summary

Like Dawkins (1998) who 'unweaves the rainbow', we have attempted throughout this book to separate out what sometimes feels like a tangle of teacher-learner, teacher-reflective thinker and reflective practitioner-learner relationships to make more explicit how different kinds of reflection can help you become an effective teacher. As Nesbit et al. argue:

> *"great teachers think strategically and act with commitment . . . it is the ways that teachers think and act at a number of different levels. . . . [which shows their] . . . deep understanding of themselves and their students, and of the organisational contexts in which they work."*
>
> *(Nesbit et al. 2004: 74)*

It appears then, that thoughtful reflection methodically directed, in turn, on varied aspects of pedagogical performance can illuminate pathways to improve practice.

Conclusion

The purpose of this chapter has been to help you to draw together what you have learned throughout this book and to recognize the power within you to be not just reflective but 'reflexive': to reflect on your reflections, knowing why you think and act in certain ways. In so doing, you are in a strong position to develop more formal, action-research forms of reflection that are at the heart of the truly reflective practitioner. As Dewey (1991: 66) indicates 'the trained power of thought' is to 'turn things over' and to 'look at matters deliberately' so that we realize what came of what we did'. By reflecting from differing perspectives, reinterpretations of incidents or happenings can enrich our learning and offer more insightful understanding to inform and steer professional judgements and behaviours. This is because 'reflection involves taking our experiences as a starting point for learning. By thinking about them in a purposeful way – using reflective processes – we can come to understand them differently and take action as a result '(Jasper 2003: 1).

Such can be your future: you have the potential to ensure that your learners have the best experience possible in your classroom by seeing yourself as a learner too.

Key learning points

- Reflexivity is a responsive form of reflection that integrates your ideas, values, beliefs and actions to inform professional development
- Action research is cyclical, involving reflective and reflexive activity (informed by evidence) that sustains personalized professional development to enhance learning and teaching.

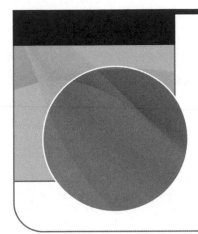

Appendix 1 QTS standards summary

Summarizing the standards required for the award of QTS (or QtT) with indications of where they are predominantly discussed in the book.

1 Professional attributes

	1	2	3	4	5	6	7	8	9	10	11	12	13	14
Relationships with children and young people														
Q1 Have high expectations of children and young people including a commitment to ensuring that they can achieve their full educational potential and to establishing fair, respectful, trusting, supportive and constructive relationships with them.	√			√	√					√				
Q2 Demonstrate the positive values, attitudes and behaviour they expect from children and young people.			√		√			√						
Frameworks														
Q3 (a) Be aware of the professional duties of teachers and the statutory framework within which they work. (b) Be aware of the policies and practices of the workplace and share in collective responsibility for their implementation.		√ √							√					
Communicating and working with others														
Q4 Communicate effectively with children, young people, colleagues, parents and carers.						√								
Q5 Recognise and respect the contribution that colleagues, parents and carers can make to the development and well-being of children and young people and to raising their levels of attainment.						√								
Q6 Have a commitment to collaboration and co-operative working.						√								

Personal professional development

Q7 (a) Reflect on and improve their practice, and take responsibility for identifying and meeting their developing professional needs				✓				✓			✓		✓
(b) Identify priorities for their early professional development in the context of induction.				✓				✓			✓		✓
Q8 Have a creative and constructively critical approach towards innovation, being prepared to adapt their practice where benefits and improvements are identified				✓		✓		✓					
Q9 Act upon advice and feedback and be open to coaching and mentoring.				✓				✓					

2 Professional knowledge and understanding

Teaching and learning

Q10 Have a knowledge and understanding of a range of teaching, learning and behaviour management strategies and know how to use and adapt them, including how to personalise learning and provide opportunities for all learners to achieve their potential.	✓		✓	✓					✓	✓			

Assessment and monitoring

Q11 Know the assessment requirements and arrangements for the subjects/curriculum areas in the age ranges they are trained to teach, including those relating to public examinations and qualifications.		✓								✓			

(Continued)

Standard						
Q12 Know a range of approaches to assessment, including the importance of formative assessment.	✓					
Q13 Know how to use local and national statistical information to evaluate the effectiveness of their teaching, to monitor the progress of those they teach and to raise levels of attainment.			✓	✓		
Subjects and Curriculum						
Q14 Have a secure knowledge and understanding of their subjects/curriculum areas and related pedagogy to enable them to teach effectively across the age and ability range for which they are trained.			✓			
Q15 Know and understand the relevant statutory and non-statutory curricula, frameworks, including those provided through the National Strategies, for their subjects/curriculum areas, and other relevant initiatives applicable to the age and ability range for which they are trained.					✓	✓
Literacy, numeracy and ICT						
Q16 Have passed the professional skills tests in numeracy, literacy and information and communication technology (ICT)		✓		✓		
Q17 Know how to use skills in literacy, numeracy and ICT to support their teaching and wider professional activities.		✓				

Achievement and diversity										
Q18 Understand how children and young people develop and that the progress and well-being of learners are affected by a range of developmental, social, religious, ethnic, cultural and linguistic influences.	✓		✓	✓						
Q19 Know how to make effective personalised provision for those they teach, including those for whom English is an additional language or who have special educational needs or disabilities, and how to take practical account of diversity and promote equality and inclusion in their teaching.			✓	✓						
Q20 Know and understand the roles of colleagues with specific responsibilities, including those with responsibility for learners with special educational needs and disabilities and other individual learning needs.				✓						
Health and well-being										
Q21 (a) Be aware of current legal requirements, national policies and guidance on the safeguarding and promotion of the well-being of children and young people. (b) Know how to identify and support children and young people whose progress, development or well-being is affected by changes or difficulties in their personal circumstances, and when to refer them to colleagues for specialist support.		✓		✓				✓		

(Continued)

3. Professional skills

Planning

Q22 Plan for progression across the age and ability range for which they are trained, designing effective learning sequences within lessons and across series of lessons and demonstrating secure subject/curriculum knowledge.

Q23 Design opportunities for learners to develop their literacy, numeracy and ICT skills.

Q24 Plan homework or other out-of-class work to sustain learners' progress and to extend and consolidate their learning.

Teaching

Q25 Teach lessons and sequences of lessons across the age and ability range for which they are trained in which they:

(a) use a range of teaching strategies and resources, including e-learning, taking practical account of diversity and promoting equality and inclusion;

(b) build on prior knowledge, develop concepts and processes, enable learners to apply new knowledge, understanding and skills and meet learning objectives;

(c) adapt their language to suit the learners they teach, introducing new ideas and concepts clearly, and using explanations, questions, discussions and plenaries effectively;

(d) manage the learning of individuals, groups and whole classes, modifying their teaching to suit the stage of the lesson.

Assessing, monitoring and giving feedback									
Q26 (a) Make effective use of a range of assessment, monitoring and recording strategies. (b) Assess the learning needs of those they teach in order to set challenging learning objectives.				✓					
Q27 Provide timely, accurate and constructive feedback on learners' attainment, progress and areas for development.						✓			
Q28 Support and guide learners to reflect on their learning, identify the progress they have made and identify their emerging learning needs.					✓				
Reviewing teaching and learning									
Q29 Evaluate the impact of their teaching on the progress of all learners, and modify their planning and classroom practice where necessary.		✓					✓		
Learning environment									
Q30 Establish a purposeful and safe learning environment conducive to learning and identify opportunities for learners to learn in out of school contexts.		✓				✓			

(Continued)

Q31 Establish a clear framework for classroom discipline to manage learners' behaviour constructively and promote their self-control and independence.			✓						
Team Working and Collaboration									
Q32 Work as a team member and identify opportunities for working with colleagues, sharing the development of effective practice with them.				✓					
Q33 Ensure that colleagues working with them are appropriately involved in supporting learning and understand the roles they are expected to fulfil.				✓					

Appendix 2 Grade criteria for the inspection of initial teacher training 2008–11

Features of trainees

Grade	Key aspects of trainees' performance: In lessons
Outstanding	Outstanding trainees: teach lessons that are mostly good, and often show characteristics of outstanding lessons ensure that all learners make good progress so that they fully achieve the challenging intended learning outcomes teach learners to be able to explain how the teaching helped them to make progress teach lessons that invariably capture the interest of learners, are inclusive of all learners, and feature debate between learners and between learners and the teacher have a rapport with learners – high-quality dialogue and questioning, guiding learning, with attention to individuals and groups monitor learners' progress to evaluate quickly how well they are learning so that they can change the approach during the lesson if necessary, and provide detailed feedback and targets to individual learners that are focused well to ensure further progress demonstrate the ability to apply their own depth of subject knowledge to support learners in acquiring understanding and skills, often showing understanding, through application of a range of different approaches to ensure that all learners make the expected progress

(Continued)

Grade	Key aspects of trainees' performance: In lessons
	demonstrate flexibility and adaptability by changing pace, approach and teaching method in a lesson in response to what learners say and do make links with other aspects of learners' development and understanding (for example, linking to work in other subjects) fully exploit possibilities to promote learners' understanding and appreciation of social and cultural diversity.
Good	Good trainees: teach lessons that are never less than satisfactory, but often good or better ensure that all learners are sufficiently challenged and achieve the intended learning objectives teach in a way that engages learners' interest so that they become fully involved in the lesson make creative use of resources use a range of different assessment methods matched well to the expected learning outcomes and show an understanding of why a particular method was chosen monitor and assess learners' achievement and provide feedback to them that is based on the specific needs of learners or groups of learners that leads to further progress show flexibility/adaptability that takes account of the progress made by learners and match their teaching to it, including by matching pace to learning and the use of a variety of teaching methods understand how to overcome barriers to learning such as low levels of literacy/numeracy use their subject knowledge to find different ways of explaining or teaching approaches work effectively with learning support and other professionals in planning, teaching and monitoring and reviewing learners' progress make links with and explore possibilities to develop learners' understanding and appreciation of social and cultural diversity.
Satisfactory	To be judged satisfactory a trainee must meet all of the qualified teacher status standards or the requirements of the appropriate learning and skills teaching qualification by the end of the course.

Grade	Key aspects of trainees' performance: In lessons
	Satisfactory trainees: teach consistently at least satisfactory lessons (by the end of their training) in which learners make progress or consolidate their learning[1] teach at a satisfactory level across a range of different contexts (for example, different ages, groups sizes, levels) respond to individual and groups of learners' questions and needs to enable learners to progress and meet the learning expectations demonstrate secure subject knowledge that develops learners' understanding and skills set clear expectations for learning and behaviour manage the learning environment and resources to enable all learners to make progress match teaching and learning activities to the intended learning outcomes plan and use resources efficiently, including the deployment of other adults, learning support and other professionals monitor learners' progress and assess their achievement, and provide feedback to learners which aids their progress begin to develop learners' wider understanding and appreciation of social and cultural diversity.
Inadequate	Inadequate trainees do not meet the characteristics to be satisfactory. They are unlikely to meet all of the qualified teacher status standards or the requirements of the appropriate learning and skills teaching qualification by the end of the course.
Grade	Key aspects of trainees' performance: Trainees' files
Outstanding	Outstanding trainees: demonstrate a clear and deep understanding of how to plan for progression – stages in learning, different rates of progress, identifying clear 'strands of progression' and the use of these to plan 'steps in learning', their teaching, dealing with barriers to learning, and through this demonstrate depth of subject knowledge and subject pedagogy

[1]Lessons judged using the Common Inspection Framework for schools or colleges and the associated evaluation schedule for *Evaluating the Quality of Teaching*.

(*Continued*)

Grade	Key aspects of trainees' performance: Trainees' files
	provide evidence of monitoring and recording learners' progress and how this the outcomes are used in subsequent planning, with a clear focus on groups and individual learners
	demonstrate the clarity of links between learning objectives, teaching approaches and assessment strategies – 'what I want learners to learn, how they will learn, and how I know that they have, what I will do next'
	show innovation within the constraints of a scheme of work/ curriculum
	maintain files as working documents – annotated as part of self-evaluation
	show high-quality self-evaluation with clear focus on learners and setting challenging targets for their own professional development – including, for example, future career progression with evidence of implementation and further review, and critical analysis and reflection, taking full account of feedback from trainers and other professionals they work with
	innovative approaches to the integration of *Every Child Matters*, and social and cultural diversity.
Good	Good trainees:
	plan lessons that take account of the needs of groups of learners and individuals, through the setting of differentiated learning outcomes, and matching these to the teaching and learning approaches and activities used – with clear recognition of how to deal with any potential barriers to learning – and through this demonstrate their own depth of subject knowledge
	plan clear links between expected outcomes and how progress and achievement will be monitored and assessed, with outcomes used in subsequent planning
	set lessons clearly in a sequence that is designed well to secure progression
	provide clear evidence of understanding the need to take responsibility for their own professional development through evaluating performance and setting challenging targets, working with trainers to refine these and to monitor their progress, then evidence of implementation, review and critical reflection.

Grade	Key aspects of trainees' performance: Trainees' files
Satisfactory	**To be judged satisfactory a trainee must meet all of the qualified teacher status standards or the requirements of the appropriate learning and skills teaching qualification by the end of the course.** Satisfactory trainees: plan lesson/s that set clear learning outcomes and indicate how the planned activities will enable learners to meet these, and how progress and achievement will be monitored and assessed – including recognition of potential barriers to learning such as low levels of literacy/numeracy evaluate their teaching and show an understanding of the need to evaluate the effectiveness of it through the impact on learners – with evidence of the use of aspects covered in training activities to secure trainees' own progress take some responsibility for their own professional development – clear relationship between targets set by trainers and trainees' own reflections and personal target-setting, and trainees' progress take account of *Every Child Matters*, and social and cultural diversity.
Inadequate	Inadequate trainees do not meet the characteristics to be satisfactory. They are unlikely to meet all of the qualified teacher status standards or the requirements of the appropriate learning and skills teaching qualification by the end of the course.

Grade	Key aspects of trainees' performance: Trainees' explanations
Outstanding	Outstanding trainees: describe the stages in progress through a topic/set of ideas and concepts/sequence of teaching – explaining what they would look for in learners can give examples of lessons, and individual/groups of learners, to illustrate this – including the identification of barriers to learning and how these were/can be overcome are able to discuss in detail individual learners' progress as well as attainment/achievement are able to use their depth of subject-specific pedagogical understanding to explain in detail why they use particular teaching approaches and why these are likely to be more successful than others

(*Continued*)

Grade	Key aspects of trainees' performance: Trainees' explanations
	demonstrate an understanding of the range of professionals that contribute to learners' overall development and their place in the 'bigger picture' – well-informed discussion about individual/groups of learners and particular needs show a depth of understanding of the implications of *Every Child Matters* across a wide range of work and how to promote learners' understanding and exploit the potential provided by social and cultural diversity.
Good	Good trainees: can give examples of how they have secured progression for groups of learners through a sequence of lessons, including how they know that learners have made progress are able to explain why they use particular teaching and learning approaches and why these work in their subject demonstrate their understanding of barriers to learning and how these can be overcome in their subject can give examples of working with a wider range of professionals to secure the overall development of learners demonstrate a secure understanding of the implications of *Every Child Matters*, and social and cultural diversity, and can apply this to their own teaching.
Satisfactory	To be judged satisfactory a trainee must meet all of the qualified teacher status standards or the requirements of the appropriate learning and skills teaching qualification by the end of the course. Satisfactory trainees: can explain how the training has enabled them to improve their teaching can explain how their lesson planning fits into a sequence that will enable learners to make progress can explain how they monitor and assess learners' achievements, and how this indicates that the learners are making progress show awareness of barriers to learning, such as levels of literacy or numeracy, and the likely impact on their subject, with some ideas for dealing with this know who they should turn to for expert advice on particular aspects of learners' overall development, specifically including child protection and safeguarding issues demonstrate a secure understanding of *Every Child Matters* and of social and cultural diversity.

Grade	Key aspects of trainees' performance: Trainees' explanations
Inadequate	Inadequate trainees do not meet the characteristics to be satisfactory. They are unlikely to meet all of the qualified teacher status standards or the requirements of the appropriate learning and skills teaching qualification by the end of the course.

Grade	Key aspects of trainees' performance: Noticeable characteristics
Outstanding	Outstanding trainees: take risks when trying to make teaching interesting, are able to deal with the unexpected and 'grab the moment' inspire and communicate their enthusiasm to learners have an intrinsic passion for learning show innovative and creative thinking – lateral thinkers have the ability to reflect critically and rigorously on their own practice to inform their professional development, and to take and evaluate appropriate actions – they are able to learn from their mistakes take full responsibility for their own professional development are highly respected by learners and colleagues and, where appropriate, parents/carers and employers have the clear capacity to become outstanding teachers demonstrate, or show the capacity to develop, leadership and management skills.
Good	Good trainees: show a willingness to try out range of approaches to teaching and learning, know how to learn from both success and 'failure', and know when/who to ask for support both in trying out new approaches and in evaluating how well they work clearly understand their own role as 'learners' and how to ensure they achieve their own learning goals systematically evaluate their own practice, including through its impact on learners, and take appropriate action have the clear capacity to become good, and possibly outstanding, teachers.
Satisfactory	To be judged satisfactory a trainee must meet all of the qualified teacher status standards or the requirements of the appropriate learning and skills teaching qualification by the end of the course.

(Continued)

Grade	Key aspects of trainees' performance: Noticeable characteristics
	Satisfactory trainees:
	tend to have a limited, but adequate, range of teaching and assessment strategies, but use these competently and with confidence
	evaluate their own practice, including through its impact on learners, and take appropriate action
	recognise that they need help with some aspects of teaching, and are willing to seek out and act on advice and guidance
	show clear capacity to become competent, and in some aspects, good teachers.
Inadequate	Inadequate trainees do not meet the characteristics to be satisfactory. They are unlikely to meet all of the qualified teacher status standards or the requirements of the appropriate learning and skills teaching qualification by the end of the course.

Appendix 3   Using progression grids for staged feedback

The following is an extract from the 'Progression grids' used at the University of Wolverhampton for the secondary PGCE. By breaking down the somewhat complex Q standards into progressive stages, the trainees are provided with a platform from which to develop and reflect on their learning. Mentors and tutors provide guidance and varied feedback at different stages of development. In the table below, Standard 25c is explained as an example. Trainees are *working towards* this standard in their first placement, and must show evidence of having made sufficient progress before progressing to the second placement. They must show clear evidence of meeting the standard consistently, in a range of contexts, by the end of the second placement. The following reflections and feedback show congruence with the trainee's stage of development:

1st November

I have researched all the key words for the topic, and I have observed this topic being taught to a parallel class, so am feeling quite confident.

15th November

Mentor	How do you think learners responded to your explanation today?
Trainee	Quite well, I think. I explained clearly and they seemed to understand.
Mentor	Yes, they answered the questions well, and you checked understanding carefully.
Trainee	They were less happy with the task though. They just did not seem to know what to do!
Mentor	That's right. They really needed you to **model** the task. Let's talk about that . . .

First School Placement October to December

Targets for the 'serial' attachment : a three week period of university and school-based days, providing time and opportunity to plan for teaching.	Fortnightly targets for the 'block' attachment: a period of six weeks with a teaching timetable of approximately eight hours per week.

Effective Teaching				
To observe good practice in teaching, taking account of the language that teachers use in demonstrating and explaining concepts to learners.	To be able to identify the key concepts and skills to be taught to pupils during the block attachment and to research ways in which these can be explained, demonstrated and practised in class.	To be able to identify what has gone well in promoting learning and what needs improving by having a developing awareness of the extent to which pupils are responding well and learning. (Q7)	To be able to evaluate, in discussion with your mentor, the extent to which your teaching is well-structured, the steps in learning are coherent, and pupils are able to follow explanations and instructions and learn from them.	25 (c) To adapt your language to suit the pupils you teach, and to introduce new concepts and ideas clearly, using explanations, questions, discussions and plenaries.

Second School Placement February to May

Serial attachment (see above)	Fortnightly targets for the 'block' attachment: a period of nine weeks with a teaching timetable of approximately 16 hours per week.

Effective Teaching				
To have gauged the language you will need to use with classes by observation of teaching, study of course text books, etc.	To use professional language, avoiding slang, and using standard English. To model the work you expect from learners, beginning with a clear idea in your own mind about what you want their work to look like.	Use a wide repertoire of approaches, explanations, and demonstrations to support the learning points you are making.	Use 'reflection-in-action' to adapt to learners' responses as the lesson progresses. To use open and closed questions, skilfully differentiated according to the needs and abilities of the learners. (Q7)	**25 (c) To adapt your language to suit the pupils you teach, and to introduce new concepts and ideas clearly, using explanations, questions, discussions and plenaries.**

25th February

I really learned the importance of modelling in my last placement; if you have a clear idea in your mind about what you want their work to look like, it is so much easier to put it into words for them to understand! This time I have such different ability groups that I will need to use different levels of language with each one. On Tuesday I go from teaching Y8 bottom set to year 12 AS level, so I will have to do a lot of reflection-in-action— 'reading' their responses to the way I talk to them and how I set up tasks.

12 March

Your explanations are very clear and the class has confidence in you. An excellent achievement after only three weeks! I notice however that most of your questions are closed: 'is that ok?' 'do you understand'? etc. You need to think now about the sort of questions that will allow you to know if they understand. What open questions could you use with this class? Think about individual students as well: could you question Adul and Mark in the same way, for example?

In these examples, the trainee's own written reflections indicate an open approach to learning and a sense of purpose, guided by the 'next stages' of development. Both mentor and trainee also have an eye to the next stage of development towards the standard, and are providing appropriate verbal (placement 1) and written (placement 2) feedback.

Appendix 4 Action plan for augmenting mentor support

Area for development	Target(s)	To be met by
Ideas drawn from reflective questions in socialization matrix (Chapter 5: Figure 5.3).		
Other reflective tools to be used.		
Other sources of support and information e.g. in-school support.		
Date to be completed	**Steps in action plan**	
	1	
	2	
	3	
	4	
Outcomes and evidence of achievement		

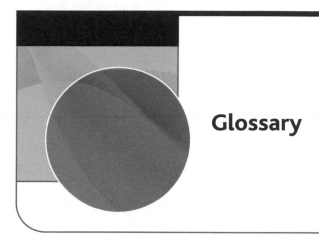

Glossary

A standards   Advanced skills teacher (AST) standards (see Chapter 9 for further details).

Action research   A form of enquiry within a social setting, such as a classroom, conduction by participants in that setting. The stimulus for action research is usually a problem to be solved or an improvement to be made. Central to the approach is 'a self-reflective spiral of cycles of planning, acting, observing and reflecting' (Kemmis 2007:168). It is most effective when conducted collaboratively, and has the potential to contribute to individual and organisational development.

Attention deficit hyperactivity disorder (ADHD)   A complex syndrome in which children display a degree of inattentiveness, disruptive or impulsive behaviour that is outside the normal range for their age. Diagnosis can be difficult as similar symptoms can be displayed for other reasons, such as lack of sleep, depression and other behavioural disorders. Children with suspected ADHD need careful evaluation.

Affective   To do with feelings and emotions. From the same stem as affection and to be affected by something.

Algorithm   Often perceived as formulaic, that is something done to a formal set of rules. May lack creativity as it is following strict, clear guidelines. Can be repetitive, a pattern of regular occurrences.

Asperger syndrome   Generally accepted as an autistic spectrum disorder, asperger syndrome was first described by Han Asperger in 1944. Behaviours of children with Asperger syndrome include: poor eye contact with others despite a generally sociable demeanour; an inability to 'read' situations, such as when they are boring or annoying others; an inability to understand humour, sarcasm and nuance because understanding is almost always literal; a focus on facts, often in a narrow sphere of interest, but with an inability to draw conclusions or manipulate information; a need for ritual and routine. Children with Asperger syndrome can be socially isolated because they appear 'strange' to other children, and may fail to thrive academically for this reason.

Banding The division of school pupils into broad teaching groups by ability. Typically a six-form entry school might have three bands, upper, middle and lower, each with 60 pupils or two classes in it.

Behaviourism A movement in developmental psychology claiming that animal and human behaviour can be learned through repetitive actions. It is 'in essence structured around reinforcing correct, repetitive, observable behaviours deemed to illustrate the learner has mastered a skill' (McGregor 2007:50). Examples in the classroom include learning maths tables, spellings or verb conjugations by heart.

C standards The core standards that all main scale teachers must achieve and maintain throughout their teaching career. (See Chapter 9 for further details.)

Cognitive skills The mental skills used in the process of acquiring knowledge, such as reasoning, perception, and intuition. Often used synonymously with 'thinking skills'. There is a strong correlation between the development of cognitive, or thinking, skills and the ability to learn.

Communities of practice Groups of people who share a common goal or passion for something they do, and interact with each other, both intentionally and unintentionally, to do things better. Pioneered by Jean Lave and Etienne Wenger (see Chapter 5).

Concept A general idea or notion: the result of combining all the characteristics of something in our mind. A mental model of something is *conceptualized.*

Constructivism A theory that humans generate knowledge and construct meaning from their experiences. Thus in educational terms a constructivist approach emphasizes learning by doing and experiencing. 'The emphasis that constructivism places on action as well as linguistic exchange is key to developing thoughtful actions alongside conceptual understanding' (McGregor 2007:65). See also **social constructivism**.

Core standards The term given in England and Wales to the criteria used to describe the core knowledge, understanding and skills of teachers. The core standards must be achieved after qualifying and during the newly qualified teacher induction period, and must be maintained throughout a teacher's career.

Core strands A term used for the most important elements of a curriculum or programme. The core strands of the professional standards are grouped as 'professional values'; 'professional knowledge and understanding' and 'professional skills'.

Creative approaches Approaches to learning that encourage an inventive or imaginative frame of mind in order to develop some element of originality. To be able to transfer knowledge to new situations, solve problems and cope with the unexpected. 'Creativity in education stresses the need to encourage experimentation and problem-solving together with reflection and critical appraisal as essential conditions for creativity to flourish in schools.' (SEED 2006: 1) Creative people are self-motivated, confident, curious and flexible. Creative approaches in the classroom should be designed to promote these characteristics. Not to be confused with the 'creative arts' as it has a more general application.

Critical incident This phrase was first coined by the psychologist John Flanagan in 1954 and defined by Jasper as 'episodes of experience that have particular meaning to. . . . any person taking part in them' (Jasper, 2003:13). Something that happens to an individual that has significance for them. It need not be a traumatic event, just something that makes you stop and think. In educational terms, it is an event, which can be mundane or unusual, usually classroom-based, that if reflected upon can lead to professional learning.

Critical reflection Reflecting on an action, its consequences or effects in a critical way. The assumption is that what has been done or happened can or must be improved in some way. Tends to be no focus; review or account of the positives or what has been done well.

E standards Excellent teacher standards. (See Chapter 9 for further details.)

Early professional development EPD is defined by the TDA as any development activity or intervention that is focused on teachers in the second or third years of their careers.

Eclecticism Drawing ideas from a broad range of sources: *she has an eclectic taste in music*. There is some agreement that VAK provides a rationale for an eclectic approach to teaching.

Ethos The characteristic spirit of a culture, era or community as manifested in its attitudes and aspirations. For example, *the ethos of this school is one where every individual is valued.*

Explicit knowledge As opposed to tacit knowledge, explicit knowledge (sometimes called propositional knowledge) is defined as knowledge that can be easily articulated (and seen or evidenced) because it is formalised and in the public domain of a work place or organisation. New knowledge can be acquired through a structured learning process, for example a school or college induction process. The inter-play between explicit and tacit knowledge is an important area for individual reflection.

Formative assessment Assessment is the collection of any data that allow us to make judgments about whether learning has taken place, for example a spoken or written answer to a question, a test, a piece of homework, a classroom task. It becomes formative if the information is acted upon to improve learning, for example if a piece of work is marked and indications about what is good, what can be improved and *how* it can be improved are given. It is also reflection-in-action on 'the minute-by-minute interactions between teachers and pupils and between pupils themselves' (Sangster and Overal 2006:21).

Ideology   The ideas and ways of thinking that influence the expectations, goals and actions of individuals, organisations and communities. Political ideologies have shaped social and education policy over many decades. For example, New Labour ideology of social justice led to the emphasis on 'education, education, education' and policies aimed to raise standards of literacy in the 1990s.

Individual education plan   Compiled by experts (teachers psychologists, medical care and social care workers as appropriate) with parents to address the specialized needs of some children. Action plans are agreed with particular targets set to support learners with SEN.

Instrumentalism   Very simply, the idea that the value of something lies in its practical usefulness. Thus an instrumentalist view of education would value technology in the curriculum more than Latin. An instrumentalist view of teacher training sees teaching as a set of technical operations that can be learned through experience.

Iterative   A process that is repeated, maybe several times, perhaps regularly. To improve an aspect of your practice you may need to try out repeated, perhaps slightly varied, approaches to solving problems, such as calming your class or grabbing attention, before you find the best way.

Learner-centredness   The principle that learning should be a meaningful experience in which the learner is actively involved. Put simply, a learner-centred lesson is one in which the teacher facilitates interaction between teacher-learner; learner-learner and learner-resources, promoting active thinking skills and opportunities to apply newly acquired knowledge in practical situations. (See also **constructivism**.)

Meta-cognitive skills   Often defined as 'thinking about thinking', or 'learning strategies' refers to the skills that help the learner to perform cognitive tasks more easily. Strategies include questioning, reflecting and evaluating what is being learned. In the classroom, learning can be made concrete through talking through ideas aloud, making concept maps and so forth.

Metaphor   When we use a metaphor, we use one concept to explain or define another concept, even though the two are not the same thing. For example, we have described training to be a teacher as a 'journey' because it is a time of new experiences that will take you to a new place in your life. We use many common metaphors every day, e.g. 'I am a night owl', which is easily understood by all. The skilful use of metaphor is an important literary device, e.g. 'The moon was a ghostly galleon, tossed upon the cloudy seas' (Alfred Noyes, *The Highwayman)*

Mini plenary   A pause part-way through a lesson to review learning so far and signpost the next step. This technique can be used several times during a lesson.

Mnemonics   Strategy to help learners remember important facts and information. Remembering the order of planets, for example the mnemonic : My Very Educated Mother Just Served Us Noodles could be used to recollect Mercury; Venus; Earth; Mars; Jupiter; Uranus; Neptune.

Norms   The way things generally are: the standard or pattern, particularly of social behaviours.

P standards   The post threshold standards that must be achieved in order for teachers to move onto the upper pay scale. (See Chapter 9 for further details.)

Pedagogical strategies   Pedagogy is the academic study of teaching. Pedagogical strategies are the different approaches or tactics that might be used by a teacher or instructor to ensure that their tutees learn.

Pedagogy   The method, practice or science of teaching; a **pedagogue** practices pedagogy (is a teacher).

Performance management   The term used for the formal monitoring of quality in the workplace through the periodic setting of targets and the provision of training to support professional development. Usually linked to pay or other incentives.

Phonics   A method of teaching reading and writing that involves helping learners to make connections between written letters, or groups of letters, and the sounds they make.

Plenary   A summary of learning, normally at the end of a lesson or learning episode, in which learning is reviewed and next steps identified.

Practitioner research   Research that focuses on your developing your own professional practice in a systematic way.

Praxis   Accepted practice or custom, as opposed to theory; often interpreted as theories in practice.

Problem-based reflection   Reflection that begins with the identification of a problem that needs solving.

Professional artistry   A term first coined by Dewey as the 'art of the teacher' and used by Schön, Fish and others to capture the essential but not easily definable characteristics of effective teaching. The view of teaching as 'artistry' is the opposite of the 'technicist' view that sees it as a set of easily definable technical operations. In reality, teachers need to display a degree of both professional artistry and technical skill at varying times or in combination.

Professional standards   The term given in England and Wales to the criteria used to describe the required knowledge, understanding and skills of teachers at five stages of their career development from qualifying to teach to advanced skills teachers.

Q standards   The professional standards that must be met and evidenced in order for a trainee to be recommended for the award of qualified teacher status.

Reflection-before-action   This involves thinking about possibilities before acting. Considering what could happen in lessons and how you will prepare for learning before delivering it is a form of reflection-before-action.

Reflective action   An act carried out after some reflection or consideration of consequences of that action. Not automatic routine action. An example could be thinking about the consequences of not allowing the class out at break, but recognizing that the mis-behaviour of some individuals warranted a response. Various possible courses of action might emerge after deliberation or reflection about the childrens' responses to your actions.

Reflective practitioner   A professional who learns from past experience to improve future performance through deliberate and focused thinking about previous and potential practice.

Reflexivity   Being able to reflectively re-act to a situation in an experiential or more informed way. Often used to indicate that although intended actions were developing in one direction, through reflection, the reflexivity resulted in a change of direction, pace or process in some way.

Routine actions   Actions that are applied or enacted in an unconscious or unthinking manner. Automatic actions which may have been developed over time might include always reading out names from the register at beginning of the lesson; always asking the first child with hand-up to answer question; always lining up the children outside a room before entry; always 'ticking' a correct answer in book; always responding to an incorrect response by saying 'no, that's not the answer I was looking for'.

Sanctions and rewards   A system for discouraging poor behaviour and reinforcing good behaviour in school. Rewards can be anything from praise during lessons to end of year prizes. Sanctions can be anything from a warning to expulsion. Knowing the system of sanctions and rewards within your school, and applying it consistently is a good first step in behaviour management.

Scheme of work   A medium to long-term planning strategy that identifies aims and learning objectives over a term, year or key stage. It is normally agreed by all involved in teaching, and identifies content, resources, assessment methods and sometimes methodology. Individual teachers draw their lesson plans from the scheme of work.

Self-efficacy   Our belief in our ability to succeed in specific situations. The concept of self-efficacy is at the heart of social cognitive theory, developed in the 1980s by the psychologist Albert Bandura. According to Bandura, people with high self-efficacy – that is a belief in their ability to perform tasks well – are more likely to tackle challenges, whereas people with low self-efficacy are more likely to avoid difficult tasks.

Seminal   From the Latin 'seminalis' meaning 'seed', it literally means 'springing from life'. Its figurative meaning (e.g. in education) relates to the origin of an idea: an idea or a piece of research is seminal when it influences the work and thinking of others in an original way. Remember a dated reference or text does not necessarily mean it is, or will be, less valid than a more contemporary source.

Setting   Putting learners of similar ability together for certain lessons. This is a flexible model that allows for a learner to be in a top set for one subject but a lower set for another. Sometimes called 'vertical streaming'.

Social constructivism   Recognizes the role that culture and society play in learning and human development. In classroom terms, social constructivism is about learning with others, in pairs and small groups, through carefully scaffolded activities that demand communication and cooperation.

Streaming   Learners of similar ability are grouped together horizontally across subjects. Typically a nine form entry school will have three streams: a top, middle and low ability. Setting may occur within the stream.

Success criteria   The 'things' that a learner indicates they can *do* to show they have achieved the learning objectives of a lesson. A lesson that states a learning objective is to understand several different fractions could be evidenced by a learner selecting half, quarter, third of the apples from a basket. The success criteria from the child's perspective would be to 'select the right number of apples to show I understand fractions'. To be most effective success criteria are usually negotiated between the teacher and the learners.

Summative assessment   Assessment is the collection of any data that allow us to make judgments about whether learning has taken place, for example a spoken or written answer to a question, a test, a piece of homework, a classroom task. It is summative when it is not directly acted upon for learning purposes and when the outcome is fixed, such as standardized assessment tasks (SATs) and GCSE results. The outcomes of summative assessment can be used as a 'ticket' to the next stage of learning, for example end of year exams might determine the set or stream for the following year; public examination results give access to further or higher education.

Tacit knowledge   As opposed to explicit, or propositional, knowledge, tacit knowledge is about all those things that we can do (or think we can do) but have never put into words why and how we do them. In contexts such as the classroom, our tacit knowledge is an accumulation of past experiences that are not consciously remembered but which form the basis of future actions (Eraut 2000: 13). Tacit knowledge can be 'picked up' or appropriated by listening and watching other more experienced and expert teachers. The interplay between tacit and explicit knowledge is an important area for individual reflection.

Teacher identity   Associated with your perception of who you are as a teacher and what sort of a teacher you perceive yourself to be, or aspire to be. Teacher identity is made up of a combination of the personal self and the professional self.

Teacher-centredness   The idea that teaching is about the transmission of knowledge from the teacher to the learner with little interaction. The learner is a passive recipient of information, and often seen by the teacher as an 'empty vessel' to be filled. For example, a lesson on the planetary system might begin with a lengthy presentation by the teacher, with learners copying a diagram into their books. It would be difficult to judge what learning had taken place in this instance.

Technical rationality   A term used by Schön and developed by Fish (1995) to describe a view of teaching as a set of technical operations that can easily be acquired. In effect, technical rationality sees teaching as the passing on of knowledge from one generation to the next, and is therefore linked to teacher-centredness. Although often viewed as an opposing view to that of the 'professional artistry' view of teaching, In reality, teachers need to display a degree of both professional artistry and technical skill at varying times or in combination.

Technicist   Technical rational approaches are sometimes called 'technicist' and the term may be used synonymously with 'instrumentalist'.

Truism   A statement that is considered to be true because it is what most people believe, although it is not necessarily true by definition of scientific proof. For example: 'Genocide is bad.'

Typology   A word, often used in academic texts, to mean classification by type.

References

Abdallah, A. (1996) Fostering creativity in student teachers, *Community Review*, 14: 52.

Alison, J. and Halliwell, S. (2002) *Challenging Classes: Focus on Pupil Behaviour*. London: CILT.

Alsup, J. (2006) *Teacher Identity Discourses: Negotiating Personal and Professional Spaces*. New Jersey: Lawrence Erlbaum Associates.

Arygris, C. (1982) *Reasoning, Learning and Action: Individual and Organizational*. San Francisco, CA: London: Jossey-Bass.

Assessment Reform Group (2002) *Testing, Motivation and Learning*. Available at http://www.assessment-reform-group.org/TML%20BOOKLET%20complete.pdf (Accessed 16 January 2009).

Atherton, J.S. (2010) *Learning and Teaching: Piaget's Development Theory*. Available at http://www.learningandteaching.info/learning/piaget.htm (Accessed 9 August 2010).

Atkinson, D. (2004) Theorising how student teachers form their identities in initial teacher education, *British Educational Research Journal*, 30(3): 379–94.

Atkinson, T. and Claxton, G. (2000) *The Intuitive Practitioner on the value of not always knowing what one is doing*. Buckingham: Open University Press.

Ball, S. and Goodson, I.F. (1985) *Teachers' Lives and Careers*. London: The Falmer Press.

Barlex, D. (ed.) (2007) *Design & Technology for the Next Generation: A Collection of Provocative Pieces, Written by Experts in Their Field, to Stimulate Reflection and Curriculum Innovation*. Whitchurch: Cliffe & Co.

Beauchamp, C. and Thomas, L. (2009) Understanding teacher identity: an overview of issues in the literature and implications for teacher education, *Cambridge Journal of Education*, 39(2): 175–89.

Beetham, H. (2005) *e-Portfolios in Post-16 Learning in the UK: Developments, Issues and Opportunities*. Available at http://excellence.qui.org.uk (Accessed 25 March 2010).

Beijaard, D., Meijer, P., and Verloop, N. (2004) Reconsidering research on teachers' professional identity, *Teaching and Teacher Education*, 20(2): 107–28.

Beresford, J. and Devlin, L. (2006) Teachers as researchers, *School Leadership Today*, 15(6): 42–46.

Black, P., Harrison, C., Marshall, B., and Wiliam, D. (2003) *Assessment for Learning: Putting it into Practice*. Maidenhead: Open University Press.

Black, P., Harrison, C., Lee, C., Marshall, B., and Wiliam, D. (2004) *Working Inside the Black Box: Assessment for Learning in the Classroom*. London: King's College.

Black, P. and Wiliam, D. (1998) *Inside the Black Box: Raising Standards Through Classroom Assessment*. London: King's College.

Black, P. and Wiliam, D. (2001) *Inside the Black Box. Raising Standards Through Classroom Assessment*. London: King's College School of Education.

Bleach, K. (2000) *The Newly Qualified Teacher's Handbook: Meeting the Standards in Secondary and Middle Schools*. London: David Fulton.

Bleakley, A. (2004) 'Your creativity or mine?': a typology of creativities in higher education and the value of a pluralistic approach, *Teaching in Higher Education*, 9(4): 463–75.

Boden, M.A. (2001) Creativity and knowledge, in A. Craft, B. Jeffrey, and M. Leibling, (eds) *Creativity in Education*. London: Continuum.

Bold, C. and Hutton, P. (2007) Supporting students' critical reflection-on-practice, in A. Campbell, and L. Norton, (eds) *Learning, Teaching and Assessing in Higher Education: Developing Reflective Practice*. Exeter: Learning Matters.

Bolton, G. (2005) *Reflective Practice: Writing and Professional Development*. (2nd edn). London: Sage.

Botton, G. (2010) *Reflective Practice: Writing and Professional Development* (3rd edn). London: Sage.

Boud, D., Keogh, R., and Walker, D. (eds.) (1985) *Reflection: Turning experience into Learning*. New York: Routledge Falmer.

Bourdieu, P. and Wacquant, L. (1992) *An invitation to Reflexive Sociology*. Oxford: Polity Press.

Briggs, J. and Ellis, V. (2007) Assessment for learning, in V. Ellis (ed.) *Achieving QTS: Learning and Teaching in Secondary Schools*. Exeter: Learning Matters Ltd.

Brighouse, T. and Woods, D. (1999) *How to Improve Your School*. London: Routledge.

Brindley, S. and Riga F. (2009) Professional knowledge learned and professional knowledge applied: a case study of two trainee English teachers, *English in Education*, 43(1): 68–85.

Brookfield, S. (1995) *Becoming a Critically Reflective Teacher*. San Francisco, CA: Jossey-Bass.

Brooks, V. (2000) School-based initial teacher training: squeezing a quart into a pint pot or a square peg into a round hole?, *Mentoring & Tutoring: Partnership in Learning*, 8(2): 99–112.

Bunton, D., Stimpson, P., and Lopez-Real, F. (2002) University tutors' practicum observation notes: format and content, *Mentoring and Tutoring*, 10(3): 233–52.

Calderhead, J. and Gates, P. (1993) *Conceptualising Reflection in Teacher Development*. London: Falmer Press.

Campbell, A. and Sykes, M. (2007) Action learning and research and inquiry methods on postgraduate courses for professional practitioners, in A. Campbell, and L. Norton (eds) (2007) *Learning, Teaching and Assessing in Higher Education: Developing Reflective Practice*. Exeter: Learning Matters.

Capel, S. (2004) *Learning to Teach Physical Education in the Secondary School: A Companion to School Experience*. (2nd edn). London: Routledge Falmer.

Capel, S., Leask, M., and Turner, T. (eds) (2009) *Learning to Teach in the Secondary School: A Companion to School Experience* (5th edn). London. Routledge.

Carter, K. and Doyle, W. (1996) Personal narrative and life history in learning to teach, in J. Sikula (ed.) *Handbook of Research on Teacher Education*. New York and London: Macmillan.

Casbon, C. and Spackman, L. (2005) *Assessment for Learning in Physical Education*. Nottingham: Coachwise.

Castro, A.J., Kelly, J., and Shih, M. (2010) Resilience strategies for new teachers in high-needs areas, *Teaching and Teacher Education*, 26: 622–29.

Chambers, G. (2007) Developing listening skills in the modern foreign language, in N. Pachler and A. Redondo (eds) *A Practical Guide to Teaching Foreign Languages in the Secondary School. Abingdon: Routledge.*

Chitpin, S. (2006) The use of reflective journal keeping in a teacher education program: a Popperian analysis, *Reflective Practice*, 7(1): 73–86.

Chitty, K.K. (2005) *Professional Nursing: Concepts and Challenges*, (4th edn). St Louis, Missouri: Elsevier Saunders.

Coffey, S. (2007) Differentiation in theory and practice, in J. Dillon, and M. Maguire, (eds) *Becoming a Teacher – Issues in Secondary Teaching*. Maidenhead: Open University Press.

Coffield, F., Moseley, D., Hall, E., and Ecclestone, K. (2004) *Should We be Using Learning Styles? What Research Has to Say to Practice*. London: Learning and Skills Research Centre.

Covey, S.R. (1992) *The Seven Habits of Highly Effective People: Restoring the Character Ethic*. London: Simon and Schuster.

Coyle, D. (2002) Towards a reconceptualisation of the MFL Curriculum, *in* Swarbrick, A. (ed.) *Teaching Modern Foreign Languages* in *Secondary Schools: A Reader*. London: Routledge.

Craft, A. (2003) The limits to creativity in education: dilemmas for the educator, *British Journal of Education Studies,* 51(2): 113–27.

Craft, A. and Paige-Smith, A. (2008), What does it mean to reflect on our practice?, in A. Craft, and A. Paige-Smith, (eds) (2008) *Developing Reflective Practice in the Early Years*, Maidenhead: Open University Press and McGraw Hill Companies.

Cremin, T. (2009) Creative teachers and creative teaching, in A. Wilson (ed.) *Creativity in Primary Education,* 2nd edition. Exeter: Learning Matters.

Cross, R. (1999) What time constraints face the junior school teacher taking on the role of student mentor? *Mentoring and Tutoring,* 7(1): 5–21.

Dawkins, R. (1998) *Unweaving the Rainbow*. New York: Penguin

Day, C., Kington, A., Stobart, G., and Sammons, P. (2006) The personal and professional selves of teachers: stable and unstable identities, *British Educational Research Journal,* 32(4): 601–16.

de Bono, E. (1992) *Teach Your Child How to Think*. London: Penguin.

de Bono, E. (2000) *Six Thinking Hats*. London: Penguin.

DCSF (2008) *Being the Best for Our Children: Releasing Talent for Teaching and Learning*. Nottingham: Department for Children, Schools and Families. Available at www.teachernet.gov.uk/publications (Accessed 30 June 2009).

DFE (2011) *The Important of Teaching: Schools White Paper*, Available at www.education.gov.uk/b00068570/the-importance-of-teaching (Accessed 1 May 2011).

DFES (2004) *Five Year Strategy for Children and Learners*. London. DFES.

Dewey, J. (1933) *Experience and Education,* New York: Collier Macmillan.

Dewey, J. (1910) *How We Think.* Boston: D.C. Heath.

Dewey, J. (1991) *How We Think.* Great books in philosophy series. New York: Prometheus Books.

DfEE (Department for Education and Employment) (1998) *Teachers: Meeting the Challenge of Change.* London: The Stationery Office.

DfES (Department for Education and Skills) (2003) *Towards a Unified e-Learning Strategy.* [online] Nottingham: DfES Publications.

Dymoke, S. and Harrison, J. (eds.) (2008) *Reflective Teaching and Learning: A Guide to Professional Issues for Beginning Secondary Teachers.* London: Sage.

Eckel, J., Kezar, A., and Lieberman, D. (1999) Learning for organizing: institutional reading groups as a strategy for change, *AAHE Bulletin,* 25(33): 6–8.

Edwards, A. (1997) Guests bearing gifts: the position of student teachers in primary school classrooms, *British Educational Research Journal,* 23(1): 27–37.

Elder, L. (2010) A reason to live, *Times Higher Education,* Available at http://www.times highereducation.co.uk/story.asp?sectioncode=26&storycode=410393 (Accessed 11 July 2010).

Eraut, M. (1994) *Developing Professional Knowledge and Competence.* London: Falmer press.

Eraut, M. (2000) Non-formal learning, implicit learning and tacit knowledge, in F. Coffield (ed.) *The Necessity of Informal Learning.* Bristol: The Policy Press.

Eraut, M. (2004) Informal learning in the workplace, *Studies in Continuing Education,* 26(2): 247–73.

Evans, T. and Nation, D. (2000) *Changing University Teaching: Reflections and Creating Educational Technologies.* Abingdon: Routledge.

Ferrier-Kerr, J. (2009) Establishing professional relationships in practicum settings, *Teaching and Teacher Education,* 25(6): 790–7.

Fielding, M. and Rudduck, J. (2002) The transformative potential of student voice: confronting the power issues. Paper presented at the Annual Conference of the British Educational Research Association, University of Exeter, England, 12–14 September. Available at http://www.leeds.ac.uk/educol/documents/00002544.htm (Accessed 11 October 2010).

Findlay, K. (2006) Context and learning factors in the development of teacher identity: a case study of newly qualified teachers during their induction year, *Journal of In-Service Education,* 32(4): 511–32.

Fish, D, (1995) *Quality Mentoring for Student Teachers: A Principle Approach to Practice.* London: David Futton.

Fletcher, J.D., Tobias, S. and Wisher, R.A. (2007) Learning anytime, anywhere: advanced distributed learning and the changing face of education, *Educational Researcher,* 36(2): 96–102.

Foreman-Peck, L. and Murray, J. (2008) Action research policy, *Journal of Philosophy of Education,* 42(5): 145–64.

Forrester, D. and Searle, J. (2003) *Making the Most of it.* Edinburgh: Center for Mathematical Education, The University of Edinburgh. Available at http://www.education. ed.ac.uk/institutes/centres-detail/ecme/research/articles/1-dutchart1a.pdf (Accessed 11 January 2009).

Fullan, M. (1993) Why teachers must become change agents, *Educational Leadership,* 50(6): 1–13.

Fuller, F. and Brown, O. (1975). Becoming a teacher, In K. Ryan (ed.) *Teacher Education* (74th Yearbook of the National Society for the Study of Education. Part 2, pp. 25–52). Chicago: University of Chicago Press.

Furlong, J. and Maynard, T. (1995) *Mentoring Student Teachers: The Growth of Professional Knowledge.* Abingdon: Routledge.

Gelter, H. (2003) Why is reflective thinking uncommon? *Reflective Practice,* 4(3): 337–44.

Ghaye, A. and Ghaye, K. (1998) *Teaching and Learning through Critical Reflective Practice.* Abingdon: David Fulton Publishers.

Ghaye, T., Gillespie, D., and Lillyman, S. (eds) (2000) *Empowerment Through Reflection: The Narratives of Healthcare Professionals.* Dinton: Quay Books.

Gibbs, G. (1998). *Learning by Doing: A Guide to Teaching and Learning Methods.* Oxford: Further Education Unit, Oxford Polytechnic.

Goodman, J. (1984) Reflection and teacher education: a case study and theoretical analysis, *A Quarterly Review of Education,* 15(3): 9–26.

Goodson, I.F. (1996) *Teachers' Professional Lives.* Oxford: Routledge Falmer.

Goulding, M. (2004) Feedback, review and self-evaluation, in S. Johnston-Wilder et al. (eds), *Learning to Teach Mathematics in the Secondary School.* London: David Fulton.

Graham, S. (2003) Learners' metacognative beliefs: a modern foreign languages case study, *Research in Education,* 70(1): 9–18.

Grainger, T. and Barnes, J. (2006) Creativity in the curriculum, in J. Arthur (ed.) *Learning to Teach in the Primary School.* Abingdon: Routledge.

Hagger, H., Burn, K., Mutton, T., and Brindley, S. (2008) Practice makes perfect? Learning to learn as a teacher, *Oxford Review of Education,* 34(2) 159–78.

Hagger, H. and McIntyre, D. (2006) *Learning Teaching from Teachers: Realising the Potential of School Based Teacher Education.* Buckingham: Open University Press.

Hall, C. and Thomson, P. (2005) Creative Tensions? Creativity and basis skills in recent education policy, *English in Education,* 39: 5–18.

Hansford, B.C., Ehrich, L.C. and Tennent, L. (2004) Formal mentoring Programmes in education and other professions: a review of the literature, *Educational Administration Quarterly,* 40(4): 518–40.

Hargreaves, A. (1995) Realities of teaching, in L.W. Anderson (ed.) *International Encyclopedia of Teaching and Teacher Education,* (2nd edn). Cambridge: Pergamon.

Hargreaves, A. (1998) The emotional practice of teaching, *Teaching and Teacher Education,* 14(8) 835–54.

Hargreaves, D. (1994) The new professionalism: the synthesis of professional and institutional development, *Teaching and Teacher Education,* 10(4): 423–38.

Hargreaves, E. (2005) Assessment for learning? Thinking outside the (black) box, *Cambridge Journal of Education,* 35(2): 213–24.

Hawkins, P. and Shohet, R. (2006) *Supervision in the Helping Professions,* 3rd edn. Maidenhead: Open University Press.

Helsing, D. (2007) Regarding uncertainty in teachers and teaching, *Teaching and Teacher Education,* 23: 1317–33.

Higgins, S. and Leat, D. (2001) Horses for courses or courses for horses: What is effective teacher development?, in J. Soler, A. Craft and H. Burgess (eds) *Teacher Development:*

Exploring Our Own Practice. London: Paul Chapman Publishing Ltd in association with Open University Press.

Hinett, K. and Weeden, P. (2000) How am I doing?: developing critical self-evaluation in trainee teachers, *Quality in Higher Education,* 6(3): 245–57.

Hobson, A.J. (2002) Student teachers' perceptions of school-based mentoring in initial teacher training (ITT), *Mentoring & Tutoring: Partnership in Learning,* 10(1): 5–20.

Hobson, A., Ashby, P., Malderez, A. and Tomlinson, P. (2009a) Mentoring beginning teachers: what we know and what we don't, *Teaching and Teacher Education,* 25: 207–16.

Hobson, A. and Malderez, A. (eds) (2005) *Becoming a Teacher: Student Teachers' Motives and Preconceptions, and Early School-based Experiences During Initial Teacher Training.* Research Report No 637. Nottingham: DfES Publications.

Hobson, A.J., Giannakaki, M.S. and Chambers, G.N. (2009b) Who withdraws from initial teacher preparation programmes and why?, *Educational Research,* 51(31): 321–40.

Hobson, A.J.; Malderez, A.; Tracey, L., et al. (2008) Student teachers' experiences of initial teacher preparation in England: core themes and variation, *Research Papers in Education,* 23(4): 407–33.

Hodges, D.C. (1998) Participation as dis-identification with/in a community of practice, *Mind, Culture and Activity,* 5(4): 272–90.

Hodkinson, H. and Hodkinson, P. (1997) Micropolitics in initial teacher education: Luke's story, *Journal of Education for Teaching,* 23(2): 119–29.

Hughes, J. (2010) 'But it's not just developing like a learner, it's developing as a person': reflections on e-port folio-based learning, in R. Sharpe, H. Beetham and S. de Freitas (eds) *Rethinking Learning for a Digital Age.* New York: Routledge.

Issacs, W. (1999) *Dialogue and the Art of Thinking Together: A Pioneering Approach to Communicating in Business and in Life.* New York: Bantam Dell.

Janssen, F., de Hullu, E. and Tigelaar, D, (2008) Positive experience as input for reflection by student teachers, *Teachers and Teaching: Theory and Practice,* 14(2): 115–27.

Jarvis, P. (2006) *The Theory and Practice of Teaching.* 2nd edn. London: Kogan Page.

Jasper, M. (2003) *Beginning Reflective Practice. Foundations in Nursing and Health Care.* Cheltenham: Nelson Thornes.

Johns, C. (2004) *Becoming a Reflective Practitioner.* Oxford: Blackwell Publishing Ltd.

Johns, C. (2002) *Guided Reflection: Advancing Practice.* Oxford: Blackwell Science.

Johns, C. with Whitehead, J. (2000) A response to Whitehead, and the reply, *Reflective Practice,* 1(1): 105–12.

Jones, M. (2005) Fitting in, feeling excluded or opting out? An investigation into the socialisation process of newcomers to the teaching profession in secondary schools in England, *Journal of In-Service Education,* 31(3): 509–26.

Jurasaite-Harbison, E. and Rex, L.A. (2010) School cultures as contexts for informal teacher learning, *Teaching and Teacher Education,* 26: 267–77.

Kelchtermans, G. and Ballet, K. (2002) The micropolitics of teacher induction. A narrative-biographical study on teacher socialization, *Teaching and Teacher Education,* 18: 105–20.

Kemmis, S. (2007) Action research, in M. Hammersley (ed.) *Educational Research and Evidence-based Practice.* Milton Keynes: Open University.

Kemmis, S. and Wilkinson, M. (1988) Participatory action research and the study of practice, in B. Atweh, S. Kemmis and P. Weeks (eds) *Action Research in Practice: Partnerships for Social Justice in Education.* London: Routledge.

Keogh, B. and Naylor, S. (2008) *Concept Cartoons in Science Education.* London: Millgate House Publishers

Kilpatrick, S., Barrett, M. and Jones, T. (2003) *Defining Learning Communities.* Available at www.aare.edu.au/03pap/jon03441.pdf (Accessed 24 March 2009).

Kinchin, G. (2007) Understanding learning, in V. Ellis, (ed.) *Learning & Teaching in Secondary Schools.* Exeter: Learning Matters Ltd.

Kolb, D. (1984) *Experiential Learning: Experience as the Source of Learning and Development.* Englewood cliffs: NJ Prentice Hall.

Korthagen, F.A.J. and Kessels, J.P.A.M. (1999) Linking theory and practice: changing the pedagogy of teacher education, *Educational Researcher,* 28(4): 4–17.

Korthagen, F. and Vasalos, A. (2005) Levels in reflection: core reflection as a means to enhance professional growth, *Teachers and Teaching,* 11(1): 47–71.

Kuit, J and Reay, G. (2001) Experiences of reflective teaching, *Action Learning in Higher Education,* 2(2): 128–42.

LaBoskey, V.K. (1993) A conceptual framework for reflection in preservice teacher education, in J. Calderhead, and P. Gates (eds) *Conceptualizing Reflection in Teacher Development.* London: Falmer.

Lacey, C. (1977) *The Socialisation of Teachers.* London: Methuen.

Larrivee, B. (2000) Transforming teaching practice: becoming a critically reflective teacher, *Reflective Practice,* 1(3): 293–307.

Larrivee, B. (2005) *Authentic Classroom Management: Creating a Learning Community and Building Reflective practice.* Boston: Pearson.

Lave, J. and Wenger, E. (1991) *Situated Learning: Legitimate Peripheral Participation.* Cambridge: Cambridge University Press.

Lawson, H. (1985) *Reflexivity: The Post-modern Predicament.* London: Hutchinson.

Lawson, T. (2008) Assessing students, in S. Dymoke and J. Harrison (eds) *Reflective Teaching and Learning.* London: Sage.

Leavy, A., McSorley, F., and Bote, L. (2007) An examination of what metaphor construction reveals about the evolution of preservice teachers' belief about teaching and learning, *Teaching and Teacher Education,* 23(7): 1217–33.

Lee Chi-kin, J. and Feng, S. (2007) Mentoring support and the professional development of beginning teachers: a Chinese perspective, *Mentoring & Tutoring,* 15(3): 243–62.

Lewin, K. (1951) *Field Theory in Social Science.* Chicago: University of Chicago Press.

Lorenzo, G. and Ittleson, J. (2005) *An Overview of e-Portfolios.* Available at http://www.educause.edu/ir/library/pdf/ELI3001.pdf. (Accessed 2 February 2010).

Loving, C.C., Shroeder, C., Kang, R., Shimek, C. and Herbert, B. (2007) Blogs: enhancing links in a professional learning community of science and mathematics teachers, *Contemporary issues in Technology and Teacher Education,* 7 (3). Available at http://www.citejournal.org/vol6/iss4/science/article1.cfm (Accessed 12 October 2010).

Lunenberg, M. and Korthagen, F. (2009) Experience, theory and practical wisdom in teaching and teacher education, *Teachers and Teaching,* 15(2): 225–40.

Mahony, P. and Hextall, P. (2000) *Reconstructing Teaching: Standards, Performance and Accountability.* London: Routledge Falmer.

Makinster, J.G., Barab, S.A., Harwood, W. and Andersen, H.O. (2006) The effect of social context on the reflective practice of preservice science teachers: incorporating a web-supported community of teachers, *Journal of Technology and Teacher Education*, 14(3): 543–79.

Malderez, A., Hobson, A.J., Tracey, L. and Kerr, K. (2007) Becoming a student teacher: core features of the experience, *European Journal of Teacher Education*, 30(3): 225–48.

Malderez, A. and Wedell, M. (2007) *Teaching Teachers: Processes and Practices*. London: Continuum.

Malm, B. (2009) Towards a new professionalism: enhancing personal and professional development in teacher education, *Journal of Education for Teaching*, 35(1): 77–91.

Martin, M. (2005) Reflection in teacher education: how can it be supported?, *Educational Action Research*, 13(4): 525–42.

Mason, J. (2002) *Researching Your Own Practice: The Discipline of Noticing*. London: Routledge Falmer.

Matthews, B. and Jessel, J. (1998) Reflective and reflexive practice in initial teacher education, *Teaching in Higher Education*, 3(2): 231–43.

Maynard, T. (2000) Learning to teach or learning to manage mentors? Experiences of school-based teacher training in mentoring and tutoring, *Partnership in Learning*, 8(1): 17–30.

McClure, P. (2002) *Reflection on Practice*, a resource commissioned by the Making Practice Based Learning Work Project, an educational development project funded through FDTL Phase 4 Project Number 174/02 and produced by staff from the University of Ulster. Available at http://www.practicebasedlearning.org/resources/materials/docs/reflectiononpractice.pdf (Accessed May 2009).

McCollum, S., (2002) The reflective framework for teaching in physical education: a pedagogical tool, *Journal of Physical Education, Recreation & Dance*, 73(6): 39–42.

McGregor, D. (2007) *Developing Thinking, Developing Learning. A Thinking Skills Guide for Education*. Maidenhead: Open University Press.

McGuinness, C. (2005) Teaching thinking: theory and practice. Pedagogy – Learning for teaching, *The British Psychological Society*, Series II(3): 10–126.

McIntyre, D. (1993) Theory, theorizing and reflection in initial teacher education, in J. Calderhead and P. Gates (eds) *Conceptualizing Reflection in Teacher Development*. London: Falmer Press.

McNiff, J. with Whitehead, J. (2002) *Action Research: Principles and Practice*, (2nd edn). London: RoutledgeFalmer.

McNiff, J. and Whitehead, J. (2005) *Action Research for Teachers*. Oxford: David Fulton.

Mezirow, J. (1998) On critical reflection, *Adult Education Quarterly*, 48(3): 185–98.

Miller, A. (2002) Communicative grammar teaching, in A. Swarbrick (ed.) *Teaching Modern Foreign Languages in Secondary Schools: A Reader*. London: Routledge Falmer.

Mitchell, J., Clarke, A. and Nuttall, J. (2007) Cooperating teachers' perspectives under scrutiny: a comparative analysis of Australia and Canada, *Asia-Pacific Journal of Teacher Education*, 35(1): 5–25.

Moon, J. (2008) *Critical Thinking: An Exploration of Theory and Practice*. Abingdon: Routledge.

Moon, J.A. (2006) Learning Journals: *A Handbook for Reflective Practice and Professional Development*, 2nd ed., London and New York: Routledge.

Moon, J.A. (1999) *Reflection in Learning and Professional Development: Theory and Practice.* London: Kogan Page.

Moore, A. (2004) *The Good Teacher: Dominant Discourses in Teaching and Teacher Education.* Abingdon: Routledge.

Morss, K. and Donaghy, M.E. (2000) *A Framework to Facilitate and Assess Reflection on Practice in Physiotherapy: The Student View.* Available at http://www.ecu.edu.au/conferences/herdsa/main/papers/nonref/pdf/KateMorss2.pdf (Accessed 4 December 2008).

NACCCE (1999) *All Our Futures: Creativity, Culture and Education* (The Robinson Report). London: DFEE.

Nesbit, T., Leach, L. and Foley, G. (2004) Teaching adults, in G. Foley (ed.) *Dimensions of Adult Learning: Adult Education and Training in a Global Era.* New South Wales: Allen and Unwin.

Newton, L.D. and Newton, D.P. (2010) What teachers see as creative incidents in elementary science lessons, *International Journal of Science Education*, 32(15): 1989–2005.

Ofsted (2008) *Mathematics: Understanding the Score.* Report number 070063. London: Ofsted.

Ofsted (2009a) *Grade Criteria for the Inspection of Initial Teacher Training* 2008–11. London: Ofsted.

Ofsted (2010) University of Wolverhampton inspection report. Reference 70084 Available at www.ofsted.gov.uk (Accessed 30 July 2010)

Olsen, B. (2008) How reasons for entry into the profession illuminate teacher identity development, *Teacher Education Quarterly*, Summer. Available at http://www.teqjournal.org/backvols/2008/3513/07olsen.pdf (Accessed 14 September 2010).

Osterman, K.F. and Kottkamp, R.B. (2004) *Reflective Practice for Educators*, 2nd edn. Thousand Oaks, CA: Corwin Press.

Otienoh, R. (2009) Reflective practice: the challenge of journal writing, *Reflective Practice*, 10(4): 477–89.

Ottensen, E. (2007) Reflection in teacher education, *Reflective Practice*, 8(1): 31–48.

Pentland, A. (2007) *Honest signals: How they shape our world.* MIT Press.

Petty, G. (2009) *Teaching Today: A Practical Guide*, 4th edn. Cheltenham: Nelson Thornes.

Phelan, A.M. (2001) Power and place in teaching and teacher education, *Teaching and Teacher Education*, 17: 583–97.

Pickup, I., Haydn-Davies, D. and Jess, M. (2007) The importance of primary physical education. *Physical Education Matters*, 2(1): 8–11.

Pollard, A. (ed.) (2008) *Reflective Teaching: Evidence-informed Professional Practice*, 3rd edn. London: Continuum.

QCA (2007) *The 10 Principles: Assessment for Learning.* London: QCA. Available at http://www.qca.org.uk/qca_4336.aspx (Accessed 15 March 2009).

Reed, M. and Canning, N. (2010) *Reflective Practice in the Early Years.* London: Sage.

Richert, A.E. (1992) The content of student teachers' reflections, in T. Russell, and H. Munby, (eds) *Teachers and Teaching: From Classroom to Reflection.* London: Falmer.

Roberts, J. (1998) *Language Teacher Education.* London: Arnold.

Roberts, J. and Graham, S. (2008) Agency and conformity in school-based teacher training, *Teaching and Teacher Education*, 24: 1401–12.

Robinson, K. (2001) *Out of Our Minds: Learning to be Creative.* London: Capstone.

Rolfe, G., Freshwater, D. and Jasper, M. (2001) *Critical Reflection for Nursing and the Helping Professions: A User's Guide*: Basingstoke: Palgrave.

Russell, T. (2005) 'Can reflective practice be taught?,' *Reflective Practice,* 6(2): 199–204

Sachs, J. (2005) Teacher education and the development of professional identity: learning to be a teacher, in P. Denicolo and M. Kompf (eds) *Connecting Policy and Practice: Challenges for Teaching and Learning in Schools and Universities.* Oxford: Routledge.

Sangster, M. and Overal, L. (2006) *Assessment: A Practical Guide for Primary Teachers.* London: Continuum.

Schön, D. (1987) *Educating the Reflective Practitioner.* San Francisco, CA: Jossey-Bass.

Schön, D.A. (1983) *The Reflective Practitioner: How Professionals Think in Action.* London: Temple Smith.

Schön, D.A. (1991) *The Reflective Practitioner: How Professionals Think in Action.* London: Ashgate.

SEED (2006) Promoting Creativity in Education: Overview of Key National Policy Development Across the UK: An Information Paper by the Scottish Executive Education Department. Available at www.hmie.gov.uk/documents/publication/hmiepcie.html#5 (Accessed 17 August 2010).

Seligman, M. and Csikszentmihalyi, M. (2000) Positive psychology: an introduction, *American Psychologist,* 55: 5–14.

Senge, P. (1990) *The Fifth Discipline: The Art and Practice of the learning organization.* New York: Barnes and Noble.

Senge, P. (2007) Give me a lever long enough . . . and single-handed I can move the world, in *The Jossey-Bass Reader on Educational Leadership,* 2nd edn. 199–204. San Francisco, CA: Jossey-Bass.

Shulman, L. (1986) Those who understand: knowledge growth in teaching, *Educational Researcher,* 15(2): 4–14.

Shulman, L.S. (1987) Knowledge and teaching: foundations of the new reform, *Harvard Educational Review,* 57(1): 1–22.

Shulman, L.S. (1991) Ways of seeing, ways of knowing: ways of teaching, ways of learning about teaching, *Journal of Curriculum Studies,* 23(5): 393–5.

Shulman, L.S. (1998) Teaching and teacher education among the professions. 38th Charles W. Hunt memorial lecture. Paper presented at the Annual Meeting of the American Association of Colleges for Teacher Education, New Orleans, LA. Available at http://www.eric.ed.gov/ERICDocs/data/ericdocs2sql/content_storage_01/0000019b/80/29/d1/9c.pdf (Accessed 21 May 2009).

Simkins, T. (2009) Integrating work-based learning into large-scale national leadership development programmes in the UK, *Educational Review,* 61:(4): 391–405.

Smagorinsky, P., Cook, L.S., Moore, C.; Jackson, A.Y. and Fry. P.G. (2004) Tensions in learning to teach: accommodation and the development of teacher identity, *Journal of Teacher Education,* 55(1): 8–24.

Steier, F. (1991) *Research and Reflexivity.* London: Sage

Stenberg, K. (2010) Identity work as a tool for promoting the professional development of student teachers, *Reflective Practice,* 11(3): 331–46.

Stenhouse, L. (1981) What counts as research? *British Journal of Educational Studies,* 29(2): 103–14.

Sternberg, R. (2003) *Wisdom, Intelligence, and Creativity Synthesized.* Cambridge: Cambridge University Press.

Stiggins, R. (2002) *Assessment for Crisis: The Absence of Assessment for Learning* USA: Kappan Professional Journal. Available at http://www.pdkintl.org/kappan/k0206sti.htm (Accessed 16th January 2009).

Stoll, L., Fink, D. and Earl, L. (2003) *It's About Learning (and It's About Time): What's in it for Schools?* London: Routledge Falmer.

Strong-Wilson, T. (2006) Bringing memory forward: a method for engaging teachers in reflective practice on narrative and memory, *Reflective Practice,* 7(1): 101–13.

Sutherland, S. (2005) e-Portfolios: a space for learning and the learner voice, in S. de Freitas and C. Yapp (eds) *Personalizing Learning in the 21st Century.* Stafford: Network Educational Press.

TDA (2007) *Professional Standards for Teachers: Why Sit Still in Your Career?* London: Training & Development Agency for Schools. Available at http://www.tda.gov.uk/upload/resources/pdf/s/standards_a4.pdf (Accessed 12 July 2011).

ten Dam, G.T.M. and Blom, S. (2006) Learning through participation. The potential of school-based teacher education for developing a professional identity, *Teaching and Teacher Education,* 22: 647–60.

Tobias, S. J. and Boon, H. J. (2009) Codes of conduct and ethical dilemmas in teacher education. Paper presented at the AARE Annual Conference Canberra, 30 November–4 December.

Tripp, D. (1993) *Critical Incidents in Teaching: Developing Professional Judgment.* London: Routledge.

Valli, L. (1993) Reflections on teacher education programs: an analysis of case studies, in J. Calderhead, and P. Gates, (eds) *Conceptualising Reflection in Teacher Development.* London: Falmer.

Van Maanen, J. (1988) *Tales of the Field: On Writing Ethnography.* Chicago: University of Chicago Press.

Veenman, S. (1984) Perceived problems of beginning teachers, *Review of Educational Research,* 54(2): 143–78.

Vygotsky, L.S. (1978) *Mind and Society: The Development of Higher Mental Processes.* Cambridge, MA: Harvard University Press.

Walkington, J. (2005) Becoming a teacher: encouraging development of teacher identity through reflective practice, *Asia Pacific Journal of Teacher Education,* 33(1): 53–64.

Wang, J., Odell, S.J. and Schwille, S.A. (2008) Effects of teacher induction on beginning teachers' teaching: a critical review of the literature, *Journal of Teacher Education,* 59: 132–52.

Weber, S. and Mitchell, C. (1995) *That's Funny, You Don't Look Like a Teacher: Interrogating Images and Identity in Popular Culture.* London: Falmer.

Webster-Wright, A. (2009) Reframing professional development through understanding authentic professional learning, *Review of Educational Research,* 79(2): 702–39.

Wenger, E. (1998) *Communities of Practice: Learning, Meaning and Identity.* Cambridge: Cambridge University Press.

Wheeler, S. and Wheeler, D. (2009) Using wikis to promote quality learning in teacher training, *Learning Media and Technology,* 34(1): 1–10.

Whitehead, J. (2007) Creating a world of educational quality through living educational theories. Paper presented at AERA 2007 in Chicago, 13th April 2007. Available at http://www.jackwhitehead.com/aera07/jwaera07.htm (Accessed 31st August 2010).

Whitehead, J. (1993) *The Growth of Educational Knowledge: Creating your own Living Educational Theories.* Available at http://www.actionresearch.net/writingw/wgek93.htm (Accessed 15 April 2011).

Wilson, A. (ed.) (2005) *Creativity in Primary Education.* Exeter: Learning Matters. (Introduction by Ted Wragg.)

Wire, V. (2005) Autistic Spectrum Disorders and learning foreign languages, *Support for Learning,* 20(3): 123–28.

Wright, T. (2008) *How to be a brilliant trainee teacher.* Abingdon: Routledge.

Yaffe, Elika (2010) The reflective beginner: using theory and practice to facilitate reflection among newly qualified teachers, *Reflective Practice,* 11(3): 381–91.

Yang, S.-H. (2009) Using blogs to enhance critical reflection and community of practice, *Educational Technology and Society,* 12(2): 11–21.

Yero, J.L. (2002) *Teaching In Mind: How Teacher Thinking Shapes Education.* Montana: MindFlight.

Young, D. and Lipczynski, K. (2007) Transferability of e-portfolios in education: phase one report, ESCalate. escalate.ac.uk/6016 (accessed 1 May 2011).

Zeichner, K. (1994) Research on teacher thinking and different views of reflective practice, in I. Carlgren, H. Gunner and S. Vaage (eds.) *Teachers' Minds and Actions: Research on Teachers' Thinking and Practice.* London: Falmer Press.

Zeichner, K.M. and Tabachnick, B.R. (1985) The development of teacher perspectives, *Journal of Education for Teaching,* 11(1): 1–25.

Index